When
Likes
Aren't Enough

A Crash Course in the
Science of Happiness

Tim Bono, PhD

GRAND CENTRAL
Life & Style
NEW YORK · BOSTON

Grand Central Life & Style
Hachette Book Group
1290 Avenue of the Americas, New York, NY 10104
grandcentrallifeandstyle.com
twitter.com/grandcentralpub

First Edition: March 2018

Grand Central Life & Style is an imprint of Grand Central Publishing. The Grand Central Life & Style name and logo are trademarks of Hachette Book Group, Inc.

The publisher is not responsible for websites (or their content) that are not owned by the publisher.

The Hachette Speakers Bureau provides a wide range of authors for speaking events. To find out more, go to www.hachettespeakersbureau.com or call (866) 376-6591.

The photos of the student with the pen in her lips/teeth on page 21 were taken by Scott Blessman.
The cartoon images "Had a Bad Day/Good Day? Go to the Gym!" (page 74) and "Introvert/Extrovert" (page 181) were created by Vic Gainor.
The author photo on page 260 is by Panit Tan.

Library of Congress Cataloging-in-Publication Data

Names: Bono, Tim, author.
Title: When likes aren't enough : a crash course in the science of happiness / Tim Bono.
Other titles: When likes are not enough
Description: First Edition. | New York : Grand Central Life & Style, 2018.
Identifiers: LCCN 2017041758| ISBN 9781538743416 (hardback) | ISBN 9781549167485 (audio download) | ISBN 9781538728093 (ebook)
Subjects: LCSH: Self-actualization (Psychology) | Emotions. | Happiness. | BISAC: SELF-HELP / Personal Growth / Happiness. | PSYCHOLOGY / Emotions. | PSYCHOLOGY / Mental Health. | SELF-HELP / Personal Growth / Self-Esteem.
Classification: LCC BF637.S4 B657 2018 | DDC 158—dc23
LC record available at https://lccn.loc.gov/2017041758

ISBNs: 978-1-5387-4341-6 (hardcover); 978-1-5387-2809-3 (ebook)

Printed in the United States of America

LSC-C

10   9   8   7   6   5   4   3   2   1

To Linda, for opening the door

To Randy, for guiding my path

Contents

Introduction   vii

1 The Holy Grail of Young Adulthood   1

2 The Common Denominator of Happiness   25

3 A Healthy Mind in a Healthy Body   47

4 Sweet Dreams   75

5 Attention Training   95

6 Failing Better   121

7 Willpower   145

8 The Time Paradox   170

9 Managing the Inevitable Bad Day   195

10 Social Connection   210

   Putting It into Practice   231

   Acknowledgments   239

   Notes   243

Introduction

Shortly after I began writing this book I was having dinner with my friend James, who asked me what had inspired this project. I told him that I was writing this book to myself—the young adult version of myself—to share the information I wish I had known in my late teens and early twenties. My transition to adulthood, I confessed, had been marked by anxiety, loneliness, and yearning. James was quick to empathize. His early adult years had been emotionally turbulent too. We'd both wrestled with heavy feelings of unhappiness, surrounded by friends who seemingly didn't. It wasn't until I'd hit my midtwenties that I started to gain some insight into the nature of these experiences and feelings—and then only because I'd set out on a career in psychology. Through my studies I eventually learned that these struggles and emotions are common in young adulthood—I hadn't been alone. And there were strategies available that could break open hope, optimism, and meaning in my life. I just hadn't had access to them. Neither had James.

Allow me to set the stage. I come from a large Italian family. Well, that's redundant. I come from an *Italian* family. I am one of seventy-five cousins just on my dad's side. With so many relatives, we gather just about every week to celebrate someone's birthday, graduation, or wedding. I have seen most of that extended family regularly throughout my life. We have a lot in common in the way of culture and traditions. But beyond our Mediterranean facial features and love for spedini and cannoli, there is a large variability in personalities and emotional states—something I noticed even as a little kid. Some of my relatives are as kind, funny, and friendly as can be, like my Grandma Rosie, whose name matches her cheery disposition. She couldn't make it to the mailbox without greeting everyone she saw on the street with a smile and a wish for a beautiful day. Others (who shall remain nameless out of fear of Mafia retaliation) are as sad, downhearted, and bitter as you can imagine, including a few who spent their entire lives clinging to decades-old grudges, ultimately estranging themselves from the family altogether. "Oh, woe is me" was their constant refrain.

Though I had a mostly happy childhood, I seemed to fluctuate between the cheery dispositions of some family members and the melancholy of others. As I made my way into my late teens and early twenties, I found the ratio shifting, my emotions becoming dominated by despair. If I had an exam coming up, I would worry nonstop. If someone angered me, I could not let it go. If I didn't have plans on a Friday night, I would wallow in self-pity. When I considered how emotions like mine affected some of my family members—the "Woe is me" types—I became resolved to halt the sweeping negativity that was invading my thinking and decision making. I didn't want to live my entire life like that. I wasn't sure what, if anything, could be done, but I at least had to find out if there was *something* that might turn things around.

From my undergraduate psychology coursework, I understood that emotion and behavior are partly determined by genetics. Considering how glum some of my relatives were, I recognized that some of my unhappiness may have been built into my DNA. However, my courses also taught me that genes do not determine our destiny. Our intentional behaviors and daily habits—the parts of our life that we choose and control—can interact with those genes to suppress or enhance their natural expression. This gave me hope. Perhaps I could find a way to quiet my gloomy thoughts and increase my happiness, even with the limitations I inherited genetically. This became my Holy Grail during my twenties.

My personal quest aligned perfectly with my professional aspirations. I was fortunate enough to be enrolled in a doctoral program in psychology at the time, which provided access to a wealth of science and the scholars in the field who could guide my inquiry. I started work toward my PhD when positive psychology, a field dedicated to the understanding and enhancement of positive emotions, was still new. In addition to satisfying the requirements for my degree, I used graduate school as a veritable sandbox. I dug my hands into as much research as I could find on the nature of human emotion and what scientists had discovered about ways to maximize positivity and psychological health in young adulthood. I gathered information with my younger self in mind, always asking questions, always pushing to identify those points of choice—where our intentions can override our genetics or circumstances.

My research provided a framework both for my own personal exploration and for the courses I began teaching shortly thereafter at Washington University in St. Louis. To answer my friend James's question, that research is ultimately what motivates this book.

———————

In 2008 I began teaching a course called The Psychology of Young Adulthood, which has enrolled between one hundred and two hundred incoming freshmen each fall ever since. As part of the course, the students complete weekly surveys in which they report what it was like to be a college freshman that week. They answer questions about their overall happiness and stress levels and tell me about the best and worst things that happen. They report how much time they spend in the library, how often they exercise, how often they get sick, and whether they feel socially connected. About eighty questions altogether gauge every aspect of how they are thinking, feeling, and behaving during each week of their transition to adulthood.

The sheer volume of data I have collected over the years has allowed me to see which variables are most closely related. Not surprisingly, more studying means better grades, and better sleep means more happiness. But not all the findings have been so intuitive. The first year I taught this class I gave special attention to how much time students spent on social media. Facebook had been on the scene for only a few years at that point, and I wanted to see how it was impacting their lives. By 2008 nearly all of the students had an account, and they were using it to organize social events, share funny videos, and peer into the lives of all the "friends" they had amassed, even those they had never actually met. One of my students called it a "miracle website" for letting him stay connected with friends from high school who had scattered all across the United States for college. The amount of time they spent maintaining their social media presence must offer a payout, I thought. With this much social connection at their fingertips, and given how much time many of them were spending on it, I assumed Mark Zuckerberg had blessed young adults everywhere with the gift of happiness.

That was, until I looked at their data.

The more time students reported spending on Facebook, the worse off they were in nearly every other aspect of their lives. Their efforts crafting perfectly manicured lives for the world to see were not only unproductive, they were actually counterproductive for their happiness. More time on social media was associated with lower self-esteem, less optimism about the week ahead, less sleep, more homesickness, and less motivation. The single strongest correlate was the most ironic of all: less connectedness to others. That's right, the more time they spent on the "miracle website" allowing them to read daily updates and live vicariously through pictures of friends and family around the world, the less socially connected they felt to actual people.

Instagram only made the problem worse. The *Washington Post* recently published the story of a teenager who carefully monitors not only which pictures she posts for her hundreds of followers to admire, but also how many likes each photo gets.[1] Those photos without at least a hundred likes she deletes altogether. She has even established a system of earning likes from others by making comments on their pictures. That's assuming they stay on her good side. As the ultimate form of revenge, she might un-like another's photo to show her disdain. What started as a means of connection has evolved into a machine for competition. Social media has become a social charade.

So if accumulating likes isn't the answer to finding sustainable happiness, where else is a young adult to turn? Reading the weekly survey responses from my Psychology of Young Adulthood course over the years has taught me a lot about the ups and downs young adults encounter as they navigate relationships, establish their independence and sense of self, and attempt to craft lives of meaning and purpose. I used what I learned from those weekly surveys to inform the topics I selected for my Positive Psychology course, which I began teaching a few years later. Since social media wasn't the solution, I wanted to offer students an opportunity to see what science had discovered about the strategies and behaviors that actually could bring about the happiness they were seeking.

I initially designed the Positive Psychology course to be a fifteen-person seminar. The student response has since been overwhelming. It has become the largest course in the Psychology Department each semester it is offered. The largest classroom I can use on campus allows seating for three hundred, which still doesn't meet the demand. A few years ago, an administrator from the IT department e-mailed me about an observation he'd made while perusing waiting-list numbers for courses throughout the university:

Tim,

I was looking at waitlist counts and saw yours. Positive Psychology is the #1 waitlist class by a pretty hefty margin. The irony is pretty funny (at least from a distance).

Jason

He attached a screenshot of my course's listing showing a waiting list in the triple digits. Similar trends occur with college classes on happiness nationwide. At UC Berkeley the waiting list for the course often grows to twice the number of seats available. At Harvard the course had to be relocated from a standard classroom to a campus theater to accommodate the eight hundred students looking to understand the psychology of well-being. And of those who enroll (at least at my own institution), few are looking just to fulfill degree requirements. Engineering, art history, architecture, finance, and English literature majors are just as common as students studying psychology. The demand for a class on happiness, though "ironic" from the perspective of Jason, my IT administrator, reflects what research on college students around the world, including findings from the National Alliance on Mental Illness, points to: young adults are yearning for well-being, and they want evidence-based solutions that they can realistically incorporate into their lives. The thousands of students who have passed through my lecture hall over the last decade have been interested in the same thing I spent my twenties grappling with: the pursuit of happiness.

What you will read in the pages that follow is what I wish I had known in my early adult years—and what I am very glad I have been able to incorporate into my life since then. I have been honored to share the science of positive psychology with young adults I have taught and advised over the years. This book shows how they have translated this information into practical strategies in their own lives. I hope it can help you do the same.

The Holy Grail of Young Adulthood

The student center was packed. It was a Tuesday night in the middle of the semester. Were free puppies being given away? Had political activists occupied the commons? No—a speaker was scheduled to talk about "Living a Life of Joy." It was part of a week of programming sponsored by the junior class to promote health and well-being for students in the throes of midterms. Not a slice of free pizza to be seen anywhere, and yet tons of students had turned out.

The event organizers invited me to say a few words about my own research on happiness to kick off the lecture. After delivering my remarks, I took a seat in the front row, eager to hear what the headliner would have to say. Within just a few minutes, I was floored. But probably not for the reasons the speaker had intended. She began her presentation with a series of lofty promises: The power to create personal happiness was ours alone. Unending joy was in our reach. It would be possible for us never to have a bad day. *Ever* again. For the *rest* of our lives. With each statement my eyes widened almost as much as my disbelief. I was waiting for her to start waving a wand of holly and phoenix feather.

It's evident why her presentation attracted such a crowd. College students want to be happy. Happiness, it seems, is their Holy Grail. This quest has apparently replaced the medieval quests for wealth and everlasting life. Nowadays, many in their late teens and early twenties just want to *feel* better. Some turn to speakers like the one who visited my campus and promised the secret solution to permanent happiness. But not even the most powerful wizard can cast that spell.

THE BEST FOUR YEARS?

Within the first decade of the twenty-first century, enrollment at American colleges and universities increased a whopping 24 percent, from 16.6 million in 2002 to 20.6 million in 2012.[1] Why are young adults flocking to the experience? Sure, college opens doors to opportunities that might otherwise not be available—students take courses that will enlighten their minds, develop strong work ethics, and prepare them for careers. But that's not all that young adults are after. There's actually something that young adults want *even more* during these formative years—and that something else turns out to be happiness. Several years ago, a team of scientists asked nearly ten thousand students in forty-seven countries around the world what they valued most in life. Happiness received the top score, beating out love, money, health, and getting into heaven.[2]

And college, they are told, is the place to find it. Somewhere in the ivory tower is the key. As comedian David Wood once said, "College is the best four years of your life. When else are your parents going to spend several thousand dollars a year just for you to go to a strange town and get drunk every night?"

The message of college as "the best four years" has been propagated ad nauseam by American culture, including television, college survival books, and of course Hollywood. By some estimates, over the last century there have been nearly seven hundred professionally produced movies depicting some aspect of college life.[3] Of course, those movies aren't in the business of telling the whole truth. As sociologist

John Conklin, a professor at Tufts University, notes in his book *Campus Life in the Movies: A Critical Survey from the Silent Era to the Present*, "Because the Hollywood dream factory exists to make money, and profits depend on entertaining the public, it isn't surprising that movies about college life dwell on the fun students have rather than the coursework they do."[4] Viewers of movies like *Animal House, Van Wilder, Old School*, and *Neighbors* (the list goes on and on) spend a lot more time following the main characters toss Frisbees in the quad, set up kegs for fraternity parties, and entertain romantic interests than watching them study, write papers, or take other steps toward fulfilling their degree requirements—never mind struggle with their mental health. These movies, according to Conklin, have seeped into the culture and dramatically affected the expectations young people develop about the college years and their transition to young adulthood.

The reality, however, can be hard to adjust to—especially as young adults enter college on a quest for the Holy Grail of happiness. What happens when "the best four years" are actually harder than they seem in the movies?

In much the same way that college enrollments have dramatically increased over the last few decades, so too has the proportion of students suffering from mental illness. Some have declared that we are in the midst of a college student mental health crisis. From all directions data are emerging, depicting a sobering scene:

- One in three young adults has experienced prolonged periods of depression.
- One in two rate their mental health below average or poor.[5]
- College students were five times as likely to score above the cut-offs for psychopathology in the early 2000s than they were in the middle part of the twentieth century.[6]
- From 2007 to 2015 the suicide rate for teenagers increased 31 percent for boys and more than doubled for girls.[7]

The psychological distress plaguing ever-increasing numbers of young adults each year is undermining progress toward their goals. A recent survey from the National Alliance on Mental Illness reported that, among students who withdraw from college, nearly two-thirds say they dropped out due to their mental health.

Professionals within higher education are responding. Many institutions have increased the number of mental health counselors available in the student health center and made the accommodations at disability resource centers more robust. Still, the same survey from the National Alliance on Mental Illness found that only half of students with a mental health diagnosis disclose their condition to their college.[8]

Whether or not they are reporting it—and whether or not they themselves are experiencing it—young adults today are feeling distress at levels never seen before. As it turns out, "the best four years" can involve navigating a lot more than cultural rites of passage like keg parties, first loves, and the freshman fifteen. But young adults are also reaching out. Whether it's attending a lecture on "Living a Life of Joy," buying books, reading articles, or signing up in droves for a nonrequired class on happiness, young adults are interested in understanding psychological health, be it for themselves or out of concern for friends, classmates, or roommates. This could explain the popularity of a psychology major at most colleges and universities today, as well as the explosion of the self-help movement. It could also explain why a trend within psychology has generated interest and enthusiasm unlike any of its other subdisciplines: positive psychology.

THE RISE OF POSITIVE PSYCHOLOGY

Over the last two decades, researchers in the field of positive psychology have embarked on a quest to understand and develop strategies for getting happier. This development in psychology came in response to the overwhelming attention the field had previously paid to providing therapy for people in distress. All of that research was important—studies investigating depression, anxiety, and fear allowed educators and clinicians to offer effective solutions to the many afflicted. However, the president of the American Psychological Association declared a call to action in the late 1990s: In addition to addressing pathology, we should also understand positivity. It wasn't enough just to fix what went wrong with a person; it was just as important to use the field's understanding of human emotion to bring people to a truly flourishing life.

By the early 2000s, positive psychology had received prominent coverage in widespread media outlets including *Time*, the *Washington Post*, the *Sunday Times Magazine*, PBS, and the BBC. Hundreds of scientific articles have since been published, advancing our understanding of the nature of happiness and how it can be increased.

Scientists weren't the only ones sharing what they knew. An even larger number of self-help gurus, journalists, and motivational speakers appeared on the scene to educate the masses. A search for happiness books on Amazon yields hundreds of returns. This overabundance of ideas on the topic makes it difficult to know which sources can be trusted and are actually useful to young adults specifically. The advantage of looking to positive psychology is that its large body of research has been conducted primarily on young adults themselves. Its ideas are based not on magic or intuition, but on systematic observations and empirically supported conclusions that have withstood rigorous scientific testing. Positive psychology offers sound evidence that can be applied toward increasing well-being today and many years into the future.

SETTING THE RECORD STRAIGHT

Before we jump into the how of getting happier, it's important to first understand a few things about the nature of happiness and its pursuit.

After all, as the science of happiness has grown, so too have misconceptions about it and criticisms of it. A few years ago, the *Wall Street Journal* published an article asking, "Is Happiness Overrated?"[9] A year later *USA Today* published an apparent response, "Final Word: Happiness Is Overrated. You Can Bank on It."[10] Books on the topic are just as snide. Consider Jeanette Winterson's memoir, *Why Be Happy When You Could Be Normal?*[11] Or Barbara Ehrenreich's book, *Bright-Sided: How the Relentless Promotion of Positive Thinking Has Undermined America.*[12] Apparently you can't be both happy *and* normal.

These books and articles are rooted in the same misconceptions that led the guest speaker on campus to tell us it was possible to never have a bad day again. They treat happiness as if it were a sacred chalice being sought by the knights of King Arthur, a remedy for all our ills and maladies. Though well intentioned, these commenters are not taking into account two important premises at the foundation of positive psychology. Let's address each of them now, to separate the science from the supernatural.

Premise #1: Positive Psychology Is Not about Being Happy All the Time

Many people believe that the goal of positive psychology is pure, uninterrupted, everlasting happiness. Even an article recently published by the *National Post* equated positive psychology with "the notion that a perpetually upbeat outlook is entirely possible once we rid our 'thought patterns' of all things negative and ugly."[13] In reality, no credible source in the field will tell you that. Scientists have studied thousands of people from all walks of life, and we have yet to find anyone who is happy all the time. It is not something we expect to find, either.

Research from the lab of Dr. Randy Larsen, one of the field's leading experts, confirms that negativity is part of life. He has collected data on thousands of college students along the full range of psychological health: those in the depths of despair all the way up to those at the pinnacle of joy. The average psychologically healthy young adult experiences positivity about 70 percent of the time. If you think back to your last ten days, and three of them were neutral or unpleasant, you're actually doing pretty well. Even the happiest students, he finds, aren't happy *all the time*. They are happy only about 90 percent of the time. So even if you are at the top of the happiness pack, at least one day of the last ten probably left you feeling down.

Aspiring to a life free of any hardship is not only unrealistic, it could also backfire, as one of my students learned:

> "I've personally struggled with depression most of my life, but during my sophomore year in college, I hit rock bottom. For years I had busied myself taking hard courses, competing in piano, and overcommitting in clubs and in my social life to avoid how I felt. I didn't realize that running away from my painful emotions would only make them come back that much stronger."

This student's experience is explained by a phenomenon psychologists call the rebound effect. As an illustration, think about your favorite animal. Develop a vivid representation in your mind of the animal's shape, size, and color. What kind of food does it eat? Where does it live? I forgot to mention one rule: the animal cannot be a polar bear. It can be anything *except* one of those cute white polar bears with soft fur and black round eyes, perched atop an iceberg waiting to dive into the water. *Don't think about that polar bear.*

Whether you were thinking of a polar bear when you began reading the last paragraph or not, you are thinking about one now. The act of trying *not* to think about something causes the thought to "rebound," making us think about it even more than we otherwise would have. The same happens with our emotions. When we have a bad day, the act of trying not to feel bad can make us feel even worse. Instead, a healthier approach is to implement strategies that manage our angst productively. As we will see later in chapter 9, putting our emotions into language by talking things over with a friend or writing them out allows us to gain new insight into our experiences and speed our recovery.

We have evolved a complex set of human emotions for a reason. Positive and negative emotions both serve important functions. Feeling afraid or anxious alerts us to parts of our environment or life that we may need to modify—they can act as an internal alarm system. Think about the last time you had a cough. It was most likely unpleasant, but it was probably improving your overall physical health: the act of coughing is a natural mechanism that helps to break apart noxious matter and send it on its way so that it won't cause further harm. Psychologically, negative emotions operate in a similar way. They can prompt us to reflect on those aspects of life that may be driving our anxiety or despair, and lead us to make changes.

Of course, negative emotions can sometimes become so severe in frequency and intensity that they render people unable to carry out their normal daily tasks. Certainly in those cases—when negative emotions become disordered—it is important to treat them with clinical interventions. But a case of the blues, a moment of anxiety, or a flash of anger may actually be providing useful information, a signal that something needs to change. One of the most common myths about positive psychology—be it found in books, news articles, or keynote speeches delivered to packed auditoriums of college students—is that the field has found a secret way to be happy all the time. That's simply not true. Bad days are part of being human. Rather, it's about minimizing the negative impact of bad days, and capitalizing on the positive impact of good days.

When people hear about this first premise—that it's not about being happy all the time—they are usually relieved. If you've had a bad day, it is because you are human. But when people hear about the second premise, they are often puzzled—at least initially.

Premise #2: Positive Psychology Is Not Even about Being Happy

When I ask my students what motivated them to enroll in my Positive Psychology course, one of the most common responses I hear is that they want to be happy. They want to know what major they need to pursue, what kind of romantic partner they need to find, and how much money they need to make one day to be happy. Unfortunately, I have to be the bearer of bad news. The course is not designed to make them happy.

Instead, it's about becoming happ*ier*.

To some that difference seems insignificant. Being happy and being happ*ier* seem like the same thing, they say. To me there is a world of difference. "Being happy" implies a destination on the horizon instead of a process we can always be working toward. Think of striving to be a good athlete. At what point do you become "good"? When you do, will you no longer work to improve your skills? Katie Ledecky won four gold medals at the 2016 Summer Olympics. But instead of hanging her swim cap on being a "good" swimmer, she is constantly striving to be *better*, breaking even her own world records. I first learned how this way of thinking affects the pursuit of happiness from psychologist Tal Ben-Shahar, who articulates this mindset in his aptly named book *Happier*:

> "'Am I happy?' is a closed question that suggests a binary approach to the pursuit of the good life: we are either happy or we are not.... We can always be happier; no person experiences perfect bliss at all times and has nothing more to which he can aspire. Therefore, rather than asking myself whether I am happy or not, a more helpful question is, 'How

can I become happier?' This question acknowledges the nature of happiness and the fact that its pursuit is an ongoing process best represented by an infinite continuum, not by a finite point."[14]

When my students ask me what they need to be happy, I tell them the first thing they need is a different way of asking the question. At any given point, circumstances or conditions may be beyond our control. By asking what we can do to become happ*ier*, we place our attention on those aspects of life that *are* in our control, which ultimately can move us forward on the happiness continuum.

Together these two premises—that positive psychology is not about being happy all the time, and that it's not even about being "happy"—provide a necessary foundation. Once we stop trying to be "happy," real strategies for strengthening our well-being become attainable.

Still, these premises don't answer the *Wall Street Journal*'s question of whether the very concept is overrated. Why should we dedicate a field of inquiry to this topic in the first place? What are the actual benefits of being happy—or being happ*ier*—especially in young adulthood?

CARRYOVER EFFECTS IN THE LONG TERM

Ancient alchemists pined for the mythical philosopher's stone partly because of its power to prolong life. They searched the world over trying to find it. But unbeknownst to the alchemists, insight into what actually can lengthen one's life was in one place they probably never thought to look: a convent.

In what has become one of the most celebrated studies in the field of positive psychology, a group of scientists in the late 1990s gained insight into one of the secrets of a long life by studying a cohort of nuns. Most had entered the religious life in the early part of the twentieth century in their late teens or early twenties. The mother superior had requested that each novice write a brief statement about herself, her background, and her motivation for pursuing the religious life. The convent kept all the statements on file, providing ideal material for a longitudinal study (one that tracks the same group over a long period).

Originally the researchers used the statements to gain insight into Alzheimer's disease. They analyzed each for grammatical complexity and idea density and found the sisters with the most sophisticated writing style were the least likely to develop Alzheimer's disease.[15] Another glance at those autobiographies, however, revealed differences in their emotional styles too.[16] Some statements were upbeat and cheerful. Others were plain and dry. Consider the following examples:

> *Sister 1:* "I was born on September 26, 1909, the eldest of seven children, five girls and two boys....My candidate year was spent in the Motherhouse, teaching Chemistry and Second Year Latin at Notre Dame Institute. With God's grace, I intend to do my best for our Order, for the spread of religion and for my personal sanctification."

> *Sister 2:* "God started my life off well by bestowing upon me a grace of inestimable value....The past year which I have spent as a candidate studying at Notre Dame College has been a very happy one. Now I look forward with eager joy to receiving the Holy Habit of Our Lady and to a life of union with Love Divine."

Although both of these women appear to be entering the convent with appropriate backgrounds, for good reasons, and with noble intentions, a stark difference separates their writing styles. The second sister didn't just spend a year studying at Notre Dame College, she spent a year that was "a very happy one." She's not just planning to enter the convent, she's looking forward to the experience "with eager joy."

Had the mother superior attached a happiness scale to each nun's autobiography, Sister 2 likely would have had a higher score than Sister 1. But this study took it a step further. Instead of looking simply at whether the nuns' emotional writing style predicted happiness right then in that moment, the longitudinal nature of this study enabled the researchers to see whether the happiness of a twenty-two-year-old could predict later outcomes, including the ultimate outcome—longevity. Sure enough, those nuns with the most cheerful and optimistic writing lived the longest. When researchers split the writing samples into four groups ranging from the least happy to the most happy, the happiest nuns outlived the least happy by an average of nearly seven years. That is an impressive difference given that the only predictor was their apparent happiness more than a half century earlier.

THE POWER OF PERSPECTIVE

The major takeaway from the nun study is that our happiness in young adulthood has implications for the rest of our lives—including our health, our well-being, and even the amount of time we have on this planet. Part of the reason this study gets so much attention is the nuns themselves. If researchers had collected data from a random group of twentysomethings and found that the happiest people lived the longest, we could come up with plausible explanations beyond their cheery dispositions. Maybe the happiest young people lived more exciting lives. Maybe their careers were more fun. Maybe they had more money.

When we are studying nuns, however, we can rule out those alternative explanations. It's not that nuns don't have exciting lives or fun careers. What they *do* have is lives that are all very similar. Their living conditions are the same. Their daily activities are the same. Their incomes are the same. Any differences that we observe in an outcome like longevity can't be caused by differences in life circumstances. Instead they're caused by how the nuns *interpreted* their daily activities, and by which aspects of their lives they gave the most attention.

As we'll see in chapter 2, our overall well-being is a result not just of our objective circumstances—how much money we have, what kind of car we drive, or how many likes our Instagram posts get—but also of those aspects of life that we choose to attend to. In most situations we can either brood over the negative or glean something more positive. Consider the hassles that go along with flying. You have to get to the airport on time, check your luggage, make sure the toiletries in your carry-on are in a bag of the appropriate size, wait in more lines at the gate, and cross your fingers that any crying babies or talkative passengers are seated as far away as possible. And that's assuming everything goes according to plan.

A few years ago, one of my students illustrated how the power of perspective can make all the difference in whether flying is delightful or dreadful. When he was on his way home for winter break, his original direct flight to Philadelphia ended up being rerouted, causing a layover in Charlotte. When he arrived in Charlotte he learned that, due to an airline error, his seat had been assigned to someone else. The airline would have to reroute him *again*, with another layover in Chicago before he could get home to Philly.

Naturally the student was frustrated to hear that his plans had been interrupted and that his wait for a home-cooked meal had been prolonged. Anyone in his situation would have been. But he also acknowledged that getting worked up about it wasn't going to get him home any sooner. So instead of allowing his emotions to spiral downward and using each layover to tweet at the airline in anger, he embraced the situation and made the most of it. He focused on positive things he would take away from the experience, like having had Chicago deep-dish pizza in O'Hare Airport, along with a cool war story he gets to tell years down the road. "Despite getting home six hours behind schedule, I enjoyed the journey," he told me. He was able to reframe the experience and was happier for it. The next time you face the "horrors" of a flight delay or long wait on the runway, think of comedian Louis C.K., who put it so succinctly to late-night host Conan O'Brien: "Did you just fly through the air incredibly, like a bird? Did you partake in the miracle of human flight...? Everybody on every plane should just constantly be going, 'Oh my God! Wow!' You're flying! You're sitting in a chair, in the sky!...People say there's delays on flights. Delays, really? New York to California in five hours. That used to take thirty years!" Travel delays are unavoidable, but putting it all into perspective can turn an inconvenience into a great story.

We cannot cherry-pick our daily circumstances, but we *can* choose how to weather them. As Maya Angelou once said, "You can tell a lot about a person by the way they handle three things: a rainy day, lost luggage, and tangled Christmas tree lights." Though it's easier said than done, having a positive mindset and a sense of humor in moments like these helps us take life's daily hassles in stride and can prevent us from blowing things out of proportion. That may have been what led the happiest nuns to live the longest. It's as if their happy demeanors allowed them to sip from the fountain of youth.

CARRYOVER EFFECTS IN THE SHORT TERM

The nun study showed us that finding happiness in day-to-day routines can carry over and affect the long run, including the length of our lives. Happiness can also benefit us in the short run.

Each week in my Psychology of Young Adulthood course, I ask the students to report the worst thing that happened to them that week. The comments cover everything from homesickness to breakups to a frozen yogurt shortage in the dining hall. Once the fifth week of school arrives, however, a darker shadow passes over the student body: *midterms*. Many students work themselves into a frenzy of all-nighters and nail-biting apprehension, furiously reviewing notes and forecasting the toll bad assessments could take on their grades and future careers. But this is not a good recipe for test performance. Such angst can be costly to mental clarity.

When facing the final minutes before an exam, a better strategy would be to stop studying altogether. Instead think of a pleasant memory or do something you enjoy. Right before each of his exams, one of my students puts down his class notes and picks up a table tennis paddle:

> "I realized that the extra thirty minutes of studying before the exam may not be the best use of my time. Instead of building up extra stress before I need to take an exam, I learned that I performed better when I took those thirty minutes to relax and do something fun. Being able to put myself in a good mood is something that has helped me out quite a bit while in college. I can be more focused while writing essays, I socialize better with other people in instances where I need to, but most importantly, I am able to perform better on quizzes or exams."

Table tennis sends him into the exam feeling relaxed instead of worried. His happier state likely accounts for his improved performance, according to research by Dr. Barbara Fredrickson, a scientist at the University of North Carolina. She finds that emotions like joy and contentment broaden our cognitive skills and enable our brains to build on their capacity to solve challenging problems.[17] This notion forms the basis of her aptly named "broaden-and-build theory of positive emotions." Fredrickson has shown that students who spend just sixty seconds calling to mind happy moments from their lives significantly improve their intellectual performance, creativity, and attention.

Dr. Fredrickson finds that the reverse is also true. Negative emotions restrict our ability to think clearly and rationally, causing performance to suffer. Getting worked up before a stressful cognitive task therefore is not only unpleasant, but also may be counterproductive. Instead find something fun to do. Think of something you are looking forward to this weekend. Listen to a playlist you love. Call or text a friend. Put down your notes and let your mind breathe. Play a quick game of table tennis. The positivity you get from any of those activities will ultimately sharpen your cognitive skills and strengthen your performance.

None of this advice is intended to condone procrastination. If you haven't put work into preparing for the exam, there won't be anything to broaden or build. But once you've put in adequate preparation, you'll be much better served by spending the moments leading up to the exam activating positivity instead of anxiety.

REVERSING THE PATTERN: THE UNDOING HYPOTHESIS

Just as positive emotion can carry over to improve our performance on later tasks, it can also be used to quiet down negativity in response to something unpleasant. A few years ago the *Washington Post* ran an article identifying America's greatest fears.[18] Twenty-two percent of those polled were afraid of bugs and snakes. Twenty-four percent were afraid of heights. But the biggest phobia the article identified was public speaking. In some polls, fear of giving a talk in front of others is rated even higher than fear of death. As Jerry Seinfeld once pointed out, "This means to the average person, if you have to go to a funeral, you're better off in the casket than doing the eulogy."

Still, like it or not, public speaking is a challenge that most young adults have to face at some point, be it for a class assignment, presentation at work, or wedding toast. So how best to tackle this challenge and the inevitable anxiety that accompanies it? Positivity. In one study college students were asked to prepare a three-minute speech they were told would be recorded and evaluated by their peers.[19] That by itself was enough to make them uncomfortable. To ramp up anxiety levels even further, they were given only sixty seconds to formulate their thoughts. Immediately following this quick prep, they were shown a short video. For some the video was pleasant—a puppy playing in nature. For others it was sad—a family in distress.

All the while the students were attached to machines measuring cardiovascular reactivity like increases in heart rate and blood pressure, which are objective measures of stress. Not surprisingly, stress levels increased significantly as the participants prepared their speeches. But for those who watched the puppy, cardiovascular reactivity was *less* than for those who watched the more distressing clip. In other words, doing something positive alleviated some of the stress the students had built up preparing for and thinking about their impending speeches. Here we find another carryover effect of positive emotion: the ability to redirect attention from negativity. Dr. Fredrickson calls this the "undoing hypothesis," arguing that positive emotions minimize the impact of negative events.[20] "Positive emotions," she says, "may loosen the hold that a negative emotion has gained on that person's mind."[21]

The next time you are feeling bummed out from a low score on an exam, an argument with your significant other, or a dessert you've attempted to make that looks nothing like it did on Pinterest, don't let that misery linger. Find something to loosen its hold. You might make plans to go out with friends, watch your favorite TV show, or watch a funny YouTube video. It won't completely take away the sting (remember, those negative emotions have a purpose), but it will at least redirect your attention. Use a similar technique when you are preparing for anxiety-provoking events. If you are studying for a major exam, practicing for a big presentation, or preparing for an important job interview, take positivity breaks. At least once an hour, get up, move around, and do something that you enjoy. When you return to your work, you'll feel refreshed, your brain will be in a better position to build on the work you've already done, and the challenge awaiting you won't seem so daunting.

After I covered this topic in my class one semester, one of my students told me how she began to make small changes to her routines:

> "Being a premed, everything is about achievement for me. Better grades, more productive studying, and more positive outcomes. Just small tweaks in the way I study have definitely made an impact: I make sure to leave time for a leisurely walk through campus on my way to exams. Instead of spending the last ten minutes cramming every piece of information I can into my head, I have started to listen to Beyoncé's 'Formation' on repeat."

Whether it's listening to your favorite song, taking the long way to class, or giving your attention to positive things happening around you, a small behavior can make the difference between a mediocre day and a happier day.

These carryover benefits also extend beyond our psychological health and into our physical health. Dr. Robert Cloninger, a noted physician who has studied the medical ramifications of well-being, recently spoke about this on St. Louis Public Radio. In response to a caller asking about the benefits of positivity and laughter on stress, he explained that humor increases the flexibility of our minds and enables us to gain new insight into our stressors. "If you're sad, you have an inflammation of your brain, there's stress that impairs memory, and there's an effect on the immune system," he said. "The whole body goes into a state of dysfunction when we don't have a sense of the joy of life."[22] In some cases, therefore, laughter really is the best medicine. It heals body and mind at the same time.

Both the nun study and the broaden-and-build framework help us understand the long- and short-term benefits of happiness in young adulthood. A positive mindset can shift our perspective and minimize the impact of negativity in our lives. It can also lead to a longer life.

The natural next question is a big one: Beyond shifting perspective, what can we actually *do* to increase our happiness? The answer is a multifaceted one (see chapters 1 through 10!) but begins with how we physically carry ourselves. The expressions we assume on our faces and the postures we hold with our bodies are, literally, positioning our sense of well-being.

WHAT'S IN A SMILE?

One of the most important decisions young adults make is whom to spend their time with, and potentially whom to spend their entire lives with. People meet in bars, at parties, and of course online. The decision to approach that cute guy or girl across the way, to message the profile picture on the OkCupid feed, or to swipe right on Tinder is a quick one based on limited information. Or so it seems. When it comes to someone's smiling face, research shows there may be more than meets the eye.

A few years ago, scientists at the University of California got their hands on 1950s yearbooks from nearby Mills College, an all-women institution in the Bay Area. They flipped to the senior class pictures and began analyzing the smile of each student. The telltale sign of a genuine smile is crow's-feet alongside the eyes. This creates a Duchenne smile, named for the nineteenth-century neurologist who discovered the role of one's eyes in displaying authentic happiness. If the corners of a student's mouth went up but her eye muscles were uninvolved, she was giving a courtesy smile, kind of like the expression I would give my grandmother when she gave me white tube socks for Christmas every year.

In their yearbook photos, about half of the Mills students exhibited Duchenne smiles. What was most interesting was the predictive power those smiles held. Shortly after the yearbook photos were taken in the 1950s, the women completed a series of personality inventories and were observed in a number of social settings such as interviews, group discussions, and mealtime conversations. Those with Duchenne smiles in their yearbook photos were also the most nurturing, caring, sociable, and cheerful. Remarkably, this effect held over the life span. At ages twenty-seven, forty-three, and fifty-two, they were still just as jovial and gregarious as they had been as young adults. What's more, those with the happiest expressions in their yearbook photos at age twenty-one had a higher likelihood of being married by their late twenties. They also enjoyed higher-quality marriages when compared to their less emotionally expressive counterparts.[23]

As we've seen with other studies so far in this chapter, happiness is not confined merely to a given moment. Young nuns who were happier went on to live longer, young adults in good moods performed better on tests, and now we see that the quality of a college student's smile predicted what kind of relationship partner she would be later in life.

TRICKING OUR BRAINS INTO HAPPINESS

An old adage tells us, "Sometimes your joy is the source of your smile, but sometimes your smile is the source of your joy." Although this saying is older than the field of positive psychology itself, it has been backed by recent scientific findings. Researchers at the University of Illinois found that when students were smiling, they rated *Far Side* cartoons as funnier than when they were frowning. The students, however, didn't even know they were smiling or frowning. Half were told to hold a pen using only their lips, and the other half were told to hold it using only their teeth. Try it for yourself. You can't hold a pen in your teeth without smiling, or in your lips without frowning.

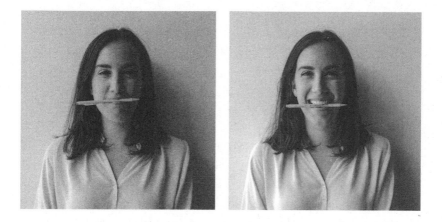

Usually we feel happy about something and then smile in response. This study shows that it's possible to reverse that pattern. Students found the cartoons funnier in the pen-in-teeth condition not because they were feeling happier, but simply because they were exercising their smile muscles. You may have heard the phrase, "Cells that fire together wire together." Because happiness activates the facial muscles that lead us to smile, the brain cells that govern both happiness and our smile muscles fire at the same time. Activating one will automatically activate the other. The simple act of smiling is enough to trigger the emotional experience of happiness.

Think about this as you go about your day. When you are walking across campus, standing in a long line at a store, or waiting for a meal at the dining hall, give a smile. It doesn't have to be over the top—in fact, if it feels forced it can backfire (kind of like forcing yourself not to think of that polar bear). But just a small grin can turn a mundane moment into something pleasant. It can also have a cascading effect, stimulating pleasant memories and putting us on the lookout for other pleasant things in the environment. Remember, the happiest nuns lived longer not because their objective realities were any different from their counterparts in the convent. Rather, it had to do with what they chose to focus on, and the mindsets that created positivity in their lives. And when happiness was hard to find, one way they may have created it was by using their smiles to be the source of their joy.

EMOTION AS A FULL-BODY EXPERIENCE

The pen-in-teeth study demonstrates that our mood can be affected simply by the movement of our facial muscles. The same principle applies to the way we stand or sit. Our emotional states manifest in our entire bodies. Researchers at Columbia and Harvard tested this by positioning forty-two college students in either high-power poses, with feet apart and arms open wide, or low-power poses, with limbs closed and hands folded in their laps.[24] To ensure they weren't primed about the study's true purpose, the students were not explicitly told they were in "high-power" or "low-power" poses. Instead they were given a cover story that this study was testing the accuracy of electrodes placed on their bodies in locations relative to their hearts. The researchers gave instructions like, "Keep your feet above heart level by putting them on the desk in front of you."[25] This ensured a high-power stance.

After just two minutes with their bodies in these positions, high-power posers reported feeling more "powerful" and "in charge." Their expansive presences also increased the production of testosterone (a hormone associated with strength and dominance), and decreased the release of cortisol (the primary stress hormone). A simple adjustment of their bodies' positions led to changes that were both psychological and biological.

GET YOUR HEAD (AND YOUR BODY) IN THE GAME

Our emotions and thoughts are full-body experiences. Mounds of evidence show how the movement and position of our bodies affect our well-being, a phenomenon psychologists call embodied cognition. One study found that young adults who flexed their muscles exerted more willpower and self-control, choosing healthy snacks like apples over unhealthy alternatives like chocolate[26]—when the body felt strong, the mind felt strong. Another study found that participants sitting upright in their chairs showed significantly greater persistence on challenging puzzles than those who slouched[27]—a confident stance led to confident performance.

Take note of your body. When you are about to go on an interview, take an exam, or ask someone out on a date, be mindful of how you are holding yourself. Standing tall, assuming an expansive stance, and donning a slight smile is literally positioning yourself for success. One of my students started doing this after a series of rocky job interviews her senior year: "I am already a pretty shy person, and during the interviews I would feel very intimidated and that I lacked authority in my answers," she said. Her feeble demeanor became a thing of the past once she learned about power posing.

"Before my next interview I went into the bathroom and stood with my arms and legs wide and my chest out and chin up. I felt much more confident and relaxed during the interview itself. I felt that I had more energy in my discussions, that I could think better on my feet, and I just felt more sure about what I was saying. More than this, it was a long day of about five interviews. It could have been tiring, but before each interview I went into the bathroom to power pose and get myself psyched."

If a smile can be the source of your joy, a power pose may be the source of your confidence. And for my student, it may also have been the source of a job offer.

————

Alchemists spent centuries looking for the philosopher's stone. They believed it would transform their lead into gold, rejuvenate their spirits, and extend their lives. Of course, no such thing exists, and attempts to find it will prove futile—much like the promises offered by the "Living a Life of Joy" speaker on my campus a few years ago. Still, in a metaphorical sense, young adults are pining for the same things the alchemists were after—a psychological wealth that allows for a long, happi*er* life. Attaining *that* kind of wealth however does not require magic. Positivity can transform hassles into something manageable, inject a dose of vitality into stressful situations, and even lengthen our very lives. Tune into your behaviors and mindsets and suddenly those things are achievable.

Now that we have established the tenets of positive psychology and that the pursuit of happiness is indeed worthwhile, let's take a tour through the behaviors and mindsets that promote authentic happiness in young adulthood. It's time to sit tall and smile.

2

The Common Denominator of Happiness

A sweet aroma filled the ice cream shop in Lower Manhattan's Chinatown. Two college students, both in New York City for summer internships, met there to catch a taste of its famed exotic flavors while they caught up on each other's lives. The first student perused the options and then selected one scoop that was bright pink and another of beautiful green.

"What flavors are those?" her friend asked with wonder.

"I don't know, I just picked them because of their colors."

The first student then scoped out the room for a table with good lighting.

"I'm gonna get a perfect shot for my Instagram," she said.

She snapped picture after picture until her culinary masterpiece started to melt. With ice cream dribbling down her hand, she began to look around the room once more. This time it was for a trash can. What good is an ice cream cone on a hot summer day if it's no longer Instagram-worthy?

IT'S ALL ABOUT THE LIKES

Documenting their lives on social media has become, for many young adults, a necessary component of any worthwhile experience. As one of my students describes it, "Social events are often so consumed by taking pictures that THAT is what the substance of the experience becomes. Taking pictures IS the experience."

Across social media platforms, students carefully monitor what they post and how it will be perceived:

> "My friends are constantly checking their Instagrams to see how many likes they received on their latest post. They are comparing the number of likes they get to the number of likes others get, along with the number of followers they have and the number of comments they receive. When we change our profile pictures on Facebook, we are sure not to do so too late at night or too early in the morning because we are concerned about maximizing the number of likes we can get. And the 'acceptable' number has increased this year; it is pretty much embarrassing to get less than sixty likes on a profile picture, and one hundred is desired."

Many studies have found a relationship between social media use and unhappiness: the more time people spend on it, the less happy they tend to be. The challenge with most of this research is that it is correlational. As any stats professor will tell you ad nauseam, correlation does not imply causation. Although it could be the case that Facebook use drives down happiness, it could just as easily follow that underlying unhappiness *prompts* a person to tap the bright blue *F* on their phones more often, to see who attended the best parties over the weekend or get a glimpse of their crazy uncle's political views.

Recently, however, a team of psychologists from the University of Michigan in Ann Arbor and the University of Leuven in Belgium developed a clever study to establish whether a causal link exists.[1] They recruited a group of eighty-two young adults, who responded to text messages sent at random times over the course of two weeks. Each asked them to report both their happiness in that moment and how much they had been using Facebook.

The longitudinal nature of this study enabled the researchers to test whether emotional or behavioral experiences at one point in time affected their emotional or behavioral experiences the next time they received a text from the researchers. Overall, when participants reported they had been spending a lot of time on Facebook, they reported lower levels of happiness the next time they were asked. The reverse pathway did not hold: feeling unhappy did not necessarily predict they would be on Facebook the next time they were asked. Because Facebook use reliably predicted subsequent mood, but not the other way around, we can take this result to mean that Facebook has a *causal* influence on well-being. The more we use it, the worse we feel.

But why? What is it about Facebook, Instagram, or any other social media platform that could damage well-being?

HEDONIC ADAPTATION

One of the basic premises of the human condition is that we are adaptable. This affects us on nearly every level, both psychological and physical. Think about the last time you spent an afternoon in a movie theater or another dark space on a bright sunshiny day. In the dark environment, your pupils would have become large to let in whatever small amount of light was available. When you stepped outside into the sunshine, the abundant daylight flooding into your large pupils likely caused some discomfort, leading you to squint and shield your eyes. After a few moments, though, your pupils automatically adjusted to a smaller size appropriate for the sunshine, eliminating the need to squint, even though there may have been just as much sunshine as when you first stepped out.

This phenomenon is due to a natural process of adaptation. Our bodies adjust to accommodate changes in our environment. When we are hot, we sweat to cool down; when we are cold, we shiver to create warmth. These are two of the body's natural ways of returning us to our baseline.

The same goes for psychological reactions to life's circumstances. Consider the last time you bought a new phone. At first you probably couldn't wait to show off your new purchase to those around you. You were so impressed with the features of its apps and quality of its camera. After a while, however, the novelty wore off and it simply became normal to have a phone with those capabilities. I remember the first time I bought a smartphone, and the sales rep tried to convince me to buy a model with 16 GB of storage. "Sixteen gigs of storage?" I asked, perplexed. "What on earth would I possibly need all of that for?" I was astonished that the least I could get was 8 GB. Compared to the storage on the flip phone I had been using up to that point, 8 GB seemed to be more than I could possibly need.

That was, until I became accustomed to the number of pictures and videos I could take so easily, and the many apps that counted my steps during the day, allowed me to download my favorite tunes, and told me if it was going to be snowing in ten days. Those 8 GB filled up quickly, prompting me to upgrade to a model with 64 GB. Just as our pupils adjust to accommodate the amount of light trying to enter our eyes, our psyche makes adjustments to accommodate the level of wealth or luxury we are experiencing...including how much storage we "need" in a mobile device. Even lottery winners—those who get enough money for a life of luxury that previously existed only in their wildest imaginations—adapt to those conditions within about a year.[2]

One of my premed students experienced this within just weeks of learning she had been accepted to medical school.

"I remember sitting in class, checking my phone, when I suddenly got the e-mail that I had dreamed about for so long—the digital acceptance letter that I had been awaiting for months. I immediately jumped out of my seat and ran out of the lecture to call my parents with the good news. I started crying hysterically because of the sheer tidal wave of happiness that overcame me."

Within a week, however, her happiness started to fade.

"As my friends congratulated me and my parents asked more and more questions, I realized that I was no longer 'happy' about my acceptance. Let me be clear—I was without a doubt satisfied with the fact that I had accomplished this tremendous life goal, but I wasn't necessarily excited or enthusiastic about it. My accomplishment seemed like the 'new normal,' not a grandiose event deserving of celebration."

A few years ago, the *St. Louis Post-Dispatch* ran a story about a local girl who at age twenty-one had achieved what many spend their entire lives pining after: a leading role in a Broadway musical. Countless young people dream of performing on Broadway, but only a select few get to live the reality. What did she have to say about her experience after just three months as star of the show, delivering nightly performances in front of thousands of people on the glamorous Great White Way? It felt, well, "like a job."

"I know how lucky I am!" she acknowledged in the same breath. "It's just, you get used to it."[3]

She's exactly right. We get used to things. Psychologists refer to this as hedonic adaptation. Even the thrill of fulfilling a childhood dream by landing a starring role on Broadway will fade with time. Some call this pattern the hedonic treadmill—no matter how much luxury and glamour we add to our lives, eventually our expectations about what we *should* have will catch up to the once highly coveted fortune that we currently have. One way of thinking about this is with the following formula:[4]

$$\text{Happiness} = \frac{\text{What We Have}}{\text{What We Want}}$$

Our happiness depends not only on what our lives are *actually* like, but also what we *want* them to be like. Mathematically speaking, we can modify our happiness in one of two ways: by increasing the numerator (What We Have) or by decreasing the denominator (What We Want). Most of us are aware of the first strategy. We work tirelessly to secure a high-paying job, surround ourselves with luxury "stuff," and post our adventures and possessions on social media to boast about just how large that numerator has become. But just as our eyes automatically adapt to the sunshine after a movie, our sense of well-being adapts to the belongings and status we have acquired. New gadgets, larger paychecks, and scores of Instagram likes on our every

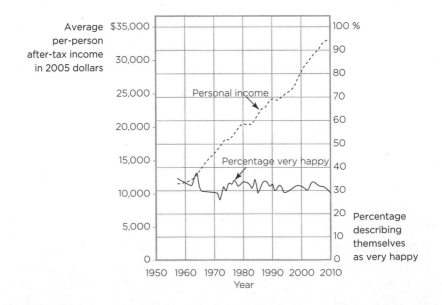

post become the new normal. What We Want quickly catches up to What We Have.

This also explains why happiness levels have remained the same even though per capita income has nearly tripled over the last fifty years, even when adjusting for inflation: yes, we have a lot more, but we also *expect* a lot more.

My dad grew up in a family of seven sharing three bedrooms, one bathroom, one telephone, one sixteen-inch black-and-white television set, and no air conditioning. The kids always looked forward to going to their uncle Sam's house, which had a *color* television and a climate-controlled home equipped with *central air*. What a treat on a hot St. Louis day.

This was a way of life in the 1960s. At the time, most homes did not have air conditioning or a dishwasher,[5] the closest thing to Instagram was a Polaroid camera, and if you had an apple or blackberry they were ingredients for a pie instead of mobile devices that allowed instant access to what was going on around the world. Nowadays most of us would not even consider a home with such austere living conditions. In fact, we would probably go so far as to say that we would be *unhappy* without air conditioning to keep us cool in the summer, or dishwashers to make cleanup after dinner a breeze. And the thought of a home without Wi-Fi offering instant GIFs of cats playing piano or blog posts revealing the missteps of celebrities? Forget about it.

Still, there was a time not all that long ago when people made do in these exact circumstances. And they were no less happy than we are today. The reason? Without lofty expectations about luxurious living standards, our parents and grandparents could maintain happiness even with very little. For the mathematically inclined, it happened the following way: the denominator of the formula on page 30 was a lot smaller, which meant it didn't take as much to bring the numerator to a happiness-yielding quotient. Our forerunners' modest lifestyles—free of smartphones, fancy vacations, and yes, even air conditioning—were enough for a happy life. Of course, our grandparents' What I Want category was not small in their eyes; it is just smaller than ours now. Even though they didn't have much by today's standards, their expectations about the good life were far more moderate—which kept the equation balanced.

WHAT YOU'VE GOT DETERMINES MY HAPPINESS

Social media, in particular, has made it easier than ever to increase What We Want. One of my students told me about a breakup her roommate recently suffered:

> "After they broke up, she had the overwhelming urge to look at her boyfriend's Facebook and Instagram pages—constantly checking to see who is 'winning' postbreakup. Who is now dating the more attractive person? Who is going on the best vacations? Who has lost the most weight? Who is happier?"

We naturally compare ourselves with those around us. Our feelings about our wealth, our material possessions, or who is "winning" a breakup are closely tied to others' experiences. Regardless of what we do have, social comparison wreaks its havoc by manipulating what we want. And with others' circumstances as our barometer, we can be led to make decisions that are *objectively* worse for us so long as they are *relatively* better than someone else's.

Consider the following scenario that psychologists Amos Tversky and Dale Griffin once posed to a group of college students:[6]

> "Imagine that you have just completed a graduate degree in communications and you are considering one-year jobs at two different magazines.
>
> "(A) At Magazine A, you are offered a job paying $35,000. However, the other workers who have the same training and experience as you do are making $38,000.

"(B) At Magazine B, you are offered a job paying $33,000. However, the other workers who have the same training and experience as you do are making $30,000."

The seemingly logical conclusion is that a higher salary would correspond with higher satisfaction. But the data did not fall into that pattern. Nearly two-thirds of the students said the position they would find most satisfying would be at Magazine B—the one with the salary that was *relatively* more than that of their colleagues, even though it was *objectively* less than the salary at Magazine A. It's worth noting that the majority said they would actually choose the option with the objectively higher salary in the end. But it was the second option that would make them feel better about their earnings. A pay cut, it turns out, was worth it so long as they were one-upping their peers.

This study was hypothetical, but scientists have also turned to data sets of actual working people to understand how comparison affects the feelings we hold toward our wealth. In 2010 a team of scientists from the University of Warwick published a study in which they measured the income levels and life satisfaction of more than ten thousand adults living in Britain.[7] They found no association between a person's salary and his or her emotional well-being, which was consistent with previous research. This study, however, dug a little deeper than most, taking into consideration another piece of the puzzle: the average income of each person's neighbors.

By analyzing the British Household Panel Survey, researchers were able to compare each person's salary with the annual earnings of others living nearby. This allowed them to take into consideration how much each person earned, and whether those wages were higher or lower than the wages of those around them. Sure enough, it was the *rank* of a person's income when compared to their neighbors, rather than total income, that predicted feelings of life satisfaction. These findings support the rank-income hypothesis, which holds that we feel good about ourselves not according to what we have, but according to how our goods measure up to what those around us have.

Earning more money or achieving more power doesn't necessarily bring more happiness when we have expectations that are based on what everyone else has. All of this helps to explain why there has been no real increase in Americans' happiness, even though their wealth continues to increase. Just as wealth has increased (which increases the numerator), so too have standards for comparison (which increases the denominator even more). Someone who lives in a four-thousand-square-foot home and drives a BMW is not guaranteed to be satisfied with his lot in life. If everyone else on the street boasts dwelling places twice the size, with Maseratis and Ferraris parked out front, the BMW owner may well feel that his accommodations are paltry—even unsatisfying—by comparison.

This is consistent with the thought experiment Tversky and Griffin asked their students to consider years ago. Their data support the notion that job satisfaction does not depend on absolute salary alone. Most of the participants in that study reported they would derive more satisfaction not from the job that *actually* pays more, but from the one that pays *relatively* more.

Satisfaction, it seems, is tied not to our actual circumstances, but instead to our sense that we are just a little better off than those around us. So it would seem that the path to happiness is simply a matter of having more than those around us, right? Well, that may not be the best approach, either.

THE PUZZLE OF SOCIAL COMPARISON

Consider a study where college students were asked to complete anagrams, allegedly because the researchers were studying cognitive performance on problem-solving tasks.[8] The students were shown sets of scrambled letters, which they were to rearrange to form actual words. YOWNS became SNOWY, NOTIX became TOXIN, and so forth. The anagrams were moderately difficult, but most people were able to solve them with enough time. Critical to this experiment was that the study participants were not alone while completing the task. Nearby, and in plain view, was another individual working on the same task. Or so the participants were told. This other person was really an accomplice of the experimenter. Instead of spending time unjumbling the word clusters, the accomplice was actually performing the most important task of the entire study.

As the real participant worked furiously on the problems, the accomplice monitored her lab-mate's progress and worked either significantly faster or significantly slower. The pace at which each was going was evident to the other person. They had both been instructed to hand each anagram to the experimenter as it was completed. This indicated how quickly each person was completing the task, which enabled the accomplice to speed up or slow down her own progress and gave the actual study participant an index of how *someone else* was doing on the task.

Therein lay the true purpose of the study: to answer the question, Does it make a difference if another person is having an easier time or a harder time attempting a task we also are working on? The answer, it turns out, depended on the participants' happiness levels. Participants had been recruited for this study based on whether they were very high or very low on happiness, which the researchers had measured in prior studies.

The happiest students felt good about their performance regardless of how the accomplice was doing. Whether she was working faster or slower, the participant's overall mood was virtually unaffected. For those on the other end of the emotion continuum, it was a different story. The unhappiest participants felt good so long as their performance was relatively better than that of the other person in the room. If they were being outperformed, however, their mood took a significant drop. In other words, whether they felt good or bad depended almost entirely on how the accomplice was performing.

One of the differences between happy and unhappy people seems to be the standards they use to judge their abilities and feelings of self-worth. Happy people are guided by internal values and standards, and are largely unaffected by others who may be outperforming them. For unhappy people the opposite is true. They are highly sensitive to how others are doing and will feel good about themselves so long as they are doing at least a little better relative to those around them. It doesn't matter how delicious their ice cream is or how high their starting salary is, what matters is that what they have is more than what everyone else has.

A MATTER OF PERSPECTIVE

Theodore Roosevelt, twenty-sixth president of the United States, once said, "Comparison is the thief of joy." Now we have scientific evidence to back his claim. Even though it may feel as if social comparison is unavoidable given the way we consume media today, there are strategies for combating this tendency that don't involve giving up your Facebook feed cold turkey. Part of what makes the happiest young adults impervious to social comparison's toxic effects is where they place their attention when they encounter someone who seems better off. Instead of wallowing in FOMO (fear of missing out), one of my students shifts her focus away from comparison:

> "If I see someone who I appreciate, who works really hard, does incredible things, and succeeds, I can easily slip into jealousy. This is a spiraling path for me—my thoughts run away from me, thinking, 'How can they handle everything, why am I not doing that, why am I not as busy, I wish I'd gotten that internship or had that idea.' But I've found that if I instead actively congratulate them, support them, and make them feel proud and valued, I actually feel a lot better

myself. Doing this positive action takes up that space where a negative thought could have filled in otherwise."

That positive action is also preventing the denominator (What We Want) from growing any larger, adding to the numerator (What We Have) instead. Numerous studies have found that people who spend just a few minutes per week focusing on the good things in their lives (what they *have*) tend to be the happiest and most satisfied. Consider this student who found a simple shift in perspective made her feel happier:

"Instead of focusing on things that I don't have, I divert my attention to things that I do have. Sunshine after days of rain cheers me up. A smile from a stranger makes my day. A message from my parents reminds me that someone is caring for me. When I stop taking things for granted, I am constantly aware of the abundance of my life and I tend to recover quickly from adversity. Finding simple pleasure in small things not only makes me happier but also makes me more willing to help others. Being grateful has made all these possible because I become satisfied more easily."

Many studies have documented a link between gratitude and happiness. However, this result begs another chicken-and-egg question: Do grateful people experience more life satisfaction *because* they have more to be grateful for, or does gratitude *itself* produce life satisfaction? To answer this question we can look to experiments that randomly assign people to reflect on good things or bad things in their lives. This design ensures that individuals from modest backgrounds are just as likely to be practicing gratitude as those who drive luxury cars and vacation on tropical islands.

One study did this by asking hundreds of young adults to keep diaries in which they maintained weekly records of their lives.[9] Some of them were specifically told to recall positive things for which they were grateful each week. The other half were instructed to think of hassles—things that bothered or annoyed them. Take a look at sample entries from students in both groups:

Gratitude:
- "Waking up this morning"
- "Wonderful parents"
- "The Rolling Stones"

Hassles:
- "A messy kitchen no one will clean"
- "Finances depleting quickly"
- "Stupid people driving"

In addition to listing weekly blessings or hassles, the students gave weekly ratings of their well-being. By the end of the study, an interesting pattern emerged. Students who spent time each week reflecting on their blessings felt significantly better about their lives overall, were more optimistic about the week ahead, and even got sick less frequently than those writing about hassles. An investment that took only a few minutes each week paved the way for health and happiness throughout the semester. This study demonstrates that happier people are not simply more likely to practice gratitude. Gratitude itself *causes* increases in well-being.

ATTENDING TO THE NUMERATOR

Let's revisit the happiness formula:

$$\text{Happiness} = \frac{\text{What We Have}}{\text{What We Want}}$$

Remember that instructions in the gratitude study did not tell the students to acquire additional positive or negative experiences each week. Students in the gratitude condition weren't increasing their numerators by actually increasing the positive things in their lives; instead they were making their numerators larger by focusing more on the positive things they *already* had. This study has become one of the most celebrated in the field of Positive Psychology because it demonstrates the powerful tool we all have at our disposal to increase What We Have: the focus of our attention.

Attention is selective. It functions a bit like a spotlight. Try this: look around you and take note of everything in your environment that is red. You will probably start to see things you hadn't noticed before. Perhaps all the books on your shelf with red spines will pop out at you. Maybe a red water bottle sitting on your desk, or a pair of scissors with red handles, will enter your awareness. A few minutes ago, if someone had asked you about them, you might not have even noticed those things were there. But now that your attention is refocused, they are nearly impossible to miss.

The same goes for positive events in our lives. We might have a hundred things that we could be grateful for right now, but if we are not actively directing attention toward them, they become like the books on the shelf or the water bottle on the desk, virtually nonexistent. Each of us could easily have been a participant in either the gratitude or hassles group in that study. Without much effort we could easily call to mind blessings or hassles we encountered over the last week. This study shows us that it's not *how many* good or bad events we encounter that determines our happiness, but *which events* we choose to give our attention.

One of my students has found keeping a gratitude journal helps her to keep proper perspective in her life:

> "Every day, I write down a few of the things that are challenging me (and if I can do anything about them) and a few of the things that are going my way. I find it highly effective. Often I'll be having what I think is a bad day, but

when I start listing out all the small things that made me
happy, I realize that the day wasn't all that bad. It helps to
make the problems seem smaller. Before practicing gratitude,
I would have considered myself a pretty negative person,
but now I find that it's easier to be positive, especially among
other negative people."

While social comparison is all about the denominator because
it directs our attention to what we *want*, gratitude is all about the
numerator because it directs our attention to what we *have*.

Another of my students writes a note about what she is grateful for
each day. She keeps them in what she calls her YOLO jar, a reminder
that life is too short to ruminate on aggravations. "Even if I've had a
crappy day, I've always been able to find one thing that I was thankful
for. That makes the day feel so much better before I go to bed, and I
sleep thinking, 'Hey, today wasn't that awful.'"

The jar is stuffed to the brim with daily recollections of everyday
pleasures that otherwise might have faded to the background. It serves
as a reminder of everything she personally has in the numerator of her
happiness formula. It also provides a concrete way to recover from life's
tribulations. "When days do get particularly bad, and I am just down
in the dumps, pulling out a note that has a good memory attached to it
cheers me up." She credits this jar for helping her mold a more positive
outlook on life, noting that her optimism is at "its all-time high."

In a similar way, another of my students used a gratitude journal to
help her recover from a challenging time. She received it as a birthday
gift from her parents. "At first I began writing in it just for fun, and
I would write in it whenever I'd remember." That changed when she
broke up with her boyfriend a few weeks later. Initially she stopped
writing in it altogether because she lacked the motivation to do anything. Eventually she became desperate to turn things around. "I was
at such a low point in my life that I was willing to try anything in order

to be happy again. I had no idea where to start, but then I remembered my gratitude journal. I started writing in it that very day."

For the first month, she wrote daily about what she was grateful for, but with no apparent results. "I found thinking of things to be grateful for tedious and difficult." Gradually, however, she noticed a change. "After a month, finding things to be grateful for became easier. I started to notice things I was grateful for throughout the day. I noticed myself thinking more positively and finding the good in everything. The more I wrote in this journal the happier I became. It really helped me change my life, and I still write in this journal today because of how amazing the results can be."

Letter writing can be another way to focus on gratitude. Take a moment to think of someone from your past who has helped you or affected your life in a positive way. Perhaps it is a coach who taught you how to lose gracefully. Maybe it's a teacher who stayed after school to listen to your problems at home, or wrote you a recommendation letter when they could have said no. Or it may have been a casual acquaintance who was there for you when you found out a grandparent had died. Whoever those people are, there is a good chance they never got to see the long-lasting effect they had on you.

A team of researchers from the University of Pennsylvania had a group of adults think of such individuals from their own lives, and then write and deliver gratitude letters to them. It is an activity that does not require much time—perhaps fifteen minutes to write the letter, and less than an hour to meet with the individual—but the effects were long lasting.[10] Participants' happiness levels increased significantly over the following week, and remained higher than usual over the next month. In fact, the researchers found that writing gratitude letters is one of the strongest ways not only to *become* happier, but also to *stay* happier for weeks on end.

The lead author of the study, Dr. Martin Seligman, describes writing gratitude letters as a powerful tool for increasing authentic happiness "because it amplifies good memories about the past, and it forges a very strong bond with an important person from your past."[11]

One of my students uses birthdays as an opportunity to write gratitude letters to her closest friends. "Conversations are useful, but writing forces you to think more about what you want to say and how to express it," she says. As we will see in chapter 9, the act of putting our emotions into language by writing them out gives them deeper meaning. "It's a great opportunity for me to reflect on how fortunate I am, and relive specific memories that I would have otherwise forgotten. I look forward to writing these cards, and find that they help build and sustain friendships."

Be it with a YOLO jar, gratitude journal, or birthday letter, you can redirect attention to positive life events in seemingly countless ways. All of these strategies are effective because they shift focus from the happiness formula's denominator, What We Want, to the numerator, What We Have.

MAKING GRATITUDE A HABIT

As we have seen throughout this chapter, what we choose to give attention to in any given moment shapes our subsequent emotional experiences. Fortunately, for the most part we have control over our attention, and directing it intentionally can increase our happiness. But it's not just our emotional experiences that change. Our thought patterns can actually physically change our brains over time. In general, the more we use a particular part of the brain, the larger it becomes.

Consider for example a study of London taxi drivers from a few years ago.[12] To become certified, taxi drivers undergo intense training. The layout of London is among the most circuitous and complicated of any city in the world, with roughly twenty-five thousand streets yielding innumerable route combinations. It can take a taxi driver years to master. This process requires the dedicated service of brain regions like the hippocampus, which facilitates navigation skills and spatial memory. For new taxi drivers navigating the streets of London, the hippocampus must be in high gear to transfer passengers from one destination to another.

A question began to intrigue scientists: Would the hippocampus grow larger to accommodate its intense use among these taxi drivers? To find out, they measured its size and structure in aspiring cabbies before their training began, and again after they had been on the job for a few years. Sure enough, the hippocampus increased significantly after their training, and the longer a taxi driver was on the job, the larger the hippocampus became.[13]

For a long time, many scientists thought that the human brain was essentially fixed during adulthood. Though it undergoes many changes as a child develops, a lot of people thought that by our late teens or early twenties we had essentially "achieved" our adult brains and that there weren't many changes taking place thereafter. However, the last two decades have seen a boom in research showing us that the brain can in fact change over the course of our lives. Those changes are affected largely by the particular regions we use. In that way the brain is like a muscle: use it or lose it.

The more we use particular regions of the brain, like those responsible for memory or finger movement, the more the neural tissue around those regions grows. Cellists, for example, tend to have larger brain regions that correspond to the fingers of the left hand. If you've ever seen someone play a cello (or if you play yourself), you know that the fingers of the left hand are the real stars of the show, dancing up and down the fingerboard to produce the intricacies of a Brahms concerto or Bach chorale. Meanwhile the right hand is just grasping the bow, pushing it back and forth along the strings. Because the neural networks that govern the left hand are more active, they grow in size and become capable of playing even more intricate melodies over time. The same principle holds for virtually every thought, every behavior, and every emotion: the more we practice them, the larger the corresponding brain regions become, and the easier it is to engage in those behaviors or thought patterns in the future.

Just like the brains of taxi drivers and cellists, which became larger in areas that correspond to the behaviors those people practice the most, our brains will also change and develop based on the thoughts and activities we spend the most time engaged in. When we regularly think happy thoughts, regions of the brain that correspond to positive emotions become larger, and it becomes easier to think more positively in the future. When we think negative thoughts, the same happens for regions of the brain dedicated to negative emotion and in turn, negative thinking becomes more automatic.

Dr. Rick Hanson, a noted psychologist, explains how this works in the brain:[14]

> "If we rest our attention routinely on what we resent or regret—our hassles, our lousy roommate, what Jean-Paul Sartre called 'hell' (other people)—then we're going to build out the neural substrates of those thoughts and feelings.
>
> "On the other hand, if we rest our attention on the things for which we're grateful, the blessings in our life—the wholesome qualities in ourselves and the world around us; the things we get done, most of which are fairly small yet they're accomplishments nonetheless—then we build up very different neural substrates."

This especially comes into play in how we interpret neutral or ambiguous scenarios throughout our day. A lot of what we experience is completely open to interpretation. In one of my favorite *Peanuts* cartoons, Charlie Brown sees two girls off in the distance and immediately starts jumping to conclusions about the nature of their conversation. He automatically assumes they are talking about him, and that their commentary must be disparaging, sending him off sulking in depression. "Why does someone always have to spoil my day?!," he exclaims.

Charlie Brown is someone we might consider the eternal pessimist. He spends much of his time complaining and worrying about his life. His brain is well practiced at experiencing negative emotion. As a result, when he is confronted with a completely ambiguous scenario like two girls chatting—about as common and ordinary as an experience can get—that information is more likely to be interpreted by those well-practiced and well-developed negative neural substrates that Hanson mentions above. Charlie Brown's interpretation would likely be much different if he were in the habit of practicing positive thinking. Just as lifting heavy weights regularly strengthens muscles to make it easier to lift heavy things in the future, practicing positive thinking regularly builds neural substrates that make it easier to interpret neutral, ambiguous events with a bit more levity and positivity in the future.

When we put ourselves in the habit of calling to mind positive moments from the day—the great lunch we had with a friend, a funny joke we recently heard, or an upcoming trip we are excited about—it becomes easier over time to take a more positive mindset during other, more difficult moments of our day. We also become more aware of good things as they happen throughout the day because we are well-practiced at identifying them.

As we near the end of this chapter I want to share one more story of a student who learned this for herself:

"A couple years ago, my best friend and I started engaging in an intentional gratitude practice that we call our 'thankful fors.' Every night, right before we go to bed, we say five things we are grateful for. And every night I fall asleep with a smile on my face. During the first few weeks of our 'thankful fors,' the practice seemed forced. When I had a bad day, the last thing I wanted to do was pretend to be appreciative. Once we got into the swing of things, though, I noticed a change in mindset. I started noticing positive things that happened throughout my day, and taking a mental note. Now gratefulness is a habit. I've realized that finding something to be grateful for isn't hard. Telling each other what we are grateful for also has the added benefits of being a good way to hold each other accountable, to catch up, and to remind each other of things we are grateful for. We still continue this practice two years later: it has become one of my favorite parts of the day."

———————

$$\text{Happiness} = \frac{\text{What We Have}}{\text{What We Want}}$$

Every so often people will ask me, based on my review of the research, what the common denominator among the happiest young adults is. They usually expect me to respond by listing off things like wealth, education, or accomplishments. But none of those things predict happiness very well, especially considering how quickly we adapt to them. Instead I tell them that the common denominator of happiness has a lot to do with the denominator itself. The happiest young adults craft lives that ensure that *what they want* doesn't get larger than *what they have*. It's not that they keep their wants or expectations needlessly low, but they do keep them realistic and they revise them when necessary. And instead of increasing the numerator by posting their every move on social media or always keeping pace with the latest trends in technology and fashion, they call attention to *what they have* with the regular practice of gratitude.

The next time you feel the urge to scroll through Facebook, take a few minutes instead to list off a few good things that happened during the past week. The next time you start comparing yourself to others who seem more talented or more accomplished than you, redirect your attention instead to your own strengths, and opportunities you may have to build on them. And the next time you find yourself at an ice cream shop scrambling to get the perfect shot for your Instagram, focus instead on how much you are enjoying spending time with your friend. In all cases, you'll be keeping your denominator low and your numerator high.

3

A Healthy Mind in a Healthy Body

A friend of mine, Mary, attended college in the 1980s. This was before the days of text messaging, social media, or even e-mail. Communication took place either in person or on the phone. Mary often learned of her incoming calls by hearing another student exclaim from the other end of the dorm hallway, "Mary, the phone is for you!" Usually someone else would shout, "Which Mary?" (This being a Catholic college no fewer than half the girls on the floor were named Mary.) The first student would yell back, "Mary Z!"

Mary Z would then pause her Hall & Oates cassette tape, walk to the end of the hallway, and take the call in the phone alcove. The amount of space it provided was small, and the amount of privacy it offered was even smaller. But it was her only option. In fact, this was a way of life for college students in the 1980s. Most dorms had just one phone per floor. If a student wanted to talk to her significant other, ask Mom or Dad for money, or arrange a taxi ride to the airport, she would have to walk down the hall. And if someone else was using the floor phone at that time, she would have to walk back and try again later.

"We didn't know any differently," Mary Z explains, "so we just made do."

Fast-forward to today and we see quite a contrast. A recent *BuzzFeed*

47

article reports "Anna Kendrick's Shower Thoughts," including this one: "If I touch my phone in the right places, a pizza will show up at my front door."[1]

Whether or not Ms. Kendrick actually came up with this thought in the shower, the idea behind it is real. Nowadays we can whip out our phones to make calls whenever we'd like. We can also use them to surf the web, check e-mail, play games, watch movies, shop, read the day's news, find out what concerts are coming to town, and, yes, even order pizza delivery. The technology of today allows us to accomplish most daily tasks with the click of a button, from the comfort of wherever we are right now, without actually *going* anywhere. And without a reason to go anywhere, many people stay seated in front of a screen all day. Mary Z's generation actually had to get up and out of their rooms to do those things. Tough break for them.

Or was it?

One study found that the amount of time young people spent idle using a computer for recreational purposes or playing video games increased by more than 40 percent between 2004 and 2009 alone.[2] That translates to the average adolescent's spending eight hours per day watching TV, using a computer, or engaging in other sedentary behaviors. The World Health Organization reported in 2017 that more than 80 percent of the world's adolescent population does not get sufficient physical activity.[3] Many find this inactivity appealing. The root of that word *sedentary* is the Latin *sedere*, which literally means "to sit." A sedentary lifestyle is ultimately characterized by a lot of sitting, a seemingly neutral (if anything, pleasant) behavior. And yet the word *sedentary* has acquired a negative connotation. But why? Can sitting be all that bad? Well, research is now showing that diminished physical activity is in fact a hefty price to pay for technology's advances. In other words, maybe it wasn't such a tough break for Mary Z's generation after all.

SITTING IS THE NEW SMOKING

In 2012 Dr. Martha Grogan, a cardiologist at the Mayo Clinic in Minnesota, told the *Wall Street Journal*, "For people who sit most of the day, their risk of heart attack is about the same as smoking."[4] Two years later, in 2014, high-profile news outlets including NBC News,[5] CBS News,[6] the *Huffington Post*,[7] and *Time* magazine[8] all featured articles claiming that "sitting is the new smoking." That same year, in an interview with the *Los Angeles Times*, endocrinologist Dr. James Levine—an obesity expert also at the Mayo Clinic—took this a step further, saying, "Sitting is more dangerous than smoking, kills more people than HIV and is more treacherous than parachuting. We are sitting ourselves to death."[9] On a physical level, extended periods of inactivity increase our risk of cancer, heart disease, diabetes, and obesity.[10] In a longitudinal study conducted by scientists at the University of South Carolina, participants who had spent more than twenty-three hours per week engaged in sedentary behaviors like watching TV or riding in a car when they were younger had as much as a 37 percent greater risk of dying from cardiovascular disease later in life.[11]

Although everyone knows that exercise is important for our physical health, many are surprised to learn the vast array of benefits psychologically. Setting ourselves into motion increases our happiness, our motivation, and our ability to stay focused on our goals.

A NATURAL MOOD BOOSTER

One of my students started playing tennis when she was a young child, and continued throughout all of grade school and high school. She estimates that she has played either competitively or recreationally "at least a couple times a week since the age of eight." However, when she left for college, she decided to leave her racket behind. "I was anxious about trying out for club tennis and not making the touring team, so I told myself it wasn't something that meant very much to me." Without all the demands and commitments that come from playing for a team—a way of life that had dominated every school year since first grade—she was in complete control of how she spent her time, crafting her schedule as she wished. "The newfound freedom and time was amazing," she said.

But within a year she began to notice that the free time in her schedule wasn't the only thing that had changed. "By sophomore year I struggled with feeling sluggish and gaining weight, which were issues I hadn't struggled with much before, considering I'd always been very active. My sluggishness led to me not wanting to hang out with friends as much outside of my suite and to my inability to pay attention to my homework. I started skipping classes out of sheer laziness." She had previously been an excellent student, and the culprit behind her indifference was evident: she was no longer physically active.

Fortunately, she turned things around during a study-abroad program her junior year. "I had a British roommate who loved working out and convinced me to get a gym membership with her. We started going to various classes and I started to understand the value of eating healthy and lifting weights." She started to feel better about herself and her ability to stay focused on her work. The benefits were so great that, in addition to souvenirs and an appreciation for a new culture, she brought back with her the desire to keep up with her exercise regimen. "I've been going to a boxing gym for about eight months now and absolutely love it. Exercising a couple of times a week has had such a positive impact. It raises my positivity like nothing else and puts me in such an upbeat mood."

This tennis player turned boxer experienced firsthand what a number of studies on the topic have found. In an analysis of nearly fifteen thousand undergraduate students from more than ninety colleges and universities across the United States, scientists from the University of Minnesota found a link between physical activity and a whole host of positive mental health outcomes. Their study asked each participant the following: "Think back over the past 7 days. On how many days did you exercise or participate in physical activity for at least 20 minutes that made you sweat or breathe hard, such as basketball, soccer, running, swimming laps, bicycling, or similar aerobic activities?" Those who had engaged in vigorous physical activity for at least three days of the last seven reported better mental health over the past month than their inactive counterparts. In particular, the active students were happier, calmer, and more confident in their ability to handle personal problems, and had an overall feeling that things were going their way. They also were less likely to report being nervous or stressed, or that insurmountable difficulties were piling up for them. These effects held regardless of the participant's sex, race, weight, year in school, or socioeconomic background, or even whether they had been physically active in high school.[12]

These findings suggest a very simple premise: engaging in vigorous exercise regularly carries benefits for you. Yes, you. It doesn't matter where you are from or what external circumstances are unique to your life, exercise will make you happier. Even if you were not physically active earlier in your life, it's not too late to get started. The Centers for Disease Control and Prevention recommend at least 150 minutes per week of moderate-intensity aerobic activity, which can even include brisk walking or light jogging.[13] The good news is that you don't have to do it all at once—you can break it into ten-minute increments throughout the week. And it doesn't matter what you do to get moving. You don't need specialized shoes or equipment or to sign up for a 10K or expensive spin class at the start. Get outside for a few minutes in between classes or meetings. Bike to your job. Catch a game of pickup basketball before dinner. Just about any activity that gets your heart rate elevated will work.* It's about finding something that you enjoy and that is realistic for you.

RESTORING ENERGY

Willie Geist, a popular TV personality on the morning show *Today*, has to wake up at three thirty a.m. to make it to work on time. He was once asked what helps him maintain energy throughout the day. His answer: exercise. "I used to find it annoying when superfit people in tight Lululemon gear said working out gives you energy and makes you feel better, but it turns out there's something to it. A workout in the middle of the day really does revive you and buy you a couple more hours."[14]

Most young adults would do anything for a couple more hours in the day. Although it is impossible to add more time, exercise can enhance your ability to capitalize on the time you *do* have. One of my students told me that exercise provides an energy boost to help her tackle the day's work:

> "As a college student, each day can be incredibly busy, but sparing even thirty minutes to exercise can make a big change in my productivity and overall happiness for the day. I've found that the energy I exert while I exercise carries through the rest of my day."

It seems counterintuitive. Usually when people are tired, the last thing they want to do is exert additional physical energy, especially

---

*According to the Centers for Disease Control and Prevention, you can calculate your target heart rate for moderate-intensity physical activity with two easy steps: First subtract your age from 220. Then calculate 50 percent and 70 percent of that value. These define your target heart rate range. So if you are 20, it should be between 100 and 140.

by exercising. However, getting up and moving around may be the best thing for anyone trying to catch that second wind. A study by scientists at the University of Georgia found that sedentary adults who engaged in low-intensity exercise for twenty minutes three times per week showed a 20 percent increase in energy and a 65 percent reduction in fatigue.[15]

These findings may be explained by the fact that exercise increases the production of mitochondria, the "energy factories" in your cells. More mitochondria means more energy. It's why Willie Geist is able to catch that second wind through exercise. When he finds it hard to keep his eyes open, a workout is what wakes him up. Though it may sound paradoxical, he is acting on what the research has shown: exercise literally creates energy in your body.

Of course, it is important not to exert *too much* energy, or the effects could backfire. Dr. Therese Pasqualoni, a behavioral therapist and personal trainer, offers the following precaution: "You should always aim to exercise in your low to moderate training heart rate range. This will prevent you from depleting your body, and help you avoid feeling fatigued, which would otherwise prevent you from getting the maximum energy benefits." One way to maximize these benefits, she says, is by eating something nutritious like a piece of fruit a few minutes beforehand. "This allows food, which is a form of energy, to be broken down and the nutrients enter the bloodstream, while preparing the body for work. The end result: You have more energy while you're working out—and more energy afterwards."[16]

SETTING THE STAGE FOR OTHER HEALTHY BEHAVIORS

Another benefit of exercising is the mindset that it creates, positioning us for other health-conscious behaviors. As one of my students told me, "When I am able to strike a balance between schoolwork and exercise I usually sleep better, eat better, and generally feel better day to day." Social psychologists have long studied priming, which is the effect that exposure to a concept has on subsequent behaviors. For example, one study found that holding a warm beverage led people to evaluate others as higher in "interpersonal warmth" than they did when they were holding something cold.[17] The warm beverage primed the person to sense warmth in others. Another study found that exposing people to words like *bold, bother, disturb, intrude, brazen, infringe,* and *obnoxious* made them more likely to interrupt the experimenter later in the study.[18] Activating rude concepts primed rude behavior.

In a similar way, exercise primes healthy living. When you make a decision to incorporate exercise into your daily routine, you are activating a mindset that leads you to make other healthy decisions. You take better care of yourself in the foods you eat, thoughts you entertain, and people you spend time with. As my student mentioned in the quote above, exercise also improves the quality of sleep at night, another important factor in our overall happiness and well-being. Studies conducted on adults around the world have shown that those who exercise regularly have an easier time falling asleep, remaining asleep, and getting better-quality sleep.[19] Taking that first run and then sticking with an exercise routine can set the stage for other behaviors that boost happiness throughout your day, and night.

AN UNEXPECTED BENEFIT

When I get to this topic in my Positive Psychology course, I ask my students to write thought papers about their experience with exercise and the impact it has on their lives as college students. Not surprisingly, many write about the benefits exercise provides in increasing their mood, health, sleep, and motivation. Those were the comments

I expected to see when I first assigned these papers. What I didn't expect was the number of students who listed *feeling sore* as a benefit. But many of them did. Apparently muscle soreness serves as a token of their progress, a physical manifestation of their hard work and what they are accomplishing. It reminds them they have done something good for themselves:

> "I really enjoy the pain and soreness that come with exercising. Feeling the soreness throughout the day reminds me that I have already done something useful before my first class. My legs hurt and yet feel amazing at the same time. I also have more confidence in myself. The simple fact that I am working my body each morning makes me feel good. Lastly, I think I sleep better on nights when I work out in the morning. I actually feel tired enough to sleep at my desired time each night. Overall, exercising is fabulous. 10/10 would recommend."

I also 10/10 would recommend. Your sore muscles will thank you.

POWERING MOTIVATION

No one ever made a decision not to exercise because they thought it was bad for them. Instead it's usually because they simply don't *want* to. One student explained last spring, "I have a very busy schedule, and it's very rare that I would even find the opportunity to go to the gym, much less the motivation when I do have the time."

This sentiment is common among young adults. They understand on an intellectual level that exercise has benefits, but they simply lack the motivation to start an exercise regimen. Often when we are down or feeling unmotivated, the last thing we want to do is lace up our sneakers and spend an hour on an elliptical or at the weight machines. Instead we want to do something that makes us feel better.

But when we are feeling low, physical activity can be one of the most effective ways to improve our mood *and* power motivation. In an experiment designed to reveal the most effective interventions for major depression, a team of researchers from Duke University randomly assigned a group of clinically depressed adults to one of three conditions: some of them met with a psychiatrist who prescribed Zoloft (a pharmaceutical antidepressant), another group engaged in thirty minutes of vigorous exercise three times per week (without taking any prescription drugs), and the final group received *both* interventions, taking Zoloft *and* establishing an exercise routine.[20]

It had already been established that drugs like Zoloft are effective at alleviating symptoms of depression. Previous research had given hints that exercise was effective at lessening the severity of mood disorders, but most studies that used exercise as an intervention were simultaneously administering other forms of therapy, including psychiatric medications. None up to that point had attempted to isolate the effects of exercise alone.

This new study allowed the scientific community to understand whether a regimen of physical exercise—by itself—could be an effective treatment. It also set the stage for scientists to see if combining exercise and drug treatment was even better. To ensure compliance with their assigned conditions, all participants were working under the auspices of qualified professionals. Those receiving Zoloft met with a psychiatrist, and those who were exercising trained with a physiologist. The researchers followed up with the participants four months later to find out how many of them were still clinically depressed and whether there were any differences in recovery rates among the three experimental groups.

A SHOCK TO THE SCIENTIFIC COMMUNITY

When examining how many patients in each group were still depressed, they found no significant differences at all. In each of the three groups, approximately two-thirds of the patients no longer met the diagnostic criteria for depression. Those who had been exercising regularly over the preceding four months were just as likely to have recovered as those who had been taking Zoloft, or those who had been doing both. This says a lot about exercise's ability to regulate mood disorders.

So far, these results fit with what we already know about exercise, that it releases neurochemicals into the brain that are important for psychological health. But the study didn't end there. What shocked the scientific community came during the six-month follow-up. One of the predictors of whether someone will become depressed is whether they have been depressed before. Therefore the researchers followed up with the participants again six months later, now ten months after they'd enrolled in the study. They wanted to see how many of the recovered patients *remained* psychologically healthy. The chart below shows the results:

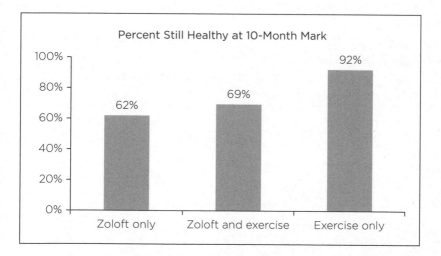

These findings left many in the scientific community astounded. Not only was exercise just as effective at treating depression as Zoloft over a four-month period, but in the long run, exercise ended up being *more* effective as a buffer against relapse. Perhaps most surprising of all, exercise was better in the long run only in the condition in which participants were *not* also taking Zoloft. Participants who had both been exercising *and* taking Zoloft saw a relapse rate comparable to the Zoloft-only condition. If anything, we would expect that two interventions would be better than one, but those exercising without taking Zoloft were best off. What might account for this seemingly counterintuitive finding?

A SENSE OF CONTROL, A FEELING OF EMPOWERMENT

The student I described earlier in this chapter—the one whose busy schedule made it "very rare" that he would have an opportunity to exercise much less the motivation even when he did—learned the hard way the consequences of an inactive lifestyle:

> "This past fall, when I wasn't exercising at all, I was also severely depressed. I couldn't muster the motivation to do any exercise, and then I felt worse about myself because I was just letting my health and body go."

Eventually, though, he found simple ways to incorporate exercise into his day:

> "I focused on small routine workouts I could do in my apartment every day. This semester I've been very consistent about exercising, and done a solid job of slipping additional small workouts into the cracks when I have some time and the resources while doing other things. It helps me feel healthy and that I'm taking care of myself."

This feeling of taking care of oneself is an important part of psychological health. Psychologists refer to this as self-efficacy, a sense that we are the masters of our own domains, capable of carrying out our work with confidence and competence. Accomplishing something in one area of our life increases our confidence that we can do other things. Feeling accomplished also offers a boost to our sense of self and overall well-being. Often, the hardest part of completing a big task is just getting started. If we can muster the strength to carry out the first step, the sense of accomplishment from that single step raises our self-efficacy. We then feel motivated to take the second step, then the third, and so on. For my student, small daily exercises may not have looked like much from the outside, but they served as stepping stones to lead him out of depression and up to a path of accomplishment.

> "When I started feeling better, it became much easier to get myself to work out every day, and now it feels almost like a safeguard. If I can keep up the good habits and do at least a little exercise every day, it means I still care about life enough that I'm not going to start feeling depressed again. And if that motivation goes away, I think I'll recognize it as a warning sign."

Part of what allowed him to recover from depression was a sense of control over his life—a feeling he got directly from exercising. Young adults trying to establish their place in the world are dealing with many variables that are out of their control. Exercise helps maintain order, balance, and routine. Another of my students incorporates exercise into her life for this very reason:

> "Not only do I feel more energized and better about myself when I exercise, but I also feel like I have done something productive for the day (even when the only other thing I may have done is watch Netflix). College can be an unpredictable time and I think everyone has moments when they feel like they don't have control of anything; I believe that exercise is important because it is an activity that is completely under my control and solely for my benefit."

THE BLOCKBUSTER DRUG
OF THE CENTURY

This feeling of self-efficacy, the sense of control and order, is precisely the explanation that Dr. Michael Babyak and his colleagues at Duke used to explain their astonishing results. What else could account for those in the exercise-only condition faring so much better than those exercising *and* taking an antidepressant? It ultimately had to do with what the participants believed, what they attributed their recovery to. For those who were exercising, it was all due to an activity they had done *on their own*. For those who had also taken a drug, it was due at least in part to a substance they'd had to get from the psychiatrist, an *external source*. Exercise yields an internal attribution for recovery. Prescription medications yield an external attribution. The scientists contend that these different attributions affected the course of the patients' recovery:

> "One of the positive psychological benefits of systematic exercise is the development of a sense of personal mastery and positive self-regard, which we believe is likely to play some role in the depression-reducing effects of exercise. It is conceivable that the concurrent use of medication may undermine this benefit by prioritizing an alternative, less self-confirming attribution for one's improved condition. Instead of incorporating the belief 'I was dedicated and worked hard with the exercise program; it wasn't easy, but I beat this depression,' patients might incorporate the belief that 'I took an antidepressant and got better.'"

Of course, it's important for us not to take these findings too far. No one should interpret them as suggesting that psychiatrists should hang up their white coats and that we should get rid of drug interventions for mood disorders once and for all. Far from it. Remember that

in the first part of the study, approximately one-third of the participants in the exercise-only condition did not recover from their depression. Hence, exercise by itself does not work for everyone. For some
people an antidepressant like Zoloft is in fact the best solution. For
many others, though, exercise is the way to go, and certainly worth
trying if you are physically able to do so.

In his bestselling book *The Science of Happiness: How Our Brains
Make Us Happy—and What We Can Do to Get Happier,* Dr. Stefan
Klein likens exercise to "a kind of natural Prozac," noting its release of
serotonin, the same neurochemical that many psychiatric medications
target due to its role in alleviating mood disorders like depression and
anxiety.[21] Other scientists and health experts agree. According to John
Ratey, a physician who has studied the physical, mental, and social
benefits of exercise, "If exercise came in pill form, it would be plastered
across the front page, hailed as the blockbuster drug of the century."[22]

But the benefits from exercise aren't confined to minimizing mental illness. Klein goes on to explain, "In contrast to medication, which
only diminishes sadness, movement also yields positive feelings,
because physical effort releases the euphoria-inducing endorphins.
This might explain why regular exercise for half an hour three times
a week is as effective against melancholy for some people as the best
medications currently available."[23]

Remember, one of the benefits of exercise—in addition to the
chemical effects it has on the brain regions associated with mood—is
a sense of accomplishment from the hard work involved with setting a
goal and working toward it.

PROMPTING PRODUCTIVITY

In 2015, two former student athletes from the University of North
Carolina at Chapel Hill filed class action lawsuits against the university. They claimed the amount of time required for their sports

commitments prevented them from engaging fully in the academic requirements of their college careers.[24] Although the case was dismissed,[25] it brought to light the intense time commitment collegiate athletes are required to make.

Earlier in this chapter, I described a student who did not want to continue playing tennis in college because of the time commitment it would require. It's an understandable reason. College athletes typically spend upward of twenty hours per week in the gym and on the field preparing for upcoming competitions. Given the demands on their time from academics and other commitments, they have to manage their schedules very carefully to fit everything in. Consider the perspective of this member of the varsity swim team: "A typical week for me involves three or four mornings up at the crack of dawn to be at the pool by six thirty, then practice most afternoons."

With a schedule like this, it's evident why some athletes who played all through grade school and high school stop once they get to college. Fitting in time for academic and social endeavors seems nearly impossible. And for those brave souls who do continue with their sport, you'd think the off-season would be a relief they await all year. Surely that would be a time of greater productivity, given the extra hours available to use however they'd like.

In fact, it's the opposite.

Many athletes report that their on-season is actually the time when they are most productive. They have no choice but to approach their academics with utmost efficiency to keep from falling behind. The swimmer who is waking up before the sun comes up to make it to the pool by six thirty has to maintain a strict schedule to fit in all her other commitments:

> "I plan my weeks out in advance, since I have finite amounts of time to do things. I know which days I'll go to the library for my break, and I know exactly how many hours I'll have to study before my eleven o'clock bedtime."

However, as soon as the off-season rolls around, it's a different story:

> "Once I stop swimming, my stress level goes way up. I notice that I struggle to get assignments done without procrastinating, which is bizarre since I have almost an entire extra day's worth of time added to my week. And, most dramatically, my mood is very different. I feel less confident in myself, and find that I have no energy. Once again, this is counterintuitive since I turn into such a bum in terms of physical activity for those six weeks."

Counterintuitive as it may be, this experience is consistent with what we know about self-efficacy. By accomplishing vigorous physical activity in one part of the day, varsity athletes position themselves to carry energy and self-confidence into tasks later in the day—along with a carefully designed schedule to ensure they complete everything efficiently. During the off-season, without the strict routine, they are less diligent about getting their work done. After all, it's not as if they have to be in bed by eleven to make it to an early-morning practice the next day.

Of course, increased productivity is not reserved only for varsity athletes. Anyone can reap similar benefits by incorporating exercise into their daily routine. Another of my students, though not a member of the cross-country team, told me that starting her days with a quick run leaves her "refreshed, empowered, and incredibly happy." Like the swimmer, she benefits from the order it brings to her entire day:

> "By running at the same time every day, I gave my life a certain rhythm and pattern that allowed me to work, eat, and socialize in a more efficient way. When doing homework, I felt a lot more motivated, and when eating, I found myself making healthier choices. My body felt lighter, less fatigued, and overall more rejuvenated. This healthy pattern raised my

self-respect a lot. The absence of exercise usually makes my life feel much less organized and I end up living with much less of a plan or efficient schedule."

So exercise is an investment. Although it takes time away that you could be devoting to other activities, it prompts you to use the time you do have remaining more efficiently. To drive home this point, I'd like to share one more story from another of my students:

"My suite-mate runs and exercises about as much as I do and we either go on runs or go to the gym together several times a week. This is quite a time commitment and when I have a lot of exams sometimes I skip a workout. I stopped running during finals week of my first semester to have more time to study. I assumed I was stressed out because of finals; however, I see now that it was also due to me not running. I saw my suite-mate leaving for a run one morning and asked her why she was running if she had so much work to do. She replied that it's the times when you don't have time to run that you need to the most because it's so easy to get depressed when you're overbooked. I realized that was exactly my problem and that not exercising was making my stressful finals week even worse. Now I make sure to carve out time to run or exercise, even if it's only for thirty minutes, during the most stressful times of the school year."

REDIRECTING OUR THOUGHTS

For many college students, the sophomore year is one of the most challenging. Whereas the first year is accompanied by orientation programs, special freshman seminars, and ongoing support to aid them in making the transition, the start of the sophomore year often leaves students feeling as if they must fend for themselves. We call the resulting disillusionment and dissatisfaction the "sophomore slump." It's that common. One of my students experienced it for himself:

> "My sophomore year was one of the most stressful years ever. I was bogged down by classwork, tests, clubs, and meetings. I was troubled with a recent breakup and with a general disappointment in myself. There were so many things in my head and I felt a huge yoke on my shoulders pushing me down. I found it physically difficult to breathe and even move. Getting out of bed was one of the hardest struggles of the day. Keeping myself moving forward in my day was the other hard struggle. Life, I thought, was very difficult."

When he talked this over with a friend, she told him that one thing that might help him feel better would be to start exercising. At first he was reluctant to take her suggestion.

> "Great. Another thing that I had to fit in my schedule. Great. Something else that I had to balance with my studies. Great. Just one more activity that I had to remember in the list of things I had to do."

Eventually, however, he got himself to do it. And although it got off to a rocky start, he began to realize its benefits.

> "The first day of running was terrible. I had to wake up earlier than usual. The run got me really winded and basically I was walking for a little less than half of the run. I got back home all sweaty and tired. I wanted to quit. This was not working. But I ran again the next day, then swimming. Then the next couple of days more swimming and running. I definitely did not get any more fit, but something that I realized was that I was no longer thinking about my worries. I was placed squarely in the present moment. I was focusing on my breath, on my stroke,

on my legs, on the floor of the pool, on the horizon. I was so zoned. It took my mind off ruminating on things that I couldn't change or things that were out of my control. It also gave me the physical energy and support to go through my day with a smile."

Though it was challenging at first, this initially reluctant sophomore discovered another benefit that exercise provides: a healthier alternative to stress and anxiety for his mind to focus on. It was just what he needed to emerge from his slump.

GETTING BACK ON TRACK

Exercise in itself is a great form of distraction. When life's stressors start to build up, they can invade the focus of our attention, propelling us into the whirlwind of a negative thinking cycle. The best way to halt racing thoughts is by doing an activity irrelevant to them, such as calling a friend, taking care of an errand, or going for a run. Exercise in particular is effective because not only is it distracting, it also releases a chemical in our brains that aids in halting those racing thoughts: an inhibitory neurotransmitter called gamma-aminobutyric acid (more commonly known simply as GABA). You can think of GABA's function as the opposite of caffeine's. Whereas a cup of coffee can worsen anxiety by making us nervous and jittery, a dose of GABA can alleviate anxiety by decreasing activation of the brain, producing a calming effect. So when we exercise, not only are we distracting ourselves with a different activity, we are also releasing a natural substance that calms our minds. One of my students has found these benefits for himself:

"Whenever I work out, I am able to compartmentalize it so that I am not thinking about anything else other than exercising in the moment. I do not worry about my problems, and I am able to recharge my batteries in a way. Because of this I can return to the 'real world' and tackle my problems with a newfound sense of calm and mental clarity. Without this feeling of therapy that I receive from exercising, I am short with people, impatient, anxious, and get annoyed very easily. Exercising is a major contributing factor to happiness in my daily life."

A bout of exercise is like hitting the brakes on our racing thoughts. As my student alludes to, it's a bit like free therapy . . . but without the need to schedule an appointment in advance.

REDIRECTING ANXIETY

During Franklin D. Roosevelt's 1933 inaugural address, he uttered a now-famous phrase that has been repeated countless times ever since: "The only thing we have to fear is fear itself." In his speech he was attempting to quell the unrest that had overcome the American people at the height of the Great Depression. He spoke as if fear itself were not so bad. Hey, if fear is all we've got to worry about, then we're OK, right?

The trouble is that for some, the fear of fear is a real hurdle to enjoying everyday life. Anxiety sensitivity is a condition characterized not just by anxiety, but also by fear of the physical symptoms of anxiety, such as a rapid heartbeat or irregular breathing. Those who suffer from it tend to construe even minor bodily arousal as catastrophic: a faster-than-normal heartbeat is interpreted as a heart attack, stomach pain as cancer, a headache as a stroke.[26] Slight unrest in the body must mean that something is wrong. As a result these people have difficulty interacting with others in social settings, or in some cases even emerging from their homes, because of the fear that they will have an anxiety attack in public.

Researchers have been looking into what can be done to help those suffering from anxiety sensitivity. The key may lie in exercise. When students at the University of Southern Mississippi spent twenty minutes running on a treadmill three times per week, they showed significant reductions in anxiety sensitivity after just two weeks.[27] Exercise improved their psychological state because it provided not only distraction, but also a new *interpretation* for physiological arousal that previously had spelled doom. Remember that for those high in anxiety sensitivity, common elements of physiological arousal—such as an increased heart rate or irregular breathing pattern—imply disaster. Exercise causes those *same* bodily reactions, but couples them with boosts in mood and self-efficacy. Over time these students came to associate a pounding heart, shortness of breath, and increased temperature with the benefits of exercise instead of the dread of anxiety.

OUTRUNNING FEAR

Many clinicians use exercise as a behavioral intervention, given its proven ability to reduce anxiety. Psychologist Keith Johnsgard touts exercise as "one of the most potent antianxiety forces available."[28] Johnsgard works with patients whose anxiety disorders take the form of agoraphobia, an intense fear of wide-open, crowded public spaces. Because the physiological arousal brought on by exercise teaches patients a new response to anxiety, he takes his patients to their worst nightmare—a crowded mall—and asks them to run sprints in the parking lot. In an earlier session, he's determined how far they can run before reaching exhaustion and breathlessness. He measures that exact distance from the mall entrance. The patients are instructed to run toward the mall, stop and catch their breath, and then turn around to walk back.

Although standing at the mall entrance previously might have triggered a full-fledged anxiety attack, the physical exhaustion from their run allows Johnsgard's patients to remain there panic-free. They now attribute the breathlessness and increased heart rate to their run and the positive benefits of exercise, when previously that same physiological arousal would have led to a panic attack—just as it would have for the Southern Mississippi students who struggled with anxiety sensitivity. In both cases exercise helped people with anxiety issues to interpret arousal sensations differently. Over time Johnsgard's agoraphobic patients were able to stay at the mall entrance longer and longer before turning around and heading back. Eventually they were able to enter the mall and walk around unaccompanied, something that had once been inconceivable. Remarkably, many of these patients were cured of their agoraphobia within only a half-dozen sessions.

In other words, exercise redirected their interpretation of physiological arousal from one of fear to one of fitness. By learning to reinterpret what's happening in their bodies, they freed their minds even of FDR's notion: fear itself was no longer to be feared. Whether it's an agoraphobia sufferer or a sophomore in an anxiety-laden slump, exercise teaches the mind and body to redirect attention to a healthier alternative.

GET ON YOUR FEET

At the beginning of this chapter, I shared with you a host of health experts who are leading the "sitting is the new smoking" movement. Among them is Dr. James Levine from the Mayo Clinic, who claims that we are sitting ourselves to death. This might be disheartening news for anyone whose job requires being at a desk all day. Fortunately, Levine has a solution. He has popularized the treadmill desk, which functions exactly as its name implies: instead of sitting in a chair, you walk on a treadmill at a leisurely pace while completing your work on an elevated surface.[29] Levine and other scientists have found that employees who use treadmill desks for just three hours a day see significant improvements in their health.[30]

As attractive as this may sound, it is simply impractical for many. The good news is that you don't necessarily need the treadmill to get the benefits. Just standing up while you work increases oxygen consumption,[31] which can strengthen cognitive performance.[32] The next time you are studying for an exam or preparing a presentation for a meeting, spend part of your time standing up with your notes in your hand. Or if you're meeting with colleagues to discuss a project, suggest that you do your brainstorming standing up at a whiteboard. If you can find a way to get yourself moving, even better. If you have an appointment with your academic adviser to discuss next semester's course schedule, ask her to go on a brief walk while you discuss your plans.

WALKING BREAKS

A number of studies have shown that even small breaks throughout the day that involve physical activity are effective. A study in the Department of Kinesiology at the University of Illinois at Urbana-Champaign tested this with fifty-two undergraduates enrolled in a class that offered a ten-minute break in its middle.[33] Some spent their breaks inside reading. Others spent them walking around campus. By the end of the semester, the students who spent ten minutes going for a quick walk in the middle of each class experienced increases in vitality and enthusiasm, and decreases in tension and fatigue.

So the next time you are in a rut, feeling unmotivated, or perhaps stressed about an upcoming exam or major assignment, get up and move around. Just a few minutes of physical activity may be all you need to quell your fears and increase your supply of energy to face the task at hand. One of my students confirms that even short exercise sessions interwoven into her day are valuable:

"As for my mind, I feel like twenty minutes of exercise can do miracles for my stress levels and creativity. It's so rejuvenating to be outside for a while and give my mind a break, and the sense of accomplishment I feel after a workout is amazing."

Another of my students puts yoga breaks in the middle of her studying, especially when exam season rolls around:

"Part of it has to do with the practice of yoga itself, but a lot of it also has to do with the fact that I'm now regularly getting off my computer and engaging in physical activity. Before exams is a great time for me to do some yoga, because it takes me down from the nervous energy that would be overflowing from me, so having an outlet for this has helped alleviate my testing anxiety."

In addition to the increase in motivation and calmness, a number of studies have also shown that study breaks spent exercising strengthen the study session itself. Researchers at the University of Ulm in Germany found that young adults who exercised three times per week experienced increases in memory.[34] A similar study at California State University, Long Beach, found that students performed 25 percent better on a memory test if they spent ten minutes taking a brisk walk outside beforehand.[35]

Throughout this chapter I have discussed how exercise releases neurotransmitters that are essentially the brain's feel-good chemicals. These neurochemicals carry benefits beyond our emotional health. They also facilitate complex cognitive tasks like learning and remembering. The brain's ability to learn new information and hold on to it for later use rests on the connections made by neurons. Those connections are strengthened by neurotransmitters like serotonin and dopamine—the same feel-good chemicals we get from exercise. So running not only makes us feel good on an emotional level, it also helps us form connections in our brains and consolidate memories.

Scientists all over the world have found that even short bursts of physical activity lead to improvements in cognitive abilities and psychological health. Whether you're exercising on a stationary bike,[36] a treadmill,[37] or the ground,[38] the results are consistent: physical activity strengthens cognitive performance and sharpens focus more than just sitting still.

GET MOVING, GET CONNECTED

Many people find that working out with others makes it easier to incorporate exercise into their routines, and also makes the exercise more enjoyable. An exercise buddy will hold you accountable and also keep you motivated. For athletes, a sense of community developed on the field often extends to the gym:

> "There is no better feeling than finishing a really hard set in our lift or doing a bunch of conditioning, and then looking over and seeing my twenty-five best friends feeling the same sense of accomplishment that I am."

Of course, you don't have to play on a formal team or even have a formal exercise routine to reap the benefits that come from exercising with a buddy. Even in a casual setting, a friend will push you in ways you might not push yourself. One of my favorite pastimes is getting together for lunch with Dr. Ruth Clark, a dear friend and faculty colleague at our School of Medicine. I know that each time I see her I can look forward to a lighthearted conversation filled with great stories and much laughter. I also know that each time I see her I need to break out my sneakers. Dr. Clark prefers to walk everywhere. If we are going to a place that is not within walking distance, she will choose a parking spot at the farthest corner of the lot from the entrance. If we take public transportation, we get off several stops before our destination to walk the rest of the way. As a physiologist she's simply practicing what she preaches in her lab and classroom: a few extra steps per day keeps the doctor away. That is, of course, unless you're having lunch with one, in which case you can be sure your "extra steps" for the day will be more than just "a few." Still, I can't blame her. She is used to incorporating physical activity into all aspects of her lifestyle. After all, when she was in college, she also had to walk down the hallway to use the phone.

———————

When we set our bodies into motion, we also set into motion psychological health, motivation to get work done, efficient structure for our schedules, and an activity that distracts us from our worries, leaving us energized and ready to tackle the day's challenges. Remember that one of the goals of positive psychology is to identify proactive strategies for increasing our happiness. One of the best ways to be proactively happy is simply to be active. Exercise is a cheap, easy, proven strategy for helping virtually everyone in almost any circumstance, whether we are recovering from a bad day, needing a second wind to power through our to-do list, or just looking to extend our good mood when we're feeling great.

This entire chapter can be summarized by a reflection one of my students shared with me about how exercise affects her life as a young adult:

"Whether I've had a bad day or a great one, exercising always makes me feel better than I did before working out. Running clears my mind while I'm pushing my body to endure a tough pace for miles on end. Lifting weights makes me feel strong when I break my record for number of reps. And scrimmaging with my team gives me the satisfaction of seeing our hard work play out on the field. Exercising takes me away from whatever frustrations or obstacles I had during the day. It gives me an addictive rush of endorphins which don't solve my problems, but at least make me feel better about them. More than anything, exercising makes me feel competent. If I can lift those weights, complete that circuit, and blow that run out of the water, I come home feeling like I can handle whatever I need to deal with. For that reason, I never skip a workout or a chance to run, even when I'm pressed for time. My brain works better and my body feels better after exercising."

And for those who prefer a visual summary:

4

Sweet Dreams

In the last chapter you met my friend Ruth Clark, who has spent the last thirty years as a professor of physiology. She has faculty appointments at both our medical school and our undergraduate biology program. She is especially popular with premed students eager to get a glimpse into their future professional training. Recently she and I appeared on a panel for incoming first-year students. The topic was "How to Be Successful in College."

Midway through the panel, an eager student in the front row raised her hand and asked, "Dr. Clark, in all the years you've been a professor, what have you noticed as the *most* important thing for students who want to be successful in college?"

"That's easy," Dr. Clark replied. "Sleep."

Not taking on a difficult course load, getting to know professors, or participating in co-curricular activities, but sleep—something that seemingly takes no effort at all.

At the end of every school year, Dr. Clark sits down with her graduating seniors to ask them about their college careers. She takes note of trends among the most successful students. Year after year the students with the highest GPAs, best job offers, and acceptances to the most prestigious graduate programs are different in most ways. They have different majors, use different study strategies, come from different financial backgrounds, traveled varying distances to attend school in St. Louis, and are involved with different sports teams and extracurricular activities. But one perennial theme among the most successful graduating students is as predictable as an entering freshman's wish to be successful in college: they prioritize sleep. The students graduating with the strongest academic records and highest overall happiness consistently get eight hours of sleep each night, or at least enough that they wake up each morning feeling refreshed.

Forget about the freshman fifteen. What really seems to matter is the freshman eight.

But eight hours of sleep each night is, for many students, something that exists only in their wildest dreams (assuming they are even getting enough sleep to be dreaming about anything at all). A *Huffington Post* article recently deemed sleep deprivation the "new college norm."[1] According to surveys by the American College Health Association, more than 30 percent of respondents had had sleep difficulties that were "traumatic or very difficult to handle" over the previous twelve months. Fifty-nine percent said they'd "felt tired, dragged out, or sleepy" on at least three of the preceding seven days.[2] When students were asked about factors that hinder academic performance, "sleep difficulties" was reported more often than alcohol use, homesickness, roommate problems, or even depression.

Many young adults are introduced to this image at some point during their college years:

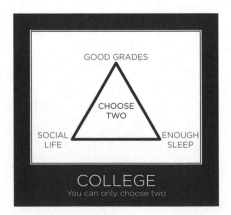

"The graphic is popular because for many people it feels true," one of my students told me. "And often, sleep is the odd man out."

Another of my students confesses, "If I could get enough sleep every night, I would probably be more focused and more productive. But then to get things done in time, I have to stay up to finish work, which cuts into my sleeping time, and makes me less focused and productive the next day. It's a vicious cycle."

This same student, however, admits that sleep deprivation can actually create a sense of unity among her friends: "On the other hand, most of my friends get just as little or less sleep than I do, so it's something we can gripe about and bond over together." Another agrees: "Losing sleep because of a last-minute paper or an upcoming exam is something we can all identify with, so when a friend complains about how little sleep they got the night before (or sometimes even the whole week), I can readily identify with their complaint."

For some, it can even become competitive: "A sort of one-upmanship occurs when discussing how little sleep one has had. It almost seems as if one gains a sort of 'street cred' for being able to 'function' on fewer hours of sleep."

Street cred or not, sleep deprivation presents a barrier to well-being in young adulthood. In many ways sleep is an enigma. Isn't it odd that we lie prone for seven or eight hours, unconscious, every day of our life, like vampires or caterpillars in cocoons? The time we spend sleeping, odd as it may seem, positions us for success in other areas of our lives. Everyone knows they feel better after a good night's sleep, but sleep is more important for your overall happiness and well-being than you may realize. Think of the inventors and artists who got solutions to problems that dogged them only after they awoke from a good night's sleep. Oftentimes what was murky becomes clear only after we "sleep on it" for a while.

But it's not just the amount of sleep we get that matters. It's also in the timing. If we align our sleep cycles with the body's natural rhythm, we can wake up feeling more refreshed. And for those nights when we can't get a full night's sleep, we can compensate (at least in part) with a power nap—if it is timed just right. Understanding the science of sleep can position us to reap all its benefits and balance all *three* legs of the "Choose Two" triangle on page 76.

SLEEP AS A FORM OF WORK

When I cover the importance of sleep in my class, one of the most common responses from the students is that there simply aren't enough hours in the day to get a full night's sleep regularly. "I have too much work to go to bed early," one student told me. Another described sleep as "a sign of laziness." Even some of the most prominent figures of the last century criticized sleep. Margaret Thatcher once proclaimed, "Sleep is for wimps." For Thomas Edison, it was "a *criminal* waste of time!"

What all of these people have in common is the belief that sleep doesn't need to be a priority. College students, politicians, and inventors alike agree there are better ways to spend our time. Why sleep when you could actually be getting work done? However, whether we realize it or not, as we sleep the brain *is* working. And it's doing a lot of important work at that.

LEARNING AND MEMORY ENHANCEMENT

The dilemma that many students face the night before an exam is how much time to spend studying. As the night draws on, a constant battle plays out: Do I sleep or do I keep working? The "Choose Two" triangle suggests that sleeping versus studying is an either-or proposition. However, a number of studies have shown us that they actually go hand in hand. In a clever study by researchers at Washington University in St. Louis, undergraduates completed a series of lab tasks that took place across two sessions.[3] In the first the students studied a list of syllables that appeared individually on a computer monitor. In the second they were told to recall as many of the syllables as they could.

Half of the participants—which we'll call Group 1—arrived to the lab at nine a.m. for the first session, and then returned at nine p.m. that evening for the second. The other half—Group 2—did the reverse: they studied the list at night and then completed the memory test the next morning. In both conditions twelve hours separated the two phases. But how those twelve hours were spent was very different.

For Group 1 (who learned the words in the morning and were tested that night), the time between study and test was filled with normal daily activities: attending class, eating meals, throwing a Frisbee in the quad, hanging out with friends, and running errands. For Group 2 (who learned the words at night and were tested the next morning), the time between study and test was filled mostly with sleep.

And it turns out that sleep is just what the memory doctor ordered. The group that slept between study and test recalled *46 percent more* of the items than the group that spent the intervening time awake. Part of the reason is that neural activity during our slumber helps us process the information we learned the day before. Skip a good night's sleep and you impede the brain's ability to retain and recall that information in the future. As I mentioned earlier, the brain is doing a lot of work as we sleep. To understand just what kind of work is taking place, let's take a look at what's happening in our brains after we've hit the hay.

THE BRAIN DURING THE NIGHT SHIFT

Deep inside the brain is a seahorse-shaped structure called the hippocampus, which plays an important role in the creation and storage of memories. When we read something in a book, learn a new task, or meet someone for the first time, the hippocampus enables us to tuck that information away and then pull it back out when we need to remember what we read, perform that task again, or recall the name of our new acquaintance. And the hippocampus is best able to do that when we are sleeping.

"When you're asleep, it seems as though you are shifting memory to more efficient storage regions within the brain," says Matthew Walker, a neuroscientist at UC Berkeley. "Consequently, when you awaken, memory tasks can be performed both more quickly and accurately and with less stress and anxiety."

This is the Catch-22 for students who pull all-nighters before exams. Although their brains take in the information when they are studying—a process psychologists call encoding—that's only the first step in committing information to memory. Inadequate sleep means they end up neglecting the vital second step—storage and consolidation. Sleep is necessary to activate regions of the hippocampus that consolidate what we have encoded in the brain, making that information available for retrieval later. It's all part of the important work the brain is doing when we sleep. Over the night, neural circuits are firing away to make sense of information we learned the day before, reactivate those memories, distribute them to key regions of the brain, and make them easy to access the next day.

"Our research is demonstrating that sleep is critical for improving and consolidating procedural skills," Walker adds, "and that you can't shortchange your brain of sleep and still learn effectively."[4]

One of my students uses this knowledge by paying attention to what her body is telling her: "Staying up past a certain point hurts my performance on an exam or productiveness in writing a paper. If I am studying and feel myself getting tired and distracted, I choose to go to sleep. Pushing myself at that point is counterproductive. Instead I choose to wake up the next morning and continue."

Another student has found that although sleeping reduces the number of waking hours he has to get things done, he accomplishes more because he is operating at full capacity: "Many times, I will lose focus in classes, meetings, or even social events because I am too exhausted or sleepy. It's ironic: when I give up sleep to do more when I am awake, I do everything in a sleepy, inhibited state. But when I take the time to get consistent and long, quality sleep I am the most happy, creative, and productive."

So contrary to what Thomas Edison, Margaret Thatcher, or even some of my own students will have you believe, sleep is not a passive waste of precious time. It's more than just a break for our bodies and minds after the day's activities. Sleep is a dynamic cognitive process. Once we go to sleep, the brain goes to work. Neural circuits keep firing away, burning what we've learned into memory.[5]

If you're tempted to pull an all-nighter, know that you'll be much better off spending at least *part* of the night asleep to give your brain an opportunity to consolidate the memories that it has stored so far. The longer you stay up, the harder it will be to concentrate on the work in front of you; the attentional resources needed to stay focused and learn new material become significantly compromised. Sometimes the more productive, efficient solution is to actually stop studying and go to bed.

SLEEP ON IT!

One of my students uses sleep as his cure-all: "Sleep is the last thing I want to sacrifice. I know that sleeping cures a lot of ailments. Worried? Sleep on it. Sick? Sleep it off. Tired? Sleep!"

The expression "Sleep on it" is actually supported by science. A number of studies show the benefits of sleep for those trying to resolve a problem or gain insight into a decision. In one study conducted at the University of Lübeck in Germany, young adults were given logic puzzles that involved a hidden abstract rule; once the puzzle solver gained insight into that rule, they were able to complete the puzzles much more quickly and easily. But it typically took some time before that insight was gained.[6] In the first phase of the study, researchers gave the students examples of the puzzles so they could become familiar with them. To find out whether sleep could hasten insight into the logic rule, the researchers manipulated the time of day when the study was administered. Like the memory study at WashU, half of the participants completed phase one at night, shortly before they went to sleep; the others did so in the morning, and were instructed to spend the rest of the day carrying out their normal activities. Everyone then came back to the lab eight hours later and was presented with more puzzles. Those who had spent the intervening time asleep were more than twice as likely to gain insight into the hidden abstract rule, enabling them to fly through a second set of puzzles much faster than their counterparts.

Importantly, the amount of time between initial exposure to the puzzles and subsequent testing period was identical for both groups. The only difference was whether the study subjects had spent their time awake or asleep. Evidently, the work the brain does while we sleep can also enhance both logic and insight. The authors of the research note, "Sleep acts on newly acquired mental representations of a task such that insight into hidden task structures is facilitated."[7] In other words, the "Eureka!" or "Aha!" moment you are searching for might be just one good night's sleep away.

THE KEYSTONE FRIEND

One of my students equates sleep to a core member of his social group: "Sleep is like that friend many of us have who does not seem to have a noticeable presence, but when absent significantly alters group dynamics. That keystone friend who quietly manages the existence and persistence of the group."

Many studies have provided insight into how sleep quietly manages our emotional health. Researchers at the Max Planck Institute for Human Development in Berlin, Germany, tested a group of more than a hundred young adults to understand the relationship between sleep and psychological well-being. For each of nine consecutive days, participants reported how many hours they had slept the night before. They also reported their emotional states throughout the day by responding to prompts on their mobile devices. On average, the participants who had gotten the most sleep the night before were best off psychologically. A full night's rest translated to higher ratings of happiness, enthusiasm, and energy, and lower ratings of anger, nervousness, or disappointment throughout the day.[8]

Here again we can understand these outcomes by looking at the work the brain is doing when we sleep. Over the course of the night we cycle through a series of sleep stages, each with its own signature patterns and functions. One of them is called REM sleep—so named not for the eighties rock band, but instead for what's actually happening in our bodies: rapid eye movement. It's also called paradoxical sleep because although it is the deepest stage of sleep, our brain waves mimic those of our awake state. Though it has some perplexing elements, scientists agree that REM sleep is an important part of the sleep cycle, especially for reducing sensitivity to emotions like fear and anger.[9]

Another brain structure, a neighbor to the hippocampus called the amygdala, plays an important role in our emotional experiences. This is the brain structure that alerts us when we encounter something fearful or anxiety provoking. When the amygdala becomes hyperactive, we start interpreting even harmless things as potential threats, and we become more likely to interpret ambiguous situations as more upsetting than they actually are. The remedy is often a good night's sleep—in particular, sleep that has a healthy dose of REM. REM sleep is associated with lower levels of amygdala activity, which essentially quell our fears and make us less reactive to potential threats. Without enough REM sleep, we are more on edge and tense the next day because of our overactive amygdala, which leads to heightened reactivity to situations that otherwise would just roll off our backs.[10]

The student who considers sleep his keystone friend knows what it is like when that chief comrade has gone astray:

"The nights that I am partially divested of sleep, I transform into a negative, cynical grumbler with an impossibly irritable disposition. Anything mildly annoying, like the sound of a ticking clock or the sound of someone opening a bag of chips on the third floor of the library, infuriates me, forcing me to angrily trudge away from my trying environment and sequester myself away from any possible minute annoyance. Sleep manages the existence and persistence of our lives, especially as college students, governing our health, sanity, cognitive ability, and emotional well-being."

When our happiness reserve is depleted and everything around us is maddening, a good night's sleep is often the best way to recharge our well-being. My graduate school adviser likened sleep to hitting the reset button on our brains, giving us a fresh start for the next day.

———

So far we've seen the benefits sleep provides: more sleep translates to mental clarity and upbeat emotions. However, translating this knowledge into a functional lifestyle can be a challenge in itself. Let's take a look at how to intentionally establish routines that can allow us to take advantage of sleep's natural benefits.

THE RHYTHM OF SLEEP

Each of us has an internal clock governed by a circadian rhythm—the term is derived from the Latin *circa dies* or "about a day," and refers to the hormonal and physiological fluctuations that occur in cycles roughly equivalent to one day. Our circadian rhythms mirror other naturally occurring daily rhythms, like that of sunlight: each morning the sun rises, and each evening it sets. Our alertness levels correspond with body temperature, which is linked to our sleep cycle. As you can see from data compiled by the BBC, body temperature is lowest during the night. This is also when alertness is low. Then both gradually rise as the morning approaches, giving us the energy we need for the day ahead. It turns out that sleep is the most productive and refreshing when it roughly follows the body's natural circadian rhythm. A bedtime of around eleven p.m. with a rising time around seven a.m. is the gold standard.

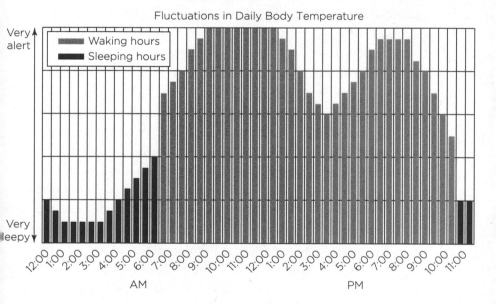

Fluctuations in Daily Body Temperature

Of course, many college students would scoff at the very notion of going to bed before midnight. The demands of their lives and living situations would prevent this; many would consider a full eight hours of sleep a rare luxury, one they could not possibly afford in light of other demands competing for their time.

One solution is to incorporate a nap during the day. As one of my students—a self-declared "morning person"—affirms: "I'm best from when I wake up until after lunch, and then I turn into a zombie. My daily nap time is around four p.m. I take a nap almost every day." This student is in good company. A recent poll found that more than half of millennials take at least one nap a week.[11]

As I mentioned in the last chapter, *Today* host Willie Geist has to wake up every morning at three thirty a.m. to make it to the studio on time. He says naps are the key to health and happiness for anyone who keeps such hours: "Don't be too proud (or too young) to take a quick nap if you need one. You might feel like an old man or lady passing out in front of *Judge Judy* at three in the afternoon, but if I have to do something at night that will keep me out past my infantile bedtime, I'll sneak a nap to push me through."[12]

Recall that sleep helped students in the WashU study recall more syllables on a memory test, and made students in the University of Lübeck study more likely to gain insight into logic puzzles. It's not just memory and insight that improve after sleep. Similar benefits are found for procedural tasks like playing the piano or learning dance choreography. Many studies have found performance improvement even after just a quick nap. Consider a study by researchers at Waseda University in Japan who taught a group of undergraduates how to juggle. After initial practice, half of the students took a two-hour nap, and the others spent two hours reading books or watching movies. Although there was no difference in juggling skills between the two groups during the initial practice phase, two hours later it was the nappers who were making significantly more three-ball-cascade juggling catches. A simple nap was enough to strengthen the motor skills of those learning this task for the first time.[13]

Of course, some people take naps that seem to leave them worse off. We've all been there—waking up feeling disoriented, as if we were intoxicated. The good news is that if timed correctly, naps can be refreshing and rejuvenating. They don't have to take much time, either. You may have heard the term *power nap*. It turns out that catching forty winks in the middle of the day can in fact be powerful—if it is timed just right. The right timing is a matter of both when in the day the nap begins and how long it lasts.

THE SCIENCE OF A POWER NAP

Let's consider first the time of the day. Some scientists have found that a nap taken at the wrong time can actually backfire, leading to more harm than good. Look back at the figure depicting the daily rhythm of our temperature (page 85). Remember that this also corresponds to our alertness levels during the day. After a fairly alert and active morning, there is a midafternoon dip, typically right after the lunch hour.

Some scientists refer to this as the midafternoon sleep gate, a name that highlights its optimal timing for a nap. It coincides with our natural dip in alertness, but it is still far enough away from nighttime that it won't reset our internal clock. Plus when you wake up, your body's temperature and alertness levels are both naturally on the rise again. So if you must nap during the day, doing so in the slot between three and five in the afternoon will capitalize on the body's natural rhythm of tiredness and alertness.

Some people become tempted to take a nap after they've had dinner following a full day of work or activities. However, these same scientists label this evening interval (from seven to nine at night) the forbidden zone of sleep because nodding off there can interrupt our circadian rhythms and prevent a full sleep period that night. Placing that nap in the midafternoon sleep gate can provide a buffer against the tiredness we would otherwise feel during the evening interval.[14] Fortunately, many college students are uniquely positioned to take advantage of this sleep gate. If you can, create a class or work schedule that leaves three to five in the afternoon open.

The second characteristic that determines whether a nap leaves us feeling refreshed is how long it lasts. Given all the benefits of sleep that we've covered in this chapter, it would seem that we should take a nap for as long as our schedule permits. If you've got a free thirty minutes, or forty-five, or sixty, you might as well use them all for sleeping, right? Why not give our brains as much time as possible to establish those neural connections that improve cognition and mood? It turns out there is a very good reason why you wouldn't want to do that. Productive naps need a strict time limit.

In much the same way that our temperature fluctuates over the course of the day, our brain waves fluctuate when we are sleeping. Take a look at the figure on page 89. This chart represents what's happening to our brain waves as we sleep. Along its vertical axis, you'll notice a series of stages, each marked by progressively slower brain waves. When we are awake, the brain waves are fast, enabling us to give full attention to whatever we are working on or thinking about. Our mental acuity is sharp and we easily process the information in front of us.

As we grow tired, our brain waves gradually become slower, and eventually we enter into stage 1 sleep. We move from stage 1 to stage 2, then into the slow-wave sleep (SWS) of stages 3 and 4. The slower our brain waves, the more deeply we are sleeping. These deep stages of sleep also happen to be the most difficult to wake us up from. If you've ever felt jolted or groggy upon being awakened by a loud sound or annoying alarm clock, it's likely that occurred during a stage of deep sleep. Your brain had to startle into action from the slow waves of stage 3 or 4 to the fast waves required for alert wakefulness.[15] Hence the perturbed feeling.

Two characteristics of this graph are important for understanding our sleep cycles. The first is that brain waves get progressively slower as we go deeper into sleep. The second is that the pattern is cyclical. After about an hour, the cycle reverses. We move from slow-wave sleep back up toward faster-wave sleep. Then it moves back down to the slower waves again.

Knowledge of this cycle can help us awaken feeling refreshed. The

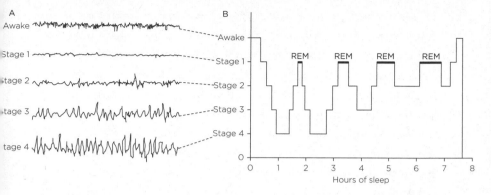

aim should always be to awaken when our brain waves are as close to our awake state as possible. As you can see, it doesn't take long for the brain waves to slow down once we have fallen asleep. Within about one hour you are in your deepest stage of sleep. This is why a one-hour nap is one of the worst things you can do for yourself. You will wake up feeling groggy and disoriented, a phenomenon scientists have termed sleep inertia, and an indication that you likely have woken up during slow-wave sleep.

In fact, this sleep inertia can appear following a nap of as little as twenty minutes. Although there is variability from one person to another, a number of studies have shown that ten minutes may be the optimal length for a power nap, one that will give you a second wind by diminishing fatigue and sharpening your focus.[16] Shorter than that might not be long enough to trigger the benefits, but much longer lands us in a sleep stage that makes it harder to awaken. That is, of course, unless you have a full ninety minutes to devote to your nap. Within ninety minutes you will have completed a full cycle of sleep, from fast wave to slow and back to fast.

Some scientists argue that the sleep inertia from waking during slow-wave sleep is even worse than sleep deprivation itself.[17] That zombie-like grogginess can impair our ability to think clearly and perform other cognitive tasks.[18] We are essentially running on diminished brainpower until the inertia subsides. So if you have only sixty minutes to nap and don't think you'll be able to wake up after only ten or fifteen, skip it. You are likely better off not taking a nap at all.

However, if you do find yourself waking from a nap in a state of inertia, a few strategies can help reduce the effect and restore a state of alert wakefulness. Expose yourself to bright lights—especially natural sunlight if it's available. Wash your face with cold water—it has been shown to counteract grogginess. If you can plan ahead, try drinking coffee or consuming other sources of caffeine five minutes before your nap. Yes, that's correct! It takes about some time for caffeine to have its alerting effect, so it won't prevent you from falling asleep, but it will kick in before your nap extends into the deep sleep stages that lead to inertia.[19]

FALLING ASLEEP

Take another look at the brain waves chart. In order for us to fall asleep, our brain waves have to slow down. Difficulty falling asleep is often due to something keeping them active: anxiety, work, or—in many cases—technology. A study at the University of Bergen in Norway found that more than 75 percent of its students use their mobile phones to play games, surf the web, or text after getting into bed to go to sleep. The more frequently they used those devices in bed, the more likely they were to report symptoms of insomnia and daytime sleepiness.[20]

Responding to a text or reading up on the latest news keeps brain waves buzzing with activity, which may be part of the reason it's harder to fall asleep. In addition, the light from these devices just inches from our face can interfere with the release of melatonin, a hormone the brain secretes to help us feel tired. If you have difficulty falling asleep, pay attention to what's in your environment that could be keeping those brain waves active and that melatonin suppressed. Close your laptop, turn off the TV, and keep your phone out of reach.

CONSISTENCY IS KEY

Another way to ensure high-quality sleep is by getting roughly the same amount each night. One of my students recalls a three-week period his sophomore year when the amount of sleep he got from one night to the next varied significantly. "Tests, papers, projects, and schoolwork overall had gotten very overwhelming, to the point where I was struggling to fit it into my schedule. Slowly, chunks of sleep started to fall off on a regular basis—to the point where I was the stereotypical college student getting only a handful of hours of sleep." To compensate for his sleep deficiency during the week, he would sleep in on Saturdays and Sundays. Though many young adults are used to racking up debt through credit cards and student loans, neuroscientists agree that there is no way to make up for sleep debt.

For my student who attempted this, the effects were harsh.

"My low levels of sleep during the week, and my change in sleep patterns on the weekend, turned me into an undesirable version of myself. My average productivity plummeted due to being tired but needing to keep working, I had no interest in seeing or interacting with other people, and my mood was hostile to the point where I would snap at my parents when I spoke to them on the phone (completely unheard of in my relationship with my parents!)."

His experience is consistent with what we have learned from research on this topic. In a study conducted at the University of Wisconsin–Madison, hundreds of adults were given Actiwatches, small devices worn like wristwatches, which detect gross motor activity and record how much sleep an individual gets each night. Participants wore them for a full week, allowing the scientists to understand how sleeping patterns relate to other aspects of one's life. They found that one of the most robust predictors of a person's psychological well-being was whether they were able to get close to the same amount of sleep each night. Those with the largest sleep variability were the most prone to stress and other negative emotions throughout the week.[21]

They note also that an irregular sleep schedule can contribute to the onset of other sleep difficulties such as insomnia: "Individuals who sleep poorly on one night may want to 'catch up' by sleeping longer on the subsequent night. Although this recovery sleep may provide temporary improvements in feelings of fatigue and sleepiness, it can result in worse sleep the following night, as overly long sleep can undermine the ability to fall asleep."

Another study at the University of California found that teenagers with highly variable sleep schedules experienced more negative moods in their daily lives than those who consistently slept well. According to the authors of this study, "Variability in adolescents' sleep time is just as important as the average amount of sleep in explaining individual differences in daily psychological well-being." In other words, it's not simply enough to get a full night's sleep *tonight*. Rather, the aim should be achieving that regularly.[22] Adults who *consistently* get optimal sleep—between six and eight hours per night—are less likely to experience depression and anxiety, and are more likely to achieve self-directed goals.[23]

After learning about the importance of sleep consistency, one of my students discovered a technique to achieve a routine sleep schedule: tracking it. "I took a biology class called Biological Clocks in which we were required to chart our sleep schedule for an entire semester. Charting it and seeing a physical manifestation of it really made me want to fix that bad habit of mine, so I began sleeping at consistent hours." In addition to a chart with fewer sharp angles, his new routine had a big payoff psychologically: "I felt more alert in the mornings, I felt like I was able to perform better (my grades certainly shot up), and

I just felt better about myself as a whole. I was able to work out early because I was up early also."

Prioritizing sleep and getting a consistent amount each night gives us the energy and focus we need to stay on task with our goals the next day. Establishing routines around sleep lays the foundation for establishing routines around other behaviors—like exercise—that also increase happiness.

———————

Many college students experience challenges balancing sleep, a social life, and good grades. But through a series of trials and errors, most figure out a system eventually. Just weeks before graduation, three of my students offered the following advice based on what worked for them.

1. For those still struggling to determine how much more they should study and when to go to bed:

> "The question is, How many more questions will you get right if you cram some more information in your head than if you go to sleep and rely on your well-rested smart brain to better analyze the test questions and pick good responses? If the answer is about equal, go to bed. Personally, the intellectual and emotional benefit of getting a good night's sleep is enormous, and I think students usually underestimate the benefits of sleeping as well."

2. For those who claim they are too busy:

> "As my senior year approached, I knew that I wanted to break the trend of sleep deprivation that persisted through my sophomore and junior years. Even though I'm a busy college student, I do not use my busy schedule as an excuse for not sleeping. I have adjusted my study habits and I've learned to go to bed before one a.m. and wake up early to study. My social interactions have been enhanced, I have become more alert, and my grades have also improved."

3. And for those Thomas Edisons and Margaret Thatchers who say they don't have enough time for regular sleep:

> "My friends are always amazed that I manage to find nine hours to sleep every night and juggle my life so well; they wonder how I have so much time. It's *because* I sleep more that I have more time. By investing the time to sleep, my awake hours are much more productive, efficient, and less stressed than most of my friends, I want to shout that from the rooftops: *Invest in your sleep!* You can get so much more out of fewer hours in the day that way, AND you don't have to spend nearly as many hours studying for each exam because you'll remember so much more (or because you were awake in class)."

A few years ago I asked first-year students in one of my classes to report how much sleep they got each week during their first semester of college. I followed up with those students four years later and found that the amount of sleep they'd gotten as freshmen correlated not only with how well rested they felt during their senior year but also with their senior-year GPA. Better sleep at the start of college was associated with better sleep—and better grades—by the end of college. Setting good sleep patterns early can position you for long-lasting success.

The young adult years are full of new experiences, information you have to retain, decisions you have to make, and insight you have to gain about where you are headed—not to mention the stress that each of those brings. You work hard to manage them while you are awake. Give your brain the time it needs to keep working on them when you are asleep. Eventually you'll find balance among *all three* legs of the college triangle. And if you find you're having difficulty getting a full night's rest regularly, just do what you can to keep three in the afternoon open on your schedule for a power nap.

Attention Training

Last spring I gave my students an assignment that has to be the easiest they've ever received. It didn't involve reading passages from a book, doing problem sets, memorizing brain structures, or writing thought papers. In fact, they didn't have to *do anything*. They were instructed simply to sit still and *do nothing* for six minutes. You'd have thought I was letting them off easy. That is, until you saw how the students reacted.

One called the assignment "particularly tough." For another it was "a real hassle." A third told me it was "extremely hard." But compared to their other assignments that semester, their instructions for this one were extremely simple:

Find a quiet space and entertain yourself with thoughts of something pleasant for six minutes. Put away any distractions such as your computer or phone, turn off the TV or radio, and sit in silence for six minutes (set an alarm), occupying yourself only with the thoughts in your head. You may think about anything you wish (going on a hike, having dinner at your favorite restaurant, being on vacation, etc.).

There are only two rules:
1) Remain seated.
2) Stay awake.

Sounds easy, right? But in today's fast-paced world of constant stimulation, I wanted to see what would happen if students were required to put down their phones, turn off their laptops, and just sit with themselves in silence. Could they last a whole six minutes, about the length of one of Jimmy Fallon's opening segments on *The Tonight Show*?

The results were startling. More than 30 percent didn't make it without checking their phones, writing something down on paper, or getting up out of their seats. Among those who did, 36 percent reported a high level of difficulty concentrating on the task. An assignment that had looked to be the easiest I had ever given ended up having the lowest completion rate I've ever seen in any course I've ever taught. According to one of my students, the time-space continuum becomes altered when you're not allowed to do anything:

> "About two minutes into the activity, I couldn't resist turning on my computer. Even though six minutes is a really short time, those two minutes felt extremely long; it felt like I was not doing anything. If I had been surfing the web or doing homework, those six minutes would have passed without me even noticing."

Even among those who had completed the assignment and lasted a full six minutes sitting in silence, 98 percent said that their minds wandered at least once from the thoughts they intended to entertain during the activity. More than half said their minds wandered a lot. One student called the task "almost impossible."

I should not have been surprised to see these results. I got the idea for this assignment from a study that had been conducted the previous year by a scientist who had done a similar experiment with undergraduates at the University of Virginia.[1] Just like my students, most of the young adults in the UVA study found it difficult to stay focused on the task without their minds wandering, and many reported that they did not enjoy the experience. The scientists found this reliably across multiple iterations of this study. People do not like being left alone in silence and would rather do almost anything else instead.

In fact, one version gave participants the option of receiving an electric shock during their six minutes of silence. Students were reminded that their primary task was to entertain themselves with their thoughts; however, the choice was available to self-administer a shock if they wanted. They already knew the shock was unpleasant because each of them had experienced it earlier in the study. Virtually all of them reported it as unpleasant. Most, in fact, said they would pay money *not* to experience the shock again in a later part of the study.

The logical conclusion, then, is that no one would voluntarily self-administer this unpleasant stimulus. But when researchers observed the number of people who gave themselves the painful jolts, the results were, well, shocking. Nearly one in four women, and two in three men, gave themselves a shock at least once during the silent thinking activity. Many of them did so more than once!

Apparently, something unpleasant (the shock) was preferable to uninterrupted solitude accompanied only by their thoughts. For some, when they are left alone with their thoughts, their minds quickly go to negative places:

"I found this to be a very difficult task. I couldn't keep myself focused on a single topic and instead my mind wandered. I started off by thinking about one of the suggested pleasant topics, having a dinner at my favorite restaurant. I thought about going there and enjoying the cheese fondue with some of my friends. However, I quickly remembered that my favorite restaurant stopped selling the cheese fondue that I really enjoyed. I tried to think about something else pleasant and recalled the last time I went to the St. Louis Comic Con. Unfortunately my mind wandered again to less positive thoughts. This year the St. Louis Comic Con is being held a week after graduation and I will not be able to attend. This is essentially how the entire six minutes went. I tried to remain focused on very positive topics, but my mind would always wander to negative things before I could stop it."

Others decide they would rather be doing anything but the task at hand.

"I chose to think about my mom and doing fun things with my mom like jamming, watching movies, and crafting. This activity was difficult for me because I could only concentrate on my mom for about thirty seconds before I started thinking about all the other things I could be doing with my time. My first distracting thought was, 'You could be doing a short workout right now,' which is insane because I would never do that."

When I polled my class the following week to ask them how they would prefer to spend five spare minutes that came up in their day (such as in between class, or in between one meeting and another), fully 89 percent of them said they would prefer to do *something* like homework, reading, or checking their phones. Only 11 percent said they would spend that time silently with their thoughts. Some might look at these results and say, "Who cares if we don't enjoy sitting silently with our thoughts?" Many consider it a waste of time, and by and large, people find it hard to do and generally unpleasant. So let's just not do that. Let's always have external tasks and activities to occupy our attention. But our thoughts can become intrusive regardless of what we are doing and when. Distractions like a phone, computer, or fidget spinner can't block out everything all the time.

Research from behavioral genetics has revealed that although genes play a significant role in our overall well-being, a full 40 percent of our happiness results from intentional acts.[2] These acts include choices in the activities that we do, like whom we spend our time with and what we do in our free time, and choices in those things we just *think* about, like where our minds go and how our thoughts affect us. Establishing control of our thoughts—especially when we are left alone with them—is one way to increase our happiness.

A WANDERING MIND IS AN UNHAPPY MIND

A study by scientists at Harvard tracked more than two thousand adults' daily thought patterns by having them respond to prompts that appeared on their smartphones at random times throughout the day.[3] In a series of questions, the participants reported not only what they were doing—such as watching TV, working, or running errands— but also what they were thinking about. The researchers wanted to know whether their attention was fully dedicated to the actual activity itself—a state psychologists call mindfulness—or if the mind had instead escaped along the scenic route through la-la land. It turns out that almost half of the time, people's minds were on something other than the task itself. Maybe they were physically present at an executive meeting at work, but their mind was traveling back to last night's baseball game that went into extra innings, or worrying about the difficult conversation they would have to have with a friend this weekend. Did it make a difference in their overall happiness if their thoughts had departed from the task at hand?

To find out, each smartphone prompt came with a question assessing the participants' happiness levels. Because of the longitudinal nature of this study, the scientists could test whether mindfulness (as opposed to a wandering mind) at one time affected happiness at another time. Sure enough, those whose minds had been fully present in whatever they were doing were significantly happier the next time their iPhones measured their well-being. If they had been thinking about something else, their happiness decreased. This effect held both for pleasant activities like having lunch with a friend and unpleasant activities like being stuck in traffic. No matter what we are doing, we are better off paying full attention to it—engaging our senses and bringing awareness to what it looks like, sounds like, and feels like—instead of surrendering to the distractions luring our minds away.

For many people, however, this tendency for the mind to wander in the middle of any given task is somewhat automatic. Consider the way another of my students reacted when asked to sit silently for six minutes:

"To be honest, this activity was difficult for me because I actually avoid sitting in silence with my thoughts at all costs. Overall, I noticed that my thoughts tended toward negative things. More specifically, when I'm left alone with my thoughts, I either worry about what I have to do or ruminate on my past mistakes. And this is why I try to keep myself busy."

Many people are like this student, aware of the unfavorable effects of their wandering minds. Mind-wandering also underlies procrastination and apathy toward goal achievement. We may have sat down at our desks to work on a project or begin an important paper, but our automatic impulses quickly draw us into our favorite social media sites, as is the case for this student:

"It has become a habit for me to check out what people are doing and saying. Sometimes I will have Facebook open in one tab and think to myself, 'I should do something else,' and I then open up another tab of Facebook."

Opening up Facebook instead of working on an assignment is the result of a mental process like the one that lets our minds travel forward or backward instead of remaining in the present moment. Both are related to an inability to stay focused. Most young adults will tell you this is one thing they wish they could do better.

> "In retrospect, I would have preferred a shock. This was a rather uncomfortable activity. Before I even sat down, I found myself procrastinating as much as possible. I probably wasted fifty minutes trying to push it off. My procrastination level reached the point in which I was searching for carry-on luggage online.
> "Finally, when I could not put it off anymore, I sat down with some yogurt and contemplated my service trip this winter. I was able to consume my thoughts with this moment in time for maybe one minute. Pretty quickly my mind had wandered. I am very aware that I need to work to become better at meditation."

The good news is that this skill can be learned.

LIVING IN THE MOMENT

I first learned about mindfulness from my friend Ginny when I was in graduate school. Ginny has spent the better part of her adult life working with young adults, helping them navigate life's ups and downs. For several years she worked at a university health center, where she incorporated mindfulness interventions into her work with therapy clients. She found that meditation was so effective at treating anxiety and reducing stress that she began offering free meditation workshops to allow even more students a chance to learn how they could benefit from the practice. Given how prevalent anxiety and stress are among college students, she initially expected the workshops to fill as soon as they were announced. Instead it was a struggle to fill them even halfway. It could have had something to do with the misconceptions many people—like this student—have about meditation:

> "I know meditation and clearing the mind of thoughts has many healthy and restorative purposes, but I just don't understand how people can take so much time to, as I describe it, 'waste time doing nothing.' I know this is a reductionist view of what meditation is, but to me I have very little time to devote to things I deem unproductive, and unfortunately, lack of activity is included in this."

One of the most common misconceptions about meditation is that it involves simply removing yourself from life's distractions, taking a break, and calming yourself down through relaxation. Although that might be a side benefit, it's more than "doing nothing," as my student first assumed. Rather, it is an exercise in strengthening our ability to focus our attention on a given task.

Ginny knew it was important to continue offering the workshops given how effective meditation had been with individual students she had worked with, not to mention the large body of evidence showing its effectiveness. The issue she faced was how best to draw students in—meditation just needed a better marketing campaign. After a few semesters an idea came to her. She didn't change a single thing about the workshop itself—each session remained exactly as it had always been. Instead she gave it a new name. She got rid of any mention of meditation in its title and description and simply called it "Attention Training." Students signed up in droves. Attendance skyrocketed from eight students to more than sixty-five in one semester.

Ask anyone who works with college students and they will tell you that one of their primary barriers to success and well-being is how easily distracted they are, and how quickly intrusive thoughts derail their attention. It's no surprise then that slots for Ginny's "Attention Training" workshops filled up almost as soon as they were announced. Even medical schools were calling, asking her to lead the workshop with first-year MD students. I jumped on that bandwagon and began incorporating her attention-training materials into my Positive Psychology class. The students loved it. Even one who was dubious at first found it valuable:

"Before last week, I didn't know what 'living in the moment' truly meant. 'Of course I'm living in the moment,' I would think to myself. 'I'm aware of my surroundings right now. Now, what homework do I need to do tonight…?' I admit, when we discussed meditation I was skeptical. But then the in-class meditation workshop really convinced me.

"As the guided meditation period ended and I opened my eyes, something was different. It was like someone had just flicked a switch and turned off the cacophony of thoughts in my head. I was completely focused on the present; the auditorium's colors were more vivid and the sounds were sharper. In many ways it was a relief. I felt alive."

THE PRACTICE OF MEDITATION

By now you may be interested in trying this assignment for yourself. Six minutes isn't that long, right? All you'll need is a quiet space and timer. Once you are seated in a comfortable position, begin by bringing attention to your body in the space that you currently occupy. Relax your muscles and then slowly bring attention to your breath. Feel the sensation of air entering your nose and leaving as you exhale. Pay attention to what it feels like as your lungs fill with air and your chest expands. Those are the experiences you are having in this very moment, and for your meditation period, those are the experiences worthy of your full and nonjudgmental attention.

Continue this pattern of mindfulness throughout these six minutes. Inevitably your mind will begin to wander. That's OK. When this happens, simply give attention to the fact that your mind led you astray, let those thoughts go, and gently bring your attention back to the task at hand, your breathing, and the feeling of your body in space.

Of course, this is easier said than done. Those intrusive thoughts are often resistant to just being "let go." However, meditation can be helpful in learning how to let them *be*. That sentiment—"If you can't let them go, let them be"—is one of the foundations of mindfulness. If negative thoughts or feelings arise and don't dissipate on their own, just sit with them. Trying to force them out is like trying not to think about a polar bear—the thoughts and feelings will rebound, becoming even more intense. Simply bring awareness to the negative emotions or intrusive thoughts in all their unpleasantness, and do so nonjudgmentally. When they just won't go away, letting them be is a far better alternative to feeling bad because you're feeling bad. Remember, positive psychology is not about "being happy all the time." Part of psychological health is knowing how to hold sadness, anxiety, fear, and anger without them taking over.

Nearly everyone who meditates reports that at some point during meditation their mind wanders off to something else. Some will even say that their mind is spending more time wandering than attending to their breathing or whatever they were choosing to focus on. Eventually they will catch their mind in the act of wandering and have to go through the steps of relinquishing their hold on those intrusive thoughts and putting their minds back on the object of their meditation.

And this is exactly what you want to have happen, and precisely why meditation is an effective way to train your attention.

The act of letting go of the distracting thoughts and placing attention back on the breath is strengthening "attentional muscles," as Ginny refers to them in her presentation. Over time meditation becomes easier and more natural because those attentional muscles become stronger. It becomes easier to detect when the mind is starting to stray, and easier to bring it back to your intended focus. In fact, recognizing when your mind is wandering and gently bringing it back to the breath is one of the most important parts of the entire meditation exercise. That moment of "bringing it back" is strengthening your attentional muscles.

This practice translates to happiness because we carry those attentional muscles with us throughout the day. When we are sitting in a meeting and we start ruminating about the dispute we had with a colleague the day before, strong attentional muscles acknowledge that our thoughts have strayed and now must come back to the meeting. When we sit down at our desk to work on a report and our fingers are opening a new Facebook window or starting to type the address of our favorite online shopping site, strong attentional muscles lead us to close the browser and direct focus to our work.

EVERYDAY MINDFULNESS

Walking down any crowded street, you've probably noticed that many people aren't looking up. Some have difficulty even walking in a straight line as they attend to text messages and phone alerts that are apparently more important than dodging other pedestrians, cyclists, or even oncoming cars. Addiction to our smartphones has become so pervasive—and dangerous—that in 2017 the city of Honolulu passed legislation to make it illegal to view a mobile device while crossing the street.[4] This distracted walking law is meant to reduce instances of oblivious pedestrians being hit in the middle of the road due to attention takeovers by their screens. Repeat offenders could pay fines of up to ninety-nine dollars for scrolling through Instagram or posting to Facebook in a crosswalk.

We have become so uncomfortable with silence as we wait for the subway, place our order at a fast food joint, or even walk down the street that our automatic reflex has become to check the mobile device in our pockets to entertain our attention. But even if it's not posing a threat to our physical safety, it is at least taking a toll psychologically. One study found that interruptions from phone alerts can increase symptoms of ADHD such as inattention and hyperactivity.[5] Another study found that the mere presence of a smartphone, even facedown and silenced, can reduce our ability to pay attention since overriding the temptation to check the phone consumes mental energy that otherwise would go to the task at hand.[6] This inattention has even slowed down business for some restaurants, where patrons don't read the menu until they have read all incoming texts and e-mails, and they can't take a bite of their meal until they've taken the perfect pictures to post on social media.

Tempting as it may be to fill the quiet, tedious, or boring spaces in your day with activity from a mobile device, you can use them instead as opportunities to practice mindfulness. As you are walking to class or to a meeting, pay attention to your surroundings—the colors of the trees and the sounds of cars driving by on the roads around you. When you are waiting for a table at a restaurant, take note of the decor on the walls and the aroma of the freshly prepared meals arriving at tables nearby. Even as you hold this book, fully experience the tactile sensation your fingers have as the cover and pages rest in your hand. Engage all of your five senses (or as many as are appropriate) in whatever experiences you are having at any given moment, and give them priority at the fore of your mind. And if you find your thoughts have drifted to something else, simply acknowledge it and nonjudgmentally draw your attention back to the present moment and the present experience. This is what keeps those attentional muscles sharp.

In her workshop Ginny explains that even stopping at a red light when driving can be done mindfully. This is an idea she first learned from the wisdom of Buddhist monk Thích Nhất Hạnh,[7] and here's how she explains it:

> "As soon as you encounter a red light, immediately *stop, smile,* and *breathe.* That's it. Stop, smile in recognition that this is a tiny opportunity you've been presented with to take a few

mindful breaths, and then mindfully take a long breath in,
and a long breath out. If you're lucky enough to be at a busy
intersection, you'll get a few complete breaths in.

"This strategy is great for those of you, like me, who tend
to get frustrated when hitting a red light. Which is so crazy,
right? Taking something personally that couldn't *be* more
impersonal—as if it saw me coming and deliberately decided
to change so that I'd be held up. Since learning this technique
I find myself much less bothered by traffic lights."

We can even do this when we are hurrying somewhere. Think
about the last time you were late to a meeting and rushing to get there.
There was probably a lot going through your mind en route. "How did
this happen? How late will I be? Will I cause a disruption when I get
there? Will other people notice I am late? Will they be upset? Should I
apologize? Will I miss something important at the beginning?" Think
about the impact these thoughts have when combined with the adrenaline rush from hurrying to get there. Once we finally have arrived,
it will take time to quiet our minds and draw our attention to the
present moment. If we had been mindful even in our rushing, paying
attention only to the sights and sounds whipping by instead of to the
potential embarrassment waiting for us upon our arrival, our mind
would already be in position to bring that same mindfulness to the
meeting itself. Cluttering our minds with the busyness and worry that
normally accompany hurrying somewhere can put us on overdrive.
When our mind is this ramped up it takes extra time to cool our jets
and calm ourselves before we can be fully present and engaged with
the next set of tasks before us.

Anxiety is born of future-focused thinking. Mindfulness is the
perfect antidote, as this graduating senior discovered:

"I've been experiencing a lot of stress and anxiety, especially
in terms of finding a job for next year while also trying to
enjoy my final year at WashU. It's a hard time of transition and

there are a lot of unknowns, but meditation helps to bring me back to the present moment and not think so much about the uncertainties of the future.

"The weeks when I don't have time to listen to a forty-five-minute guided meditation session (which happen to be just about every week), I do try to incorporate mindfulness into every day. Even if this is simply taking a few deep breaths before starting the day or replaying positive quotes in my head, I try to stay in the present moment, react carefully, and think before I speak. Oftentimes when I feel anxious or overwhelmed, I try to use the techniques of mindfulness by breathing and letting the thoughts go. It is quite simple and easy, and most times it is actually very helpful."

One of the most popular activities Ginny does during her workshop involves individually wrapped chocolate candies. Normally college students would devour these as soon as they got their hands on them. But for this exercise the students are told to simply hold the chocolate in their hands and take note of it, following Ginny's mindfulness instructions. "What does it look like? What does it feel like? How much does it weigh? Put it up to your ear and shake it. Does it make any sound?" Then the students are invited to slowly pull away the foil, listening to the metallic crinkling that finally breaks open the sweet aroma of chocolate. They bring the delectable treat to their noses to take in a full whiff and then finally are invited to bite into it, paying added attention to each sensation as they taste and chew.

Some of them will have spent more time with this one piece of chocolate than they did earlier in the day with their entire lunch. Eating is a prime opportunity for mindfulness when we consider how much goes into preparing meals, and the fusions of ingredients that produce distinct tastes. Many people report that when they bring mindfulness to their eating, they enjoy the food more, find it more satisfying, and often will even end up eating less because they are taking their meal at a slower pace. So for those looking to create a healthier relationship with food, and maybe to lose a pound or two, mindful eating could be one step toward these goals.

One of the advantages of meditation is that it can be done nearly anywhere. A number of free apps are available that can enable a quick meditation. I use the Insight Timer, which allows you to set meditation sessions of any length and provides a soothing bell to begin and end each session. It also keeps statistics on how frequently you meditate and lets you see who else around the world is meditating "with you" at the start and end of your session. (This morning I meditated with Ryan from Idaho Falls.) I also listen to the guided meditations and evening talks available from dhammatalks.org, most of them led by an American Buddhist monk at the Metta Forest Monastery outside Valley Center, California. Each talk provides insight into the practice of meditation and how to calm the mind to minimize suffering.

A WORD TO THE SKEPTICS

Of course, the entire realm of calming the mind and maintaining control of one's thoughts has garnered many critics. Ruth Whippman offers an unfair indictment of mindfulness in a recent *New York Times* article wherein she lambasts it as a "special circle of self-improvement hell."[8] In her tirade she laments that "on the face of it, our lives are often much more fulfilling lived outside the present than in it," and goes on to say, "Surely one of the most magnificent feats of the human brain is its ability to hold past, present, future and their imagined alternatives in constant parallel, to offset the tedium of washing dishes with the chance to be simultaneously mentally in Bangkok, or in Don Draper's bed." Here Ms. Whippman is illustrating one of the most common myths about meditation, that the practice is somehow intended to prevent us from replaying a previous vacation or imagining a parallel universe. Let me assure you, meditation is not about preventing you from dreaming about backpacking through Thailand or a secret rendezvous with your celebrity crush. As we will see in chapter 10, we can get a lot of happiness from anticipating future events and re-living past experiences (be they real or imaginary).

There is a key difference, however, between self-driven reflection and unrestrained mind-wandering. The issue is not *where* our thoughts end up (be it past, present, or future), but *how* they got there. Did we direct our thoughts there on our own, or did they crop up in a time and space that was originally intended for something else? If we are making a conscious decision to direct our attention to the party we are throwing a friend next month, or to an argument we had last night that we are still trying to figure out, that mental activity can be useful. But when such thoughts pop into our minds on their own when we are working on a project or trying to pay attention in class, the effects can be detrimental to our overall well-being.

Practicing mindfulness at the kitchen sink, therefore, is not about giving undue attention to stubborn lasagna stuck to the bottom of a casserole dish, but instead about practicing mind control. The same attentional muscles that redirect attention to the suds along our skin also are capable of redirecting attention away from the tumultuous thoughts wreaking havoc in our minds. Remember that negative thinking patterns, which are among the hallmarks of depression and anxiety, can intrude without warning and take on a life of their own, spiraling downward in a vicious cycle. When they start going, we need the capacity for mind control to slow them down. Focusing on the here and now during a simple household chore, and preventing our minds from going anywhere else, is developing a skill that can put the brakes on a negative thinking cycle in the future. As with any other skill, the more we practice it, the more easily we can implement it.

Developing this skill was at the heart of Ginny's workshops, and it is easy to see why they became so popular. If you can get past the new age misconceptions about meditation, "attention training" has benefits that can improve many domains of life. Just in the last few years a large body of research has found that mindfulness meditation may be effective in treating myriad hindrances affecting young adults, including anxiety,[9] depression,[10] binge drinking,[11] eating disorders,[12] OCD,[13] sleep dysfunction,[14] and procrastination.[15]

A LESSON IN SELF-FORGIVENESS

As beneficial as meditation can be, people often wonder if they are doing it correctly. To ease such concerns, Ginny would always start the workshop with a definition of mindfulness from one of the field's leaders, Jon Kabat-Zinn: "Paying attention on purpose, in the present moment, nonjudgmentally." This sounds so simple, but as the research described earlier demonstrates, our minds often spend a lot of time in places other than the present moment. Even if we *are* in the present moment, the odds of our being there nonjudgmentally are slim. How quick we are to criticize our work, our relationships, or our body image for not being good enough. For some, letting go of judgment is the biggest challenge:

> "The hardest part of meditating was following the instructions. The soothing voice told me to allow thoughts to drift through my mind without judging them or focusing on them—letting go of thoughts of 'You should be working on that problem set' or 'You should be rehearsing organic reaction mechanisms' felt impossibly difficult."

Like those new to any skill, first-time meditators often encounter self-doubt. Although many people understand on an intellectual level the benefits of meditation, it can be challenging to put into practice. But like most things, the way to become better at it is through practice.

After I guided my students through meditation training in class, one told me about his attempts to do it alone:

> "It was more difficult than I anticipated. I got frustrated at how easily I distracted myself during the exercise. However, at some point near the end, I reached an epiphany. The true purpose of meditation is not to train oneself to prevent distraction; it is to forgive oneself for getting distracted in the first place. The next time I sat down to meditate I realized that the faster I could let go of a thought the quicker I could get back to thinking about my breathing. Meditation is not hard to do, but it can be difficult to understand."

This student's epiphany gets at the core of the meditation practice. Although we will never be able to clear our minds entirely of obtrusive thoughts, we can learn how to manage them. Remember, the goal is to strengthen our attentional muscles. We make them stronger the same way we make any muscles stronger: by using them. Just as pumping iron at the gym makes your biceps capable of lifting heavier things, bringing your mind back to whatever you are focusing on makes your attentional muscles capable of maintaining focus for longer periods. The more you exercise them, the stronger those muscles become, and the more you can use them in the future. It gets easier over time, even for the student who initially had difficulty following the instructions without being swept away by thoughts of her chemistry homework:

> "I found that the more frequently I did it, the more rapidly I could enter the state of calm. I could do shorter meditations, get into a calm state faster, and be able to resume my studying in a much more relaxed state—a state that would enable me to learn more and feel better about it."

The benefits extend far beyond the meditation period itself. Recall the student I described earlier who was initially dubious of the practice but opened his eyes to feeling alive after the in-class workshop. He soon began incorporating meditation into his daily habits:

> "The greatest benefit comes from being able to concentrate on a task, which saves time. I decided to meditate before doing homework tonight, and while I still had urges to browse social media and surf the web, I was able to catch myself moving my cursor to the web browser, stop myself, and refocus on homework. I cannot believe it has been only an hour since I meditated, because I rarely get this much done in one hour!"

Meditation is a lot like sleep or exercise. Many are reluctant to devote large amounts of time to it because it feels like a waste of time. Those behaviors, however, position us to use our remaining time more efficiently, ultimately allowing us to be more productive in the long run.

PRACTICE FOR STANDARDIZED TESTING

As we've seen, mind-wandering is one impediment to the productivity and efficiency of many young people. Attention training is important for everyday tasks, but the ability to maintain your focus becomes especially important under a time crunch. This may strike a chord for anyone who has applied to college or is considering graduate or professional school. Entry into these highly selective programs requires strong performance on a standardized test like the SAT, GRE, LSAT, or MCAT. The market for private tutoring and test preparation—including companies like the Princeton Review and Kaplan that offer courses and materials aimed at improving test takers' scores—generates billions of dollars annually.[16] To be sure, taking practice tests and getting a tutor can be helpful. But another strategy—proven especially useful for improving performance on the reading comprehension passages—is as free as the air we breathe: meditation.

Consider the challenges of the reading comprehension section. Test takers must digest a passage of unfamiliar text in a short time and then answer questions about its ideas and themes. Completing this section successfully requires steadfast attention to the most relevant details throughout the test. Given the time constraints, intrusive thoughts can be costly to one's score. After I introduced meditation in my Positive Psychology course one semester, one of my premed students began meditating as part of his preparation for the MCAT. Like other students, he also was initially skeptical, but found that his attentional muscles got stronger with practice:

"My mom had been telling me for as long as I can remember to try meditation and I had blown it off, thinking, 'Why would I just sit there doing nothing? That seems stupid.' But I began to meditate every night and I've noticed some subtle yet important changes in my mindfulness.

"On the first two days, I found myself losing focus several times a minute, and found it frustrating to have to let go of the thought and drag myself back into focus each time. But each day thereafter, it became less and less of a hassle, and last night I only lost focus twice over a span of ten minutes.

"The result of this improved control over my focus has been clear to me as I'm taking practice tests of the MCAT. Like we discussed in class, I found that comprehending passages has become somewhat easier. My thoughts flow much better and I am able to grasp the author's argument without too much effort."

His inspiration to begin meditating as part of his MCAT prep came from a study we had discussed in class that tested this technique with undergraduates at the University of California, Santa Barbara. Each student completed the reading comprehension section of a GRE (the standardized test required for entry into many PhD programs).

Half of them began integrating mindfulness and at least ten minutes of meditation into their daily activities. In as little as two weeks, these meditators saw significant increases in their scores. Meditation had strengthened their working memory, which is the mind's capacity for processing information efficiently. Meditation and mindfulness also reduced the number of intrusive or unrelated thoughts that popped into their minds when they were taking the test.[17] Just as meditation can prevent our emotions from spiraling out of control, it also can boost our attention spans to help us concentrate on our work. Intrusive thoughts that otherwise would impede our reading comprehension are less likely to emerge once we have trained the mind to focus.

MEDITATION AND DEPRESSION

A common characteristic among people who suffer from anxiety and depression is rumination, the intrusion of thoughts that either deprecate the self, replay negative experiences from the past, or cause worry about bad things that may happen in the future. Halting negative thinking cycles is often at the heart of therapies for psychological distress like depression and anxiety.

Meditation is one strategy for diminishing the impact negative and intrusive thoughts can have on us. The sad irony is that people who suffer from anxiety are often the most reluctant to attempt meditation, as was the case for one of my students:

> "I used to be an 'avoid sitting in silence with my thoughts at all costs' type of person. Therefore, when it was initially recommended that I try meditation to cope with my anxiety, I was extremely resistant. This practice seemed so counterintuitive to me—if I was plagued by negative thoughts that disrupted my daily functioning, why would I sit in silence with nothing but my thoughts for large amounts of time?"

For people who are depressed or highly anxious, those negative thoughts will often spiral out of control. Meditation teaches how to simply bring awareness to those thoughts, acknowledge them non-judgmentally, and then let them go, so you can carry on with the rest of your day. Even small doses of meditation can set you on a path toward psychological health. Eventually my anxiety-prone student agreed to a regimen of five-minute exercises at the start and end of each day:

> "While at first those five-minute sessions were excruciatingly long and most certainly increased my anxious thoughts, over time the positive effects began to appear. Instead of being bothered by my intruding thoughts, and interpreting these thoughts as a sign of failure, I began acknowledging the thoughts, accepting them, and allowing myself to refocus as the thoughts passed.
>
> "I envisioned the thoughts as leaves floating through a river. Instead of standing in the middle of the river and trying to single-handedly halt the flow of the river, I decided to let the water pass. I metaphorically placed each thought on a separate leaf and watched as it calmly floated down the river. It was important for me to learn that one, I could not 'fail' at meditation, and two, meditation didn't require that I eliminate all thoughts from my mind, but simply that I stop allowing these thoughts to control me."

More and more clinicians are recommending meditation as an intervention, and the effects are significant. In the book *The Mindful Way through Depression*, a team of psychologists and brain scientists who have studied the impact of meditation on mood disorders discuss how bringing awareness to negative emotions is the first step in mitigating their impact. As the authors note, "Our reactions to unhappiness can transform what might otherwise be a brief, passing sadness into persistent dissatisfaction and unhappiness."[18] Their ideas are consistent with an ancient Buddhist teaching that uses the analogy of two arrows to describe suffering. It tells us that when we get hurt by something or someone, there is pain, as if from an arrow hitting us. The first arrow is bad enough. But responding with anger, vengeance, or rumination is only self-inflicting additional suffering beyond the initial pain. Such a reaction to that first arrow is, in effect, shooting ourselves with a second.

Meditation quiets the mind, halting the emotional havoc anxiety and depression can cause. One of my students reported that meditation was the most effective intervention he had ever tried for his psychological health:

> "I've struggled with anxiety, stress, and some depressive symptoms throughout college, and meditating has helped give me peace and control over my thoughts more than anything else (including counseling). This was totally unexpected, and I didn't realize thirty minutes a day of sitting quietly and guiding my thoughts could impact the rest of my life so much. The day or two after meditating I feel significantly better, and am a better person to the world and my friends around me—it's started to feel like something necessary to do for my well-being."

As another passage from *The Mindful Way through Depression* highlights, "The problem is not the sadness itself, but how our minds react to the sadness."[19] Learning to let something *be* prevents the second arrow—"suffering"—from being shot.

A ZEN HEALTH BOOSTER

Meditation also has medicinal properties, causing changes in the brain that can improve both physical and psychological health. Consider this student who used meditation as an intervention during a rough patch she encountered in college:

> "I started meditating last summer after an absolutely terrible
> semester. I was really unhappy with being premedicine,
> and I had just ended an extremely awful relationship. I was
> quite depressed, and was prescribed antidepressants to get
> back on the wagon. However, even in my depressed state,
> I knew that the drugs would just be a quick fix and that the
> real problem was my thought patterns. So I looked up ways
> to combat depression and one of the ways was meditation.
> So I decided to throw myself into meditation in lieu of the
> medicine. It was such a freeing experience. I relearned things
> about myself that I had forgotten, and I was exposed to new
> feelings that I had kept bundled up inside of me. I called
> meditation my crash course in self-love."

One of the leading scientists in the study of meditation and its impact on our physical and psychological well-being is Dr. Richard Davidson, a faculty member at the University of Wisconsin–Madison. In one of his landmark studies, he trained a group of adults in mindfulness meditation, which they then practiced on their own for an hour per day over the next eight weeks. At the end of the study, they exhibited less anxiety and a decrease in other negative emotions, and there was even evidence that their immune systems were stronger. In other words, the benefits of meditation took place on both psychological and physical levels.[20]

Importantly—and impressively—meditation even changed the physical structures of the participants' brains. Since the late 1990s scientists have been accumulating evidence in favor of neural plasticity, the idea that the brain can physically change in response to repeated behaviors and thought processes. One brain region in particular that happiness researchers are interested in is the prefrontal cortex. This part of the brain governs aspects of the self that make us uniquely human: abstract reasoning, complex decision making, and impulse control. It also plays a role in our emotional well-being. The prefrontal cortex is subdivided into two halves, one in the brain's left hemisphere and one in the brain's right hemisphere. Using measures of the brain's electrical activity (known as electroencephalography or EEG), scientists have found that people who are the happiest tend to have a higher level of activity on the left side of their prefrontal cortex relative to their right side.

Remarkably, Davidson's study found that meditation is one such strategy for increasing that ratio of left-to-right prefrontal cortex activity. Just eight weeks of the practice was enough for brain function to change in ways that were associated with both physical and psychological well-being. My student who used meditation as a crash course in self-love encountered these benefits in about as much time:

> "My depression started to slowly dissipate as I learned to move past old pains and to not judge myself or my feelings. I learned to focus on my breathing and to just observe sounds, feelings, and thoughts. In doing this I learned to appreciate not just myself, but also the world around me more. I woke up.
>
> "Before, I was just living life by going through the motions; I was practically a zombie. When arriving at school this past fall, I was determined to keep up with my meditations since I had experienced the benefits firsthand. I had legitimately helped myself without any medications. I now meditate as often as possible because it helps center and calm me, and it allows me to set an intention for the day. I have also noticed that I'm happier and more myself when I meditate. It's a time that I look forward to because it rejuvenates me."

A NEW APPRECIATION FOR LIFE

Last spring when I asked my students to spend six minutes silently with their thoughts, an alarming proportion of them could not do it. For many it served as a wake-up call, exposing the destabilizing potential of their wandering minds. It also provided an impetus for some to begin incorporating meditation into their routines:

> "I had done absolutely no work over spring break and when, upon my return to school, I had to face the consequences of my laziness, I felt completely overwhelmed. Thus, trusting in the positive benefits of mindfulness and meditation that this class advocated, I decided to make meditation a habit.
>
> "Not knowing where to begin, I downloaded a guided meditation app. My expectations were pretty low—my attempt at the 'six minutes with your thoughts' task hadn't gone so well, so I didn't really think I'd be cut out for the meditation life. But three minutes into the guided meditation, feeling the most relaxed, focused, and at peace that I had been in months, I was gladly proven wrong.
>
> "Since then, I have tried to meditate every day, and have mostly been able to stick to this goal. Although it's only been a few weeks, I do feel that I am already less stressed—in the midst of the chaos that is midterms period, I've managed to stay surprisingly calm and happy. These positive changes in my life, and in my attitude toward life, motivate me to continue meditating. Moreover, I truly enjoy the process of meditation, and savor those few minutes of feeling deeply in tune with my body and in touch with my environment. I never thought I would be one to say something as cheesy as this, but meditation has brought a new appreciation for life that I hadn't experienced before."

Who knew a six-minute homework assignment could offer such long-lasting benefits?

6

Failing Better

Years ago, Forbes.com reported a list of kids' dream jobs.[1] Children say they want to travel through space as astronauts, score winning goals as professional athletes, save lives as firefighters, and perform to sold-out crowds as rock stars. Of course, as they grow up they get a better understanding of the (incredibly low) odds of becoming the next Taylor Swift or David Beckham. Aspirations they may have set at a young age mature as they do. They eventually develop a more realistic understanding of where their strengths may lead them.

The dream job that tops the list, however, doesn't seem to fade after the naïveté of the kiddie years: treating injuries and illness as a physician. According to the Higher Education Research Institute, of the 1.5 million students entering college each year, about 20 percent self-identify as premed.[2] That equates to roughly three hundred thousand hopeful physicians starting college each fall. How many of them actually make it through the premed requirements and go on to apply to medical school? Only about fifty thousand. How many of that group get accepted? Around twenty thousand.[3] That leaves us with a meager 8 percent of the initial pack who will go on to don the coveted white coat. NCAA baseball players have better odds of being drafted by the MLB.[4]

The sharp drop in premeds from freshman year to graduation day says a lot about the demands of the premed curriculum. The courses are daunting and the workload is intense. Even students who previously had been academic superstars encounter difficulty. One of my former students—a member of the 8 percent who eventually make it to medical school—told me about how his journey there got off to a rocky start: "During my freshman and early sophomore year, my grades were not what they could have been. Unfortunately, I suffered from poor class selection and an inability to balance my extracurriculars with my coursework. I was working hard every day, but I just wasn't getting the results that I was hoping for." No matter how hard he studied, it seemed, his performance was mediocre at best. "I didn't get it; in high school, working harder in my classes always seemed to give me better grades."

The hard reality many students face is that success in college—especially when one is confronted with the rigor of a premed curriculum—requires an approach that is different from what may have worked in high school. My premed student's expectations about what would lead to academic success were going to have to change.

It's not just those applying to graduate and professional schools who encounter such reality checks. One of my students experienced similar struggles when he was applying for summer internships during his sophomore year. He applied to more than a hundred jobs. Only two potential employers gave him an interview. Neither offered him a position. "I was extremely discouraged and I could not for the life of me figure out why no one wanted to hire me," he said. "After all, I was clearly smart, as demonstrated by my test scores and the fact that I went to a good college. So why wouldn't anyone hire me?"

After a bit of soul-searching and consulting with his father, he came to understand that success does not come as easily as he—and countless young adults like him—had been led to believe. "For years I had relied on intelligence to do well without effort; in fact, I even took pride in how little I had to try to succeed. But now, for the first time, I ran into a challenge I could not outsmart: job hunting. Success without hard work had warped my expectations."

But where did those expectations come from? What was it going to take to turn them around and onto a path toward success? And what led them to become warped in the first place? When expectations and reality don't line up, there is room for despair to sneak in. Plans that go awry can often be interpreted as the ultimate form of defeat, a sign that we should give up altogether. Although no one likes to fail, everyone encounters it eventually. But it need not spell doom or be the final verdict. There are ways to *fail better* that can leave us stronger and positioned for success in the long run—including, perhaps, a white coat or job offer.

A "FULL" TANK

One way to begin exploring expectations is to look at how we arrive at them. What signs and signals are we following to understand our place in the world—and our future success or failure? I like to frame it for my students using a simple story from my own college experience.

During my last two years of college I was a resident adviser in an undergraduate dorm, charged with enforcing quiet hours, helping students who had lost their keys, and planning study breaks during midterms. In the weeks before school started, all RAs went through an intensive fourteen-day training. We learned how to cure homesickness, put out small fires, intervene for suicidal freshmen, and perform all the other responsibilities that a fresh-faced twenty-one-year-old is obviously capable of handling. It was an intense two weeks, but a reprieve came right in the middle, when we got to leave campus for three days of RA camp, an opportunity for quiet reflection and bonding with each other. To ensure that it was a true break from the busyness of training, it was always held at a rural campsite about two hours south of campus.

Well, it was *supposed* to take two hours to get there. As we were traveling down a windy road in rural Missouri, the old yellow school bus carrying sixty excited college students came to an abrupt stop. Confused, we all began looking at each other. The administrators on board were just as puzzled. "This isn't camp," we all thought. "Why are we stopped here?" Our attention then turned to the bus driver. He nervously hit the gas and turned the key in the ignition. The motor sputtered out a few tired coughs but wouldn't turn over. "This can't be," he apologized.

It turns out the culprit was a faulty gas gauge whose needle had been stuck on "Full" the entire trip. By all signs (or at least the most important one) there was plenty of gas in the tank. But that sign was misleading. In fact, we were without the most important element to get us where we needed to go. Although a nearby farmer was able to get us enough gas to complete the trip, the stuck gas gauge was, in a way, an appropriate analogy for the very people the bus was transporting. Our own meta-phorical needles had been stuck on "Full" from the time we learned to read the words "I am special" in kindergarten. And instead of parents, teachers, and coaches putting metaphorical gas in our tanks, they kept pushing our needles to the "Full" position, leading us to believe we had everything we needed for a smooth, easy ride to a successful future. Little did we know how bumpy the road was up ahead.

A TROPHY FOR EVERYONE

All the RAs riding the bus that day, including myself, grew up during the advent of the self-esteem movement, sanctioned by government officials in the 1980s. This initiative aimed to bolster how kids felt about themselves. Politicians and educators believed societal problems including teen pregnancy, drug abuse, and crime were rooted in adverse upbringings.[5] Kids who were hoisted up and told how great they were, it was believed, would become adults who abstained from deviant behavior. To this end, we were bathed in messages of how *special* we were and how we could do *anything* we set our minds to. Posters on classroom walls encouraged us to dream big and told us that nothing could stand in our way. Teachers handed out recognition certificates simply for completing assignments. Sports coaches distributed trophies for simply showing up to the games.

I suppose you could make a case that I earned the academic certificates that spent years collecting dust in my parents' basement. I always excelled academically. But trophies and ribbons recognizing my athletic abilities? That's a different story.

When my brothers and I played catch in the backyard, I would spend more time analyzing the baseball itself, calculating the number of stitches along the ball's circumference, than actually throwing it. Suffice it to say they didn't invite me to play with them very often. When my kindergarten soccer coach told me that I would be playing left fullback and pointed to my assigned territory, I stood in that specific spot of the field the entire game, never straying beyond the twelve square inches surrounding it. If other kids dribbled directly past me, I might have a go at the ball, but I spent the remaining 99 percent of the game staring at the scoreboard, doing mental arithmetic to determine how many seconds remained before it was over so I could stop by the concession stand and get nachos or Fun Dip. When I ran the hundred-yard dash in middle school, I almost always ended up in the bottom tier of finishers. That was, until one race day when an unusually low number of runners left only three people in my heat instead of the usual eight. This was great news for me—I got to tell everyone that I came in third instead of eighth!

I have similar anecdotes for nearly every sport I attempted as a child. So why was *I* collecting trophies and ribbons recognizing my athletic accomplishments? Wouldn't it seem that the kids who were scoring goals on the soccer field and breaking the finisher's tape on the track would be the only ones going home with the hardware in hand? Well, the reason I was showered with praise without actually earning it on the athletic field was that *every* kid was going home with a trophy and ribbon. It didn't matter who won. It didn't matter who lost. It didn't matter what the score was (that is, if we were even keeping score at all). All that mattered was that no kid suffered the agony of defeat or the disappointment of not coming out on top.

Although it may have felt good at the time, those awards from our coaches—just like the posters and certificates from our teachers—were pushing our self-esteem needles to "Full." And as the bus driver taking us to RA camp would have attested, that's a dangerous place for a needle to get stuck.

It's no secret that adversity is unpleasant. Research by Dr. Mark Seery at the University at Buffalo has confirmed that, not surprisingly, people who experience the highest levels of lifetime adversity are the worst off: their lives as adults are the most stressful and the least satisfying.[6] Impairments to their physical and emotional health interfere with their daily activities. In other words, extreme levels of adversity in childhood leave people in bad shape later in life.

It makes sense, then, that the self-esteem movement of the 1980s aimed at making children's lives as easy as possible. Even pop artists jumped on the bandwagon, wanting kids to always feel good about themselves. Take a look at the opening lyrics of the hit song "The Greatest Love of All," popularized by Whitney Houston around this same time, in 1985:

I believe the children are our future . . .
Show them all the beauty they possess inside
Give them a sense of pride to make it easier

These lyrics simply describe the goals of parents, teachers, and coaches at the time: make children aware of their inner beauty. Make them feel proud. *Push their self-esteem needles to "Full."* On the surface this seems like a wonderful notion. Who doesn't want children to feel good about themselves? If we fill children with a sense of pride—with armfuls of trophies and certificates to showcase it—their lives should be easier, right?

But there's a question of how far is *too far*. In fact, the desire of so-called helicopter parents to clear every pebble from their children's paths sometimes doesn't end in middle school or even high school. Many continue to intervene even when their children enter college. In their book *Letting Go*, Karen Levin Coburn and Madge Lawrence Treeger provide examples of how this unfolds: "Some parents even try to have dorm rooms switched, or show up at the meetings for students and advisers, or make special requests to the RAs to look out for their children."[7]

One could argue that these parents are simply heeding the advice of Whitney Houston to "make it easier" for their students. But if life becomes easier, does it really become better? According to Coburn and Treeger, the answer is a resounding no. "All of these actions, no matter how well-intentioned, make it more difficult for the new freshmen to separate and assert their independence," they say.

And these barriers to self-sufficiency are only the tip of the feel-good iceberg.

UNINTENDED AFTEREFFECTS OF THE SELF-ESTEEM MOVEMENT

Take a look at the following article that ran in *Time* magazine a few years after the launch of the self-esteem movement:[8]

"A standardized math test was given to 13-year-olds in six countries last year. Koreans did the best. Americans did the worst, coming in behind Spain, Britain, Ireland and Canada.

"Now the bad news. Besides being shown triangles and equations, the kids were shown the statement 'I am good at mathematics.' Koreans came last in this category. Only 23% answered yes. Americans were No. 1, with an impressive 68% in agreement.

"American students may not know their math, but they have evidently absorbed the lessons of the newly fashionable self-esteem curriculum wherein kids are taught to feel good about themselves."

There's no denying it. And if you were a kid growing up in the 1980s or 1990s, there was no escaping it. You were taught to feel good about yourself. Your self-esteem needle was planted firmly in the "Full" position. However, feeling good about yourself all the time, especially when it's not warranted, will eventually take its toll.

Psychologist Jean Twenge has examined personality characteristics of thousands of young adults over several generations and found significant increases in narcissism from the 1970s to today. She wrote a popular book summarizing her findings—*Generation Me: Why Today's Young Americans Are More Confident, Assertive, Entitled, and More Miserable than Ever Before.*

The title explains it all. The praise young people were showered with growing up has translated to negative outcomes as they enter adulthood. As Twenge explains in the companion website to her book, "Today's young people have been raised to aim for the stars at a time when it is more difficult than ever to get into college, find a good job, and afford a house. Their expectations are very high just as the world is becoming more competitive, so there's a huge clash between their expectations and reality."[9] This clash may account for the warped expectations of my student on the job market who came to expect success without hard work, or the premed who struggled with science classes but expected to do better just by trying harder.

Such a discrepancy between expectations and reality also represents another misfortune of the self-esteem movement. Here we have two young adults who, as children, likely got trophies or were told they were special just for showing up—for putting in the *minimal* amount of effort. These messages fostered a mindset that became problematic in young adulthood. They had to learn the biology lab and interview room were not the soccer field. Just showing up was no longer enough to guarantee they would go home with the prizes they sought.

Though rooted in good intentions, the self-esteem movement left out three essential elements that are at the core of success and well-being:

1. Perseverance in the face of adversity
2. The ability to glean wisdom from setbacks
3. A willingness to lean into life's challenges

Fortunately for my students, they eventually learned the first of those elements on their own. Both could easily have thrown in the towel at the first job rejection or poor chemistry grade. Many in their situations would have. But there was something—a critical outlook—that kept them trudging along. Ultimately it's what led to their success.

STARING FAILURE IN THE FACE

That critical outlook was at the core of a study conducted by Professors Jonathon Brown and Keith Dutton at the University of Washington.[10] Everyone knows what it feels like to get good feedback, but what about a situation where you've been knocked down and the temptation to throw in the towel rears its head? To find out how mindset affects reactions to failure, the professors had more than three hundred undergraduates solve a series of word puzzles that were rigged so that half would enjoy an easy victory and the others would suffer an agonizing defeat. Each puzzle consisted of three words. Solving them required identifying a fourth word that related to the other three. For example, they might see "duck—fold—dollar," for which the solution is "bill" (duck*bill*, *bill*fold, dollar *bill*).

See if you can think of the word that fits the bill for each of these puzzles:

1: cream—skate—water
2: home—sea—bed

The answers are below.* If you are like most people, you had an easier time coming up with the answer to the first puzzle than the answer to the second. Now imagine that you had to answer a whole series of these puzzles, and they were all either as easy as the first set above, *or* as challenging as the second. Enter Professors Brown and Dutton. This was the design of their experiment. Half of the students were given easy puzzles, allowing them to enjoy effortless success. The other half were given the more challenging type, all but guaranteeing imminent failure—and also providing the most interesting reactions to observe.

Recall that the self-esteem movement was about making us feel good, making life easy, and making success preordained. But a true test of someone's self-esteem actually comes when they *fail* at something. In other words, self-esteem—*authentic* self-esteem—is not merely a matter of feeling good all the time. It's not just about having your needle pointing to "Full." Merely telling a kid that she is great, irrespective of her actual abilities, leads to artificial self-esteem, the kind that many educators, politicians, and parents have been propagating unknowingly for years. It's what has driven increases in narcissism. It's the reason American students believe they are so good at math. It's why, as a child, I thought I was a star athlete (trophy cases don't lie, right?).

Authentic self-esteem, on the other hand, involves knowing how to rebound when you encounter adversity. It's what keeps you going when faced with the harsh reality that, contrary to what your needle is telling you, you are actually running on empty.

As this mindset played out in the study, everyone in the condition with easy puzzles felt good about their performance. No surprise there—it feels good to succeed. For those in the more challenging condition, left to surrender worksheets peppered with unsolved word puzzles, nearly all showed a dip in happiness and self-worth. No

_____

* 1) Ice: ice cream—ice skate—ice water; 2) Sick: homesick—seasick—sickbed

surprise there, either—it feels bad to fail. But some who failed were hit especially hard by the crushing feedback.

What predicted the severity of the sting among those unable to complete the task? Their *authentic* self-esteem. If it was low, they were devastated. If it was high, though they were somewhat upset, they had the psychological wherewithal to prevent being dragged down by the failure. In other words, *authentic* self-esteem provides a psychological buffer that can soften the blow when we take hits to our egos. It's not simply a matter of being told how great we are regardless of the circumstances; that leads to *artificial self-esteem* and an unrealistic view of our abilities. *Authentic self-esteem* is about knowing how to pick ourselves back up when things don't turn out well.

As Brown and Dutton explain, "Self-esteem plays its most important role in guiding people's self-relevant emotional responses to negative outcomes. Consequently, it will be most closely tied to behavior when responses to failure, disappointment, or rejection are involved."[11] The movement from decades ago—the one interested in developing a child's self-esteem to ease adult anguish—prevented children from facing failure head on. Without ever having confronted it, they never got to learn how to guide their emotions beyond those negative outcomes. Think back to the three essential elements at the core of success and well-being. The first is about knowing how to respond when life hands you lemons, or, for that matter, word problems you can't solve.

PRESS ON!

For my premed student who encountered struggles early on in his college career, it was ultimately high authentic self-esteem that helped him turn things around. "At first, this was hard. It was easier for me to just wallow in self-pity or blame it on other factors rather than actually do something about it." This initial response is like that of the low self-esteem students who failed at the word puzzles in the Brown and Dutton study: their feelings of self-worth and overall happiness had taken a hefty hit by the end of the experiment. Fortunately for my student, his authentic self-esteem eventually came through and provided a buffer. Instead of giving up and resigning himself to low grades and improbable odds for his postgrad dreams, he kept going.

"I forced myself to look inward and truly analyze my performance," he said. "I made appointments with premedical advisers, spoke with successful colleagues, and focused on a more active approach to an intense workload." The wisdom he gained by speaking to faculty, administrators, and students just a few steps ahead in the premed curriculum helped him identify what he had been doing wrong and what would be necessary to succeed. His new approach paid off. Beginning the following semester, he improved his grades and maintained strong performance even in the most rigorous courses. Most importantly, he developed a mindset that will serve him beyond his undergraduate days: "I now have confidence that I can tackle difficult classes because of my work ethic and ability to adapt to the class itself." Making a hard self-assessment and identifying room for improvement left him motivated to push harder, instead of confused as to why his usual approach was no longer working.

In a similar way, the student who had more than a hundred failed job interviews kept persevering on account of his high authentic self-esteem. A conversation with his dad led him to this insight from Calvin Coolidge:

"Nothing in this world can take the place of persistence. Talent will not; nothing is more common than unsuccessful men with talent. Genius will not; unrewarded genius is almost a proverb. Education will not; the world is full of educated derelicts. Persistence and determination alone are omnipotent. The slogan Press On! has solved and always will solve the problems of the human race."

This was just what he needed to hear. "I went back on the internship hunt with new vigor," he told me, "and I managed to land one that positioned me to get my dream job my senior year."

Most successful people will tell you that en route to their accomplishments, it was necessary to take risks and be open to the possibility of failure. Even when things didn't turn out well, they learned lessons that proved valuable for them in the future. Importantly, they came to see failure as par for the course, an expected part of the journey.

Consider J. K. Rowling's message to Harvard graduates in 2008:[12] "It is impossible to live without failing at something, unless you live so cautiously that you might as well not have lived at all—in which case, you fail by default." Looking back on her young adult years, she considered herself an epic failure: divorced, jobless, a single parent, and "as poor as it is possible to be in modern Britain, without being homeless." But she had a buffer to protect her: authentic self-esteem. Staring failure in its formidable face, she kept going. "Rock bottom became the solid foundation on which I rebuilt my life," she said. It also became the foundation for the most successful book series of all time.

DEVELOPING AUTHENTIC SELF-ESTEEM

The premed, the job hunter, and the children's novelist all behaved according to what research on authentic self-esteem has shown. When the first approach doesn't work out, people with high self-esteem search for another way. They keep at it. Quite a contrast from those on the low end of the self-esteem continuum. For them the agony of defeat squashes any interest in an opportunity to bounce back. It's not just a hit to self-worth in the moment that affects low self-esteem people. Even more unfortunately, failure also makes them less likely to take risks and put themselves out there in the future. As Brown and Dutton (of the word puzzle study) describe, "They may become more concerned with protecting the self from the pain of failure rather than risking success. . . . Low self-esteem people will not undertake the same behaviors high self-esteem people undertake because they (correctly) anticipate that a negative outcome will be so aversive."[13]

Failure is an inevitable part of life. Trying to eliminate it altogether will prove futile. What actually matters is how we *respond* to failure. That's why the students with the more challenging word puzzles in Brown and Dutton's study were the most interesting to observe: if you really want to gauge someone's authentic self-esteem, you don't want to look at how they are doing when the sun is shining, their needle is on "Full," and everything is going their way. Instead you'll want to see how they respond after they've *failed* at something. Everyone feels good after a success. It's in the aftermath of a stumble or a fall when you really get a sense of someone's psychological strength.

Of course, some criticize the very idea of building up one's authentic self-esteem. It teaches young people to chase dreams they have no chance of fulfilling, these critics contend. A student who fails one chemistry exam after another may still cling to dreams of being a doctor because his high self-esteem tells him—irrationally—to keep at it.

A fine line, however, separates perseverance and stubbornness. Another characteristic of authentic self-esteem is a sense of realism: the level-headedness to understand the steps that are required to achieve a desired outcome, and whether you have the capacity to fulfill them. In other words, authentic self-esteem isn't about having a needle pointing always to "Full," or always to "Keep at it." Instead it's about persevering toward goals that are realistic and picking yourself back up after getting knocked down—while also adjusting plans as needed, aligning them with your actual potential.

Still, the educators and politicians who developed the self-esteem movement were on the right track. It's true that self-esteem is worth developing in a young person. Self-esteem is necessary for persevering in the face of adversity and helping you discern whether you need to modify your goals. But it doesn't come just by forcing the needle to "Full." Instead it is a skill that is developed just like any other—through experience. This brings us to the second essential element of success and well-being: understanding that adversity presents opportunities to become even better at your trade. The self-esteem movement omitted this message from its curriculum. Fortunately, the pop music scene picked up the slack.

———————

Kelly Clarkson, the celebrated winner of *American Idol*'s first season, is known for her Billboard-topping hits exploring relationships and personal empowerment. She is regarded as the most successful winner of any *American Idol* season, having sold tens of millions of albums and singles, far more than any of her peer front-runners in the singing competition series. Her concerts play to sold-out crowds, and she has been showered with awards from the National Academy of Recording Arts and Sciences, Billboard, the Country Music Association, and nearly every other organization that honors top musical talent in her genre.

Her popularity may well be the result of her ability to provide a musical backdrop to the many emotions we feel as we dream of a lover, get over a broken heart, or bounce back from hard times. Her most popular single, "Stronger (What Doesn't Kill You)," has sold more than five million copies worldwide. What accounts for its extraordinary success? Perhaps it comes from how easily the listener can identify with the lyrics:

> *What doesn't kill you makes you stronger, Stand a little taller...*
> *What doesn't kill you makes a fighter, Footsteps even lighter...*

This sentiment makes for an inspirational lyric, but is it actually true? Could this hit song be more than just a catchy tune? Might there be something about facing challenges that, so long as they are not fatal, can actually leave us standing taller, with footsteps lighter, and—cue Ms. Clarkson—even *stronger*?

Let's revisit that study conducted by Dr. Mark Seery, which showed that adults who had faced extreme adversity growing up suffered poor psychological outcomes later in adulthood. This surely was not a surprise. In fact, your reaction was probably along the lines of, "They actually had to do a study to show that?"

Well, there was a lot more to the study than simply showing that severe hardships herald negative outcomes. As you might imagine, there was considerable variability in the amount of adversity the participants in the study had encountered. Some had endured a lifetime of hardship marked by severe adversity of every kind; others had made it to adulthood free of any real misfortune. Many were in the middle, having endured *some* lifetime adversity, though an amount that was manageable. At first glance, those who had experienced no prior adversity in their lives seem like the lucky ones. They never had to bear the burdens of serious illness, financial instability, or losing a loved one. Shouldn't we all be so lucky— to make it to adulthood unscathed by hardships of any kind?

Or should we?

In the first round of analyses, Seery found that extremely high adversity meant extremely low psychological well-being. As I described earlier, this is not surprising. This might leave some to extrapolate that less adversity would be better for us. And that's true, but only up to a point. Here's where Seery's findings become, to many, counterintuitive.

The people who ended up with the best outcomes—most satisfied with their lives and functioning best in their relationships and at work— were not the individuals who had *never* encountered adversity growing up. Rather, it was the adults who had experienced *some* adversity who were the best off.[14] A bit like Goldilocks, when it comes to lifetime adversity, you don't want too much, but you also don't want too little. A "happy medium" yields the best outcomes. And in this case that's not just a phrase. Many studies are showing that those who have to cope with "medium" hardship in fact turn out to be the "happiest."

The benefits of experiencing some lifetime adversity were not simply a matter of stronger psychological health and functioning years down the road. A person's amount of childhood adversity also predicted how well they were able to cope with adulthood adversity.

Because this study was tracking people over the course of several years, the scientists were able to monitor how the participants responded to hardships that arose in that time: some of them got divorced, others were fired from a job, and several suffered the loss of a close friend or relative. All the while they were providing updates on their well-being, giving the scientists a glimpse into how these recent hardships affected them and how quickly they recovered.

What predicted their ability to bounce back from recent adversity? The same thing that predicted their psychological health in the first round of analyses: previous adversity. Those who had recovered from hardships earlier in life were fastest to rebound compared to those whose past contained none. That previous adversity, it turns out, provided them with the psychological wherewithal to pull through. According to Seery, "In moderation, experiencing lifetime adversity can contribute to the development of resilience."[15] Part of the silver lining of adversity is that it teaches coping skills that indeed make us *stronger* in the face of future adversity.

A LEARNABLE SKILL

Much like playing the piano, tying your shoes, or speaking a new language, coping with adversity is a skill developed with practice and repeated exposure. A child who never practices his scales on the piano will never develop the skills necessary to master a Beethoven sonata. Likewise, someone who never has to overcome hardship early in life will not develop the psychological strength necessary to persevere through severe relationship woes or career stress.

According to Seery, knowing how to overcome adversity is important for our overall well-being:

"Experiencing low but nonzero levels of adversity could teach effective coping skills, help engage social support networks, create a sense of mastery over past adversity, foster beliefs in the ability to cope successfully in the future, and generate psychophysiological toughness. All of these qualities should contribute to resilience in the face of subsequent major adversity. Such qualities should also make subsequent minor daily hassles seem more manageable rather than overwhelming, leading to benefits for overall mental health and well-being."[16]

J. K. Rowling's message to the 2008 Harvard grads had a similar refrain. "Failure taught me things about myself that I could have learned no other way," she told them. "You will never truly know yourself, or the strength of your relationships, until both have been tested by adversity. Such knowledge is a true gift, for all that it is painfully won, and it has been worth more than any qualification I ever earned."[17]

So it seems Kelly Clarkson is correct. In moderation, what doesn't kill us *does* make us stronger. Of course, Clarkson's lyric, as it stands right now, tells only half the story. Adversity makes us stronger so long as we engage our social support networks and reflect on the experience to glean strength and confidence for the future. Although we might have difficulty getting her to rewrite the song, it still offers an important lesson. It gives us permission to embrace hardship. An exam that goes poorly or a job application that is rejected can teach us how to study for the next test or what to say in a future interview.

Extracting a learning opportunity from our failures is the second essential element of success and well-being. Remember from the early pages of this book that well-being is not about being happy all the time. A core component of psychological health is knowing how to respond to negativity. We all fail from time to time. Having the coping mechanisms to get back on our feet will help to minimize its impact.

This doesn't change the fact that no one likes to fail. It does bring to light, though, the third essential element of success and well-being. Whereas the first two elements are about *dealing with* challenges—finding the psychological strength to persist, and gleaning whatever lessons can be attained—the third is about *leaning into* life's challenges. Instead of responding to them as they come up, the most successful people actually seek them out.

———————

Last spring I asked my students to write about a time they encountered a challenge. One wrote about a physics class that was so challenging she initially assumed there was no hope for her. In fact, by the time she walked into the first lecture, she had already made up her mind that she was not cut out for it. "Give me a neuron or a redox reaction and I was fine, but circuits and electromagnetism left me completely befuddled," she admitted. "My mind just didn't work like a physicist's, and so my only goal for the class was to struggle through it and pass."

Like many others, this student interpreted her challenges in the class as a sign that she was simply not good at the subject. What intrigued me about her story, though, wasn't just the fact that she'd thought she wasn't good at something. It was *why* she'd thought she wasn't good at it. From her perspective, the aptitude to complete a physics problem set was an either-or proposition: either you are smart enough to do it or you aren't. She spent the first few weeks of the course relying on friends to explain answers to her. She did poorly on the first exam and felt completely lost—both seeming confirmations of what she'd felt on the first day of the class: she just wasn't cut out for this.

Fortunately, by semester's end she had turned things around completely. She approached her assignments with confidence and her performance on exams had skyrocketed. The turning point, she found, was not just about learning the rudiments of circuits and electromagnetism. In addition to relying on authentic self-esteem to lean into the challenge, she also mastered another important characteristic that highly successful people bring with them into adverse situations: the right mindset.

GROWING INTO SUCCESS

Dr. Carol Dweck, a noted psychologist at Stanford University, has identified two distinct mindsets that influence how people approach challenging situations.[18] The first is called a fixed mindset. Students with this mindset are primarily interested in the outcome of a task and whether it was successful or not and less so about the process that led them there. All that matters to the student with a fixed mindset is that they get an A. On top of that, the A should come easily, because performance reflects raw intellect or talent. People who are talented shouldn't have to work hard at something. If things don't turn out well, it's because the person is not smart and is doomed to fail in future attempts. Consider a student who gets a low grade on their first college assignment or paper. The fixed-mindset student would say, "I'm not smart enough to take this class," or "I'm not good at writing papers," or "This grade means I won't get into graduate school." They would see poor performance as a reflection of their abilities, with no potential for change or improvement. This student would choose easy courses in which they could consistently receive good grades, protecting their self-concept that they are "smart."

The second is the growth mindset. With this mindset, people acknowledge that effort and hard work are necessary for success. When things don't turn out well, the individual with a growth mindset reflects on the approach and considers what might be done differently next time to achieve a more desirable outcome. This person is energized in the face of challenge because it presents a learning opportunity. A low grade on an English paper would prompt them to strengthen their approach moving forward by seeking out assistance from the instructor, tutors, or other resources. This student would choose the most challenging courses available so that they could expand both their knowledge of the subject and the work ethic necessary to tackle such challenging material.

My dismayed physics student started the term with a fixed mindset:

the either-or thinking, the idea of a mind that "just didn't work like a physicist's," the reliance on others to carry her through. The course topics were intimidating and she didn't believe she had what it took to master them. After doing poorly on the first exam and being completely lost on several homework assignments, however, she decided to go to the professor's office hours. "I was hoping to just get some quick answers and get out of there." What she got instead proved to be a lesson about the opportunities available for growth that come from challenging situations.

Within minutes of working through one of the problems inside the professor's office, she stumbled on a moment of sheer embarrassment. "I had to explain that I had forgotten how to take derivatives." As this knowledge is a prerequisite for enrolling in the course at all, the instinct to quit loomed large. The professor, unbothered by her paltry derivative-taking skills, took her back to the drawing board to provide a refresher. He coached her through a series of practice problems until she understood the material. In that moment he was teaching her not only physics, but—more importantly—how to respond to adversity. He was teaching her that getting stuck was an acceptable, even necessary, part of the process. He was, in essence, teaching her the growth mindset. "That moment made me realize that with a little extra work and some extensive coaching, I could solve physics problems on my own."

From then on, when she encountered a problem she couldn't do, she no longer interpreted it as a signal that she wasn't good at physics. Instead she knew this meant that she had to go back to the drawing board and try it another way. "I started going to office hours regularly, asking the TAs for help on homework questions, and seeking out study groups to cement my knowledge of the topics. Instead of giving up, I found myself trying new methods and ideas to work out a problem. If I was really stuck, I would set the problem aside and come back to it later instead of just quitting. By the end of the class, I had raised my C to an A minus, all because I changed my mindset. I went from believing there was nothing I could do to change my lack of physics ability to acing exams and solving problems on my own."

GLEANING SKILLS

Whereas authentic self-esteem helps you overcome life's challenges, a growth mindset gives you the wisdom to realize that challenges are not merely incidents to be overcome. They are, in fact, necessary for mastering key skills. Those with a growth mindset understand this and look forward to challenges, knowing how much they will learn from them. According to Dweck, these people don't just seek a challenge, they thrive on it. "The bigger the challenge, the more they stretch," she says.[19]

Consider another of my students who failed time and time again attempting to find an internship during college. Although he wasn't gaining employment, his growth mindset helped him understand that he wasn't leaving the process empty-handed, either. He came to appreciate just how much he had gained when applying for full-time jobs later in college: "I had failed so many times that I knew every wrong and right answer to give in an interview. I knew all the wrong and right ways to prepare. It was crazy how grateful I felt for failing so many times the year prior so I knew how to not make the same mistakes when it mattered even more. I succeeded in this job search, almost entirely from my misfortunes and mistakes a year prior."

In a similar way, my physics student was able to turn around her course performance by shifting from a fixed mindset ("I'm not good at physics") to a growth mindset ("I need to take a different approach"). When the course inevitably became more challenging, she understood that getting stuck didn't reflect an inability to do a problem set. Instead it was an opportunity to engage the work ethic and social network she had developed to help her along.

Be mindful of the feedback you get either from yourself or from others when you complete a task. When things go well, it's tempting to celebrate the victories and rest on your laurels. When times are tough, it's tempting to quit prematurely and brood over your shortcomings.

But if you can get yourself to focus on the *process* of how you got to where you are—or how you came up short—you'll be developing the growth mindset, ensuring greater perseverance in the future. It's also what positions you for that third essential element of success and well-being—a willingness to lean into life's challenges.

———

My fellow RAs and I ended up stuck in an old yellow school bus because it was out of gas. Unfortunately, the driver had no way of knowing this because the gauge was stuck on "Full." Psychologist Dr. Matthew Lieberman likened a car's gas gauge to self-esteem in an article he wrote for *Psychology Today*:[20]

> "If your car is running out of gas, what should you do? Here's what you shouldn't do. Break the glass on your dashboard and manually move the needle on your gas gauge from empty to full. That won't put any more gas in your tank and it might leave the next person thinking they have gas in the tank when there is almost none. The right thing to do is to fill up the gas tank itself. It's essential that the gas gauge is calibrated to the actual amount of gas in the tank, otherwise it's pretty useless.
>
> "All of this is true for self-esteem as well. As a society, for the past 25 years we have exerted tremendous effort to move the needle on the self-esteem gauge without necessarily putting more gas in the esteemability tank. Self-esteem without esteemability represents a dangerous miscalibration in which people think they can master hard things with ease (because everyone has told them that their middling performances are exceptional) and it deprives those individuals of the chance to know that they are not yet exceptional but perhaps could be with hard work."

What Lieberman was calling "esteemability" I have been calling authentic self-esteem throughout this chapter. We strengthen our authentic self-esteem—or fill our "esteemability tank"—by developing the capacity to bounce back from adversity.

Whether you're a premed who gets knocked down by the rigor of a daunting course schedule, a graduating senior who gets rejected from dozens of jobs, or a physics student with problem sets that seem unsolvable, challenges are part of life. It's not just feeling good about yourself that enables you to persevere. It's not just being handed a participation trophy on the soccer field, or accumulating hundreds of likes on Facebook posts and thousands of followers for your Instagram account, that will see you through life's challenges. Showering a child—or an adult, for that matter—with indiscriminate praise only produces an artificial sense of self, much like the broken gas gauge that was supposed to take us to RA camp. What really counts is having a realistic grasp of one's capabilities, and the strength to forge ahead on the roads to success and well-being. We get there by developing three essential elements: the capacity to persevere in the face of adversity, the ability to emerge from hardship even stronger, and the willingness to opt for challenges that will prompt us to strengthen the first two.

These lessons are hard won, often emerging only when we reflect on previous setbacks. Though it may be comfortable to always go with the easy option or have others solve our problems for us, it's only in negotiating life's hardships that we strengthen our authentic self-esteem. Otherwise we end up like RAs stranded in an old school bus on their way to camp. We might think we have what it takes to navigate life's challenges, but it will be a precarious trek if we don't know how much gas is actually in the tank.

7

Willpower

On January 25, 2016, Mark Zuckerberg returned to work at Facebook after a two-month paternity leave following the birth of his daughter, Max. Many decisions awaited his first day back: which projects would get his attention, which employees he would meet with, and how late he would stay before returning home to his family. Some of these decisions required more deliberation than others.

But one decision was far easier than any other: what he was going to wear. The thirty-one-year-old billionaire, with the means to sport a custom-made Versace suit and Prada leather shoes, chose a gray shirt and blue jeans instead. Really, it wasn't a decision at all. It's the same outfit he wears almost every day. He even posted a picture of his closet that morning, publicly acknowledging his daily uniform.

A little more than a year before, he'd addressed the topic during a public Q&A.

"I really want to clear my life to make it so that I have to make as few decisions as possible about anything except how to best serve this community," he said, adding that he prefers not to waste time on minor decisions that could be tiring and consume energy.[1]

Zuckerberg is not alone in his fixed work attire. Steve Jobs, the late cofounder of Apple, wore the same black mock turtleneck and jeans to the office every day. It turns out that wearing the same thing all the time isn't evidence of a lack of fashion sense, but a life hack practiced by some of the most productive thinkers and leaders of our

Mark Zuckerberg 😊 feeling undecided.
6 hrs · Palo Alto · 🌐

First day back after paternity leave. What should I wear?

time. When we preserve mental energy in one area of our lives, more remains for other areas. Fortunately, wearing the same outfit every day is not the only way to do this.

A FINITE RESOURCE

If there's one thing young adults love, it's free food. One group of researchers capitalized on this by inviting college students to eat as much of it as they wanted in what was advertised as a study of taste perception.[2] To ensure the students would arrive hungry, they were told to skip one meal before the experiment and not eat anything for at least three hours before. As they entered the lab, they were greeted by the aroma of freshly baked chocolate chip cookies wafting through the air. The delicious snacks awaited them in plain sight. Little did they know the researchers had cooked up more than treats for this study—they had designed an experiment that would revolutionize our understanding of willpower.

Next to the warm, tantalizing cookies lay a different kind of snack: radishes. Bitter, cold, raw radishes. Half of the students were invited to indulge in the chocolate chip cookies. The others were instructed to eat the bitter vegetables. All students were told to eat at least two samples from their assigned food and to leave the other untouched.

After digging in, tasting either cookies or radishes for five minutes, an experimenter explained they would need to wait fifteen minutes before moving on to the next phase to allow the food's sensory memory to fade. To help pass the time, the students were given puzzles to solve. They were told to trace shapes like the ones below without retracing any lines or lifting their pens from the page.

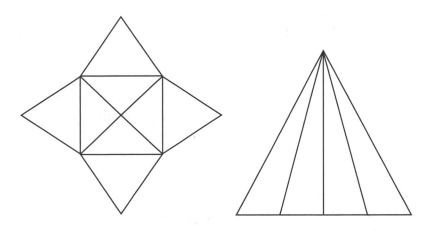

As motivation to dedicate as much effort as possible, their performance would be compared to that of local high school students. But there was a catch. The puzzles were impossible to solve. Did you try to trace either shape above without retracing any lines or lifting your pen? No solution exists. The same experimenters who had just forced half of these hungry college students to eat an entirely objectionable vegetable were now taunting them with impossible geometry problems.

As you may have guessed by now, the researchers had been hiding their true purpose from the get-go. This was not a study on taste perception at all. The researchers didn't care what the students thought of the cookies and radishes. Their performance on the puzzle task wasn't going to be compared to that of local high schoolers. The fifteen-minute puzzle task wasn't just meant to pass the time, either. In fact, the puzzle task was the most important part of the entire study. More specifically, the researches cared about how *long* the participants persevered in this impossible task.

The ability to solve a challenging problem requires willpower. When we are tempted to give up, willpower keeps us going. The amount of time the students were willing to put into the puzzle task and the number of times they were willing to try again after getting stuck tells us how much willpower they had at their disposal. But one half of the students were at a disadvantage. The unlucky radish-eaters had already spent some of their willpower by forgoing the chocolaty goodness before them. And when these students were given challenging puzzles to solve, they spent less than half as much time and made 43 percent fewer attempts than those who had been eating the cookies earlier.

This study illuminated an important insight into the nature of willpower: *it is a finite resource.* If we spend some of it on one task, less will remain for others. Compared to those eating the radishes, the cookie-eaters approached the task with willpower reserves intact, which explains why they were able to spend more time and effort on the puzzle task. You can think of willpower as being like the physical energy in our muscles. When runners train for a marathon, they usually take it easy for a day or two before the big race. If they helped a friend move instead of resting right before attempting 26.2 miles, they would tire much more quickly because some of their energy would already be spent. By conserving their energy ahead of time, they approach race day with a full tank.

Although Mark Zuckerberg doesn't run a marathon every day, his job requires his full engagement. By eliminating small taxing actions like choosing which outfit to wear, he can retain a full tank of willpower to spend on business matters. But this is not to say that he never expends willpower on small tasks at all. In fact, as we'll see in the next section, you have to exercise willpower in the short term in order to build it in the long term.

WILLPOWER IN THE LONG TERM

"Since coming to college, I have found myself to be increasingly lazy and unmotivated," a college senior admitted to me. "In high school I was extremely driven and completed my work well in advance, performed tasks when they were given, and did countless extracurricular activities. Nowadays, I push my work off till the last minute, don't study if I could be hanging out with friends, and even find it difficult to motivate myself to run, which is strange for someone who has loved running cross-country all her life." How could a student who was previously so astute now struggle to meet deadlines and keep practicing her beloved sport?

After some reflection the reason for my student's plunge in motivation became apparent to her. "I'm not forcing myself to stay motivated in other areas of my life." She had stopped running on the cross-country team and no longer had to regulate her diet, water intake, or sleep, or manage an intense training schedule. She also was not enrolled in any of the rigorous science courses that previously had been a staple in her schedule and required her to log long hours at the library. She also had stepped down from her leadership position in her sorority and no longer had to put in extra time and effort to keep the sisterhood functioning. "By allowing myself to slack off in other areas of my life, I found myself growing lazier with every aspect of my life."

When she was in high school, the strict schedule and lifestyle demanded by her rigorous course load and sports regimen required willpower that carried over to other aspects of her life. In college, an easier schedule meant her willpower needn't be quite as sharp. A mediocre willpower reserve for academics and sports meant a mediocre capacity to meet deadlines and find time for activities she enjoyed, like running. My student's experience illustrates another way willpower is like a muscle: the more we use it, the stronger it becomes; and the less we use it, the weaker it becomes.

This analogy of willpower as a muscle may seem counterintuitive when we consider the previous study with cookies and radishes, which taught us that using willpower now means we will have less available later. Shouldn't an easier schedule leave a student with plenty of willpower to do everything else she needs to complete? The cookies-and-radishes study, however, was dealing with willpower in the *short term*. Doing a challenging task now will make *immediately* doing another task harder. It's like working out at the gym. If you pump iron for forty-five minutes, you will be physically tired right after and unable to carry out other physically strenuous activities in the short term.

But in the *long term*, after a few months of working out at the gym, your physical muscles will become stronger and capable of more vigorous activity. Hard labor that may have burdened you before will be much easier to carry out. Willpower works in a similar way. Yes, if you have to forfeit a large amount of self-regulatory strength by finishing a report that is due at noon, you will have a harder time choosing carrot sticks over chocolate cake at lunch. But by repeatedly expending willpower through hard work and meeting deadlines, you strengthen your long term willpower and can stay focused on even more challenging work in the future—just like the gym junkie whose biceps get larger with each bench press.

As a bonus, once willpower is strong in one domain of life, it carries over to just about everything else we do.

FLEXING THE WILLPOWER MUSCLE

Consider a study from Macquarie University in Australia, in which psychologists Megan Oaten and Ken Cheng gave undergraduates a free gym membership with access to treadmills, free weights, and aerobics classes.[3] Students could go as often as they wanted. As you can see in the graph below, the students initially went to the gym only about once per week, but by the end they were going three to four times per week. They reported that it became easier to do so. Just as their physical muscles were getting stronger, enabling them to add heavier weights to their lifts, so too were their willpower muscles, enabling them to override the impulse to stay at home on the couch.

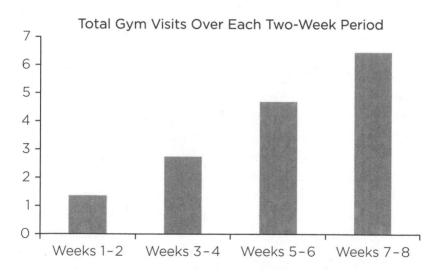

Total Gym Visits Over Each Two-Week Period

But the willpower they gained along the way wasn't just helping them get to the gym. Throughout the study the researchers also noticed changes in the students' self-regulatory behaviors that had nothing to do with the gym per se. They ate less junk food, smoked fewer cigarettes, drank less alcohol, spent less money on impulse buys, missed fewer appointments, watched less TV, studied more, lost their tempers less often, and even left fewer dirty dishes in the sink. They also showed more concentration and less distraction on a computer-based lab task.

Even though none of those other behaviors required the *physical* strength they were gaining at the gym, they were manifestations of the *willpower* strength they were developing by getting up from the couch to spend thirty minutes on a treadmill. It turns out that willpower is not domain specific: when we practice willpower in one area of life, we get the benefits of stronger willpower in many other areas as well. According to Oaten and Cheng, these results bear important implications: "In an overconsuming society, where food and attractive nonactive leisure activities prevail, perhaps nothing is more important to health than improving self-regulation. It could be a most important 'medicine' for our times."[4]

Other research has also found that practicing self-control in one area of life can strengthen self-control in others. In a study at the University at Albany, adults who ate as little dessert food as possible for two weeks performed significantly better on a subsequent lab test of self-control than people who had been making no self-regulatory modifications to their diets.[5] They find similar effects for participants who squeezed hand grips for as long as they could twice daily for two weeks. Repeatedly saying no to a slice of cake and enduring the discomfort of a strenuous physical task both involve overriding the temptation to do the opposite. Though taxing in the short term, such self-regulations strengthen the capacity for willpower in the long term.

Opportunities abound for strengthening willpower. Turn down a piece of candy the next time one is offered. Resist the urge to check how many people liked your latest Instagram post. Spend a few extra minutes studying for an exam or do extra exercises at the gym. Even correcting your posture throughout the day and making an effort to sit up straight and walk tall strengthen willpower.[6] Each of these behaviors is the "medicine" Oaten and Cheng described. Cough syrup doesn't always taste great, but it will make us feel better in the longer term. Flexing willpower muscles, though challenging today, is a practical way to be more productive, cut stress, get better grades, and make better choices tomorrow.

WHEN WILLPOWER IS IN SHORT SUPPLY

Even if we use every strategy available to increase our willpower capacity, there will still be times when we just don't feel like continuing our work. We become tired, frustrated, or indifferent. Even in those situations, however, not all hope is lost. Scientists have identified two ways we can muster strength to persevere even when it feels as if the willpower well has run dry.

The first is by developing a sense of autonomy around your work. Remind yourself why you, personally, chose to do this. In one variation of the cruel cookies-and-radishes experiment, half of the students were made to feel they had a choice in the matter: "We ask that you please don't eat the cookies. Is that okay?" The others were handed an unyielding directive: "You must not eat the cookies." Even controlling for the differences in mood that could arise from either set of instructions, those who felt they had a say in the matter held on to more of their willpower, outperforming their controlled counterparts in a later test requiring self-control.[7]

The authors of this study offer the following advice based on these results: "Dieting or quitting smoking or any other self-control activity is easier and less depleting when you want to do it for yourself or if you really believe in the outcomes than when it is forced on you."[8] So in those moments when you are feeling at your lowest in motivation, remind yourself why you chose to complete this task, and why it is important. Reframing it as a personal choice can give you the little extra you need to keep going.

Of course, not every task you have to complete will be one you actually want to do or personally believe in. What about a project you're doing solely because it is a course requirement, or a mundane assignment from your boss?

That brings us to the second strategy: remind yourself of your long-term goals.

One of my students aspires to be a doctor. Her premed curriculum is full of assignments that do not always excite her. But she has found a way to power through when her motivation begins to slip: reminding herself what is waiting for her at the end of her schooling. She specifically wants to become a pediatrician and work one day with Doctors without Borders, an organization that provides health care to underserved communities. By keeping that goal in the back of her mind when she is studying for a tough biology exam or working on a particularly tricky organic chemistry problem set, she stays on task.

Numerous studies have found that college students who reflect on their most important core values and overarching goals show greater performance on tests involving self-control. Calling to mind your guiding principles actually provides a buffer against willpower depletion.[9] It's part of a growing body of research showing that with proper motivation, anyone can overcome low willpower.

When a group of forty-three college students from the University at Albany were asked to solve impossible geometric puzzles after performing a challenging willpower-depleting task earlier in the experiment (another variation of the experiment with cookies and radishes), only *half* saw a reduction in their problem-solving skills. Why did the other half of these students keep going even when their willpower had been diminished? They were told that findings from this study could help scientists develop interventions for patients suffering from Alzheimer's disease. When benefits for a noble cause are on the line, even the most fatigued college student can muster the psychological strength to forge ahead. Sure enough, their persistence and effort on the puzzle task were just as strong as those of a control group whose willpower had not been depleted earlier.[10] As the authors of this study explain, "Depletion of self-control strength does not prevent the subsequent exertion of self-control. Individuals can still exert self-control when they are depleted, provided they are sufficiently motivated."[11]

Motivation is especially effective when it is altruistic in nature. Advancing Alzheimer's research or working with Doctors without Borders are both examples of *self-transcendent goals*, which involve using one's skills to strengthen the lives of other people or a community.

One study primed a group of high school students in California to adopt a self-transcendent mindset by asking them to reflect on how they could make the world a better place.[12] The students were also shown survey results suggesting that most students are motivated to perform well academically to develop skills that will both help them in their personal careers and benefit others. Another group of students in the study were told to think of a concept that didn't promote a self-transcendent mindset—how high school is different from middle school. Those in the first group, with the self-transcendent mindset, saw a significant increase in their math and science grades by the end of that grading period. The same study found that college students who had a self-transcendent mindset toward their work spent twice as much time reviewing practice questions for an upcoming exam and completed 35 percent more math problems on a lab-based assignment, even when given the option to quit at any time. This research offers a powerful strategy for remaining motivated during even the most tedious tasks: The next time you become frustrated or tired before you've completed your work, and motivation is hard to come by, shift attention away from how boring or challenging it is. Focus instead on how it is bringing you one step closer to achieving your long-term goals. Better yet, think about how your work will contribute to something bigger than yourself. Such self-transcendent reflection can keep the mind steadfast, even when willpower is lacking.

WILLPOWER-SAVING STRATEGIES

We've seen that willpower is a finite resource, willpower can be strengthened and then made easier to incorporate in all areas of your life, and you can compensate for low willpower by reframing your work as a personal choice or by focusing on self-transcendent goals. But some of the people who *seem* to have the most self-regulatory strength don't necessarily have any more than anyone else—extra willpower wasn't something they were born with or taught by their parents. Instead they may have just crafted a life that requires as little willpower as possible. Remember that Mark Zuckerberg didn't start off with a closet full of the same clothes. Rather, he intentionally created this condition for himself. A number of studies have shown that we can preserve willpower by developing good habits and selecting the right environments.

THE POWER OF HABIT

The first willpower-saving strategy involves creating routines. In one study psychologists Brian Galla and Angela Duckworth asked thousands of young adults how much willpower they'd used the last time they exercised, studied, ate healthy snacks, made it to bed on time, or meditated. The young adults also reported how long it had taken to decide in favor of each behavior, and how difficult it had been to resist temptations luring them off track. For some these tasks were incredibly laborious, requiring a huge expenditure of mental energy and self-regulatory strength; for others the tasks were no-brainers, leaving the wellspring of willpower intact.

Galla and Duckworth identified a key ingredient that predicted where along that spectrum each young adult fell: those who had spent the least willpower had developed *habits* around those good behaviors.[13] For example, the researchers found that when college students established daily routines for their studying—such as completing their homework in the same location around the same time of day—they persisted more, got less distracted, and ultimately got more done. With no loss of mental energy from deliberating over whether, where, or when to study, more willpower remained for the task at hand. The same principle applied for making it to the gym, eating healthier foods, getting to bed at a reasonable hour, and waking up on time. The more habitual those behaviors became, the less willpower they required.

William James, one of the pioneering figures in the field of psychology, once wrote, "There is no more miserable human being than one . . . for whom the lighting of every cigar, the drinking of every cup, the time of rising and going to bed every day, and the beginning of every bit of work, are subjects of express volitional deliberation. Full half the time of such a man goes to the deciding, or regretting, of matters which ought to be so ingrained in him as practically not to exist for his consciousness at all."[14]

When a behavior becomes habitual—occurring as a regular part of your routine—it requires less psychological strength to start and there's no need to waste additional time deciding or regretting the action. It's like brushing our teeth. This morning, did you weigh the pros and cons to determine if today would be a day you located your toothbrush and scrounged around for a tube of toothpaste so you could leave home with a minty-fresh mouth? No, this behavior is so ingrained into our morning routines that we can do it half-asleep. We know exactly where to reach for our toothbrush and toothpaste, and the entire activity happens almost automatically. Think about the last time you felt your shoe getting loose—did you deliberate about whether you would tie your laces? No, you reached down and did it without even thinking about it. You probably didn't feel even remotely tired afterward, either. When something becomes automatic, it requires very little in the way of mental energy or psychological strength to execute.

Make it a habit to study, exercise, or practice a new skill at the same time on set days of the week. Eventually those behaviors will also become automatic and occur without any internal deliberation and wasted willpower.

THE INFLUENCE OF ENVIRONMENT

The second way to preserve willpower is by choosing the right physical surroundings for particular tasks. One study found that college students achieved their study goals most successfully when they minimized environmental distractions.[15] They turned their phones off (or put them in another room altogether), used online apps that blocked social media sites, or set up shop in the library or another environment conducive to studying. These simple modifications reduced the amount of temptation in each study session, minimizing their need to expend energy blocking out distractions.

In an interview with Kathie Lee Gifford and Hoda Kotb on *Today*, one student explained that even the position of her adjustable dorm room bed affected how much she studied. Initially, she kept hers low to the ground, making it easy to "plop down" at any given moment. But she quickly realized how easy this made it to abandon her studies in favor of catching a quick nap or watching TV. After she and her roommate saw the toll this was taking on their studies, they made some changes.

"Having your bed right there is a distraction in itself, just like a cell phone," she explained. "This year, we realized the higher the bed, the higher the GPA." With the bed situated in a position that made it more difficult to climb into, she was removing part of the temptation that had steered her away from her books. "When you raise it high...you have to get up into bed if you want to go to sleep [you can't just 'plop down'], and so it actually keeps you at your desk and keeps you working."[16] Changes as small and easy as lofting your bed, shifting your desk, or moving your television into a new location can actually lead to better grades. When you remove temptations, good behaviors occur naturally. No willpower needed.

BREAKING GOALS INTO SMALLER STEPS

One of my students had a problem with procrastination during his freshman year. The workload was so overwhelming that it left him psychologically paralyzed. "I would have so much work that I wouldn't know where to start, so I wouldn't do anything. This resulted in many late nights, lower scores than I would have preferred, and a lot of stress." He knew this approach would not be sustainable throughout his college career.

Stress is everywhere. You don't need this book to tell you that stress levels among college students are at an all-time high, especially during high-pressure moments like finals period. And stress is another variable that gets in the way of exercising self-control, making it harder to stay focused on our work. The sad irony is that finals time is exactly when students are most in need of self-control to accomplish all the studying and paper writing necessary for a strong finish to the semester. Academic stress can also lead to emotional and behavioral disarray. It becomes difficult to maintain other positive behaviors that require self-regulatory strength, such as exercise, good study habits, and healthy food choices.[17] Fortunately, one study found a strategy capable of curbing this tendency for stress to wreak havoc during critical moments, while also leading to overall academic improvements.

Early in the semester, students came to a lab session with their class schedules in hand and a timetable cataloging all due dates for major exams and assignments. The researchers helped the students break each of these major projects into smaller goals, setting deadlines for each step along the way. For a term paper due in early December, a student might decide to choose the topic by September, conduct initial research by mid-October, create an outline by the end of October, write an initial draft by mid-November, and revise the final draft by the end of November. The students also established a study program, identifying particular dates and times each week they would dedicate to completing their work.

Compared to a control group, students who had taken time early on to break down their work into smaller goals with set deadlines spent *twice* as much time on their studies throughout the semester.[18] The deadlines held them accountable. For students especially motivated to achieve their goals, these deadlines prompted them to modify other parts of their daily routines to stay on course. For example, one student wrote, "In order to stick to the program I have to get out of bed an hour earlier so I can get the study hours in."[19]

But the benefits of this strategy didn't end with improved academic discipline. Remember that overriding an impulse to stay in bed is exercising the same willpower muscle necessary for carrying out other good behaviors. Sure enough, in addition to being more engaged academically, these students also showed improvements in virtually all other habits relevant to well-being throughout the semester. They ate less junk food, watched less TV, procrastinated less, lost their temper less frequently, and drank less alcohol. Even stress levels, which have been shown to skyrocket for students during exam season, were kept low when they had taken time on the front end to map out their academic commitments and set intermediary deadlines for major projects.

One of my students has incorporated this strategy into her own semester planning:

"I put all the major assignments and meetings and events that I know I will have into my schedule toward the beginning of the semester. This allows me to see what major assignments and other commitments will cluster together so that I can plan to work on each assignment earlier so that I am not overwhelmed when in one week I have three assignments, a test, and two events that I need to prepare for. I've found that this is very helpful in getting me to manage my time. By starting my assignments earlier than I otherwise would have this allows me to be mostly finished with everything by the week that everything is due. By the time the due dates roll around I find that I only have minimal work to do each night instead of spending the week pulling all-nighters every night. This greatly decreases my stress and increases the time I have to enjoy myself."

Likewise, for my other student whose college workload initially left him psychologically paralyzed, things turned around when he broke his assignments into smaller tasks with specific goal intentions for each. Eventually he made some changes that proved useful:

"I decided to start making smaller lists of tasks to accomplish every day and take everything one step at a time. By focusing on smaller tasks rather than everything all at once, my homework seemed much less intimidating. It was satisfying and rewarding to complete assignments and cross them off my agenda with a clear light at the end of the tunnel. I still procrastinate once in a while, but for the most part this method has motivated me to tackle large workloads in less time and with relative overall ease, which translates to less stress and a greater sense of control."

Part of what happens when we accomplish even a small, rudimentary task is an increased sense of confidence in our ability to complete our work. The confidence we get from completing one task inspires us to tackle the next, cycling us upward on the spiral of productivity.

Admiral William H. McRaven, commander of the United States Special Operations Command from 2011 to 2014, addressed nearly eight thousand students graduating from the University of Texas at

Austin on this very topic just months before his term ended in 2014. His speech outlined ten lessons he'd learned from his experience in the military, which he believed could help them change the world. His first piece of advice: make your bed.[20] As simple as that task sounds, it positioned him and his fellow trainees for success and mental sharpness throughout the day.

> "Every morning in basic SEAL training, my instructors, who at the time were all Vietnam veterans, would show up in my barracks room, and the first thing they would inspect was your bed. If you did it right, the corners would be square, the covers pulled tight, the pillow centered just under the headboard and the extra blanket folded neatly at the foot of the rack. If you make your bed every morning you will have accomplished the first task of the day. It will give you a small sense of pride, and it will encourage you to do another task and another and another. By the end of the day, that one task completed will have turned into many tasks completed."[21]

Often the hardest part of completing a challenging task is just getting started. Instead of thinking about how challenging the entire task will be, it's far better to summon the motivation to take just the first step. One of my students describes starting off small and going on to larger tasks "snowballing," declaring it one of his best tools to ward off procrastination:

> "I start off by finishing something that takes little effort or that I can finish relatively quickly and then I move on to the next assignment. I feel like this works for me because I build motivational momentum as each assignment is finished. It's nice being able to look back over the day and see all the work I have accomplished. It helps me manage my time better by making me more focused and determined to finish my work.

I might finish an assignment weeks before it's due when I'm snowballing."

Ultimately, stress arises when we feel we won't be able to accomplish everything we need to in a given time. By breaking our work into individual steps, we make the work less intimidating. The prospect of writing a twenty-page report might feel overwhelming, leaving us stuck in our tracks. Creating a one-page outline (the first step toward the report) is a specific and simple task, and something we can start right away. And when we've finished that first step, we can move on to the next, and then the next. Breaking our work into smaller parts and tackling them one at a time makes even the most daunting tasks manageable.

To keep yourself motivated, reward yourself after you've completed a certain number of steps toward your goal. Remember that one way to save willpower is by developing good habits. *New York Times* reporter and bestselling author Charles Duhigg has written extensively on the science of productivity and explains that rewards can turn any behavior into a habit:

> "If you want to start running each morning, it's essential that you choose a simple cue (like always lacing up your sneakers before breakfast or leaving your running clothes next to your bed) and a clear reward (such as a midday treat, a sense of accomplishment from recording your miles, or the endorphin rush you get from a jog)....Only when your brain starts *expecting* the reward—craving the endorphins or sense of accomplishment—will it become automatic to lace up your jogging shoes each morning."[22]

Knowing that a reward is coming can help you power through toward the end of the series of steps and keep you pushing ahead to the next. Think back to the broaden-and-build theory of positive emotions we discussed in chapter 1. The reward will boost your mood, which will help you work faster, more creatively, and with greater attention. So not only do intermittent rewards break the work into manageable steps, they also prime you to tackle the next series of steps with greater gusto.

If you love candy, here's a practical way one student stays motivated with his reading assignments. After he reads each section, he gets a reward.

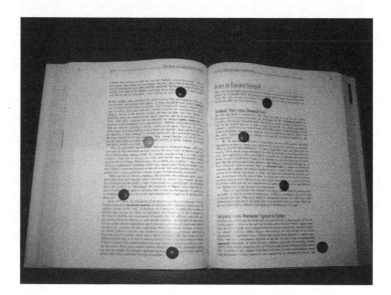

STAYING ON TRACK WITH
IMPLEMENTATION INTENTIONS

Of course, it can still be challenging to stay motivated even when you've broken your goal into smaller, more manageable steps and linked them to rewards. Fortunately, other research has provided insight into what you can do to actually stick to the plans you make.

In 2011, NYU psychologist Peter Gollwitzer, together with a team of psychologists from England and Germany, invited young adults to complete a concentration task involving a series of arithmetic problems that appeared individually on a computer monitor.[23] Before they began, each participant was instructed to write down a goal intention: "I will try to find as many correct solutions as possible!"[24]

The math problems were simple, yet tedious, the kind that would make watching paint dry a welcome reprieve. However, the participants had just made a promise to themselves to answer as many as they could. A few minutes in, a lost student appeared, asking for directions to the experimenter's office. This other student was actually an accomplice of the experimenter, setting up the most important part of the study: How much time would the participants spend helping her? They all had just set out to achieve a particular goal—to answer as many math problems as possible. Would they help the lost student quickly and then get back to work, or would they dawdle, allowing the interruption to become drawn out?

The answer had to do with a simple exercise the participants did immediately before beginning the task. Just after they established their goal intention—to find as many solutions as possible—half were asked to identify *implementation intentions.*

Implementation intentions are detailed plans that keep us on task toward our goals. One common form is the "if-then plan." First you think of any obstacles that could get in your way. Then you establish contingency plans in case any of those come up.

If I get tired, *then* I will stretch for thirty seconds and get right back to work.

If I get the urge to check social media, *then* I will remind myself that is a waste of time.

If I get hungry, *then* I will have a small piece of fruit instead of potato chips.

By establishing implementation intentions ahead of time, you have a plan already in place if an obstacle comes up—no need to expend mental energy on the fly to figure out how to respond. For the students in Gollwitzer's study, that plan looked like this:

"*If* I get distracted, *then* I will concentrate on the test even more!"[25]

Sure enough, when the accomplice came wandering in, the students who had *not* considered how they would respond to an interruption took significantly longer to get back on track. Those who formed implementation intentions spent 40 percent *less* time responding to her. Because they'd already considered what they would do if a distraction arose, they were able to quickly redirect their attention back to the math problems.

Beyond just completing more math problems, implementation intentions can keep us on track toward important long-term goals in our lives. For example, when university students in the United Kingdom were asked to establish implementation intentions regarding their dietary habits, they ate significantly more fruits and vegetables over the next three months.[26] If they ate out, had dinner with friends, or started to talk themselves out of making healthy choices, they always had a plan to incorporate fruit into their meals. By considering ahead of time how they would respond to potential distractions from their health goals, they became less likely to give in to such temptations when they arose.

A MATTER OF TIME AND PLACE

Implementation intentions can also come in the form of specifying in advance the precise time and location of a particular behavior. One study asked undergraduates at the University of Sheffield to identify how much time they would spend outside of class studying and doing other work relevant to their courses in the upcoming week.[27] The students also rated how much that time would contribute to their overall performance in the course, along with their confidence that they would complete the amount of work they'd set out to do. Their responses to these items formed their goal intentions. Naturally, students with ambitious goal intentions were more productive than those with less ambitious goal intentions. Approaching a workweek with high expectations, optimism, and confidence corresponds with the ability to actually fulfill those aspirations.

But half of these students were at an even greater advantage. They fulfilled their goals with the greatest success of anyone in the study. Their success was stimulated by responding to one simple item at the start of the week: "Decide now where (e.g., library) and at what times (e.g., 2–3 p.m. and 4–5 p.m.) you will do your independent study in the next week."[28]

It was an implementation intention requiring them to plan specific details of their goal intention. It took only moments to establish, but offered a huge return on the investment. The graph below illustrates the differences in overall studying time based on goal intentions and implementation intentions.

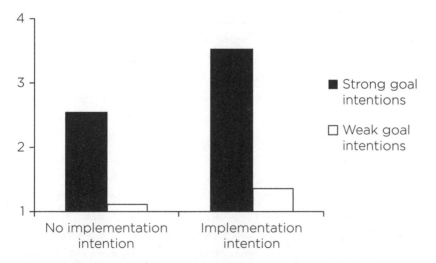

For students with weak goal intentions, it didn't matter whether they had established an implementation intention or not. If they said they weren't going to spend much time studying, and they approached the very prospect pessimistic that it would even pay off, they were headed for an unproductive week regardless. But a strong goal intention (confidence they would be productive and complete a lot of work) combined with a specific implementation intention (how and where they were going to do it) appeared to be the golden ticket, offering a significant boost to overall study time.

Importantly, the implementation intentions did not affect motivation. When they followed up with the participants at the end of the week and asked them how motivated they had been to complete their work, how interested they were in their studies, and how effective they found their studying to be, there was no difference between one group and another. So it's not the case that implementation intentions work because they increase motivation. Both groups were equally motivated. The implementation intentions were effective because they created a specific plan that triggered goal-directed behaviors throughout the week. The next time that you have difficulty finding willpower or motivation, see if you can at least find the right environment, and then schedule time to complete particular tasks in that location.

"Even when I know I'm going to be in the library until the sun comes up studying for some nasty exam, I'll take ten minutes to schedule my time," explains one of my students. "One a.m. to two a.m. review homework solutions, two a.m. to three a.m. review notes, three a.m. to three twenty a.m. take a break, and so forth. My plans hardly ever end up being completely accurate, but they give me comfort that I'll get everything done and that I'm going to leave the library at some point. Since I can see that, I stay motivated." This student understands that establishing detailed implementation intentions for his work can override both the limits of willpower and the fallibility of self-regulation. Even when the work isn't carried out exactly according to plan, creating good habits, selecting the right environments, and establishing implementation intentions can still offset lapses in psychological strength and accelerate overall progress toward goals.

One of the barriers to our well-being is that we are often unmotivated to adopt behaviors and mindsets that will reduce stress and increase happiness. We know exercise is good, but lying on the couch all night is more comfortable. We know more sleep will make us feel better, but staying up scrolling through social media is more entertaining. We know that spending more time working on a report will help advance our careers, but binge-watching Netflix is more fun.

To overcome these temptations, use what we have learned from the science of willpower to your advantage: Clear out other tasks that might be vying for your willpower capacity (those other tasks are your radishes). When you aren't pressed to use willpower, find opportunities to exercise it to keep it strong for the long term. When it's in short supply, remind yourself why you chose to do this task and how it's helping you achieve bigger goals. For your biggest projects, break them into small steps and take them one at a time. Let the sense of accomplishment you get from completing the first step snowball your motivation toward completing the others. Develop a specific plan for not only what you're going to do, but also when and where you're going to carry it out. Identify on the front end the barriers that could distract you and have implementation intentions in place to counteract them.

With that approach, you no longer need to worry about wearing the same outfit every day or forgoing chocolate chip cookies.

8

The Time Paradox

In the first week of April each year, I do something really mean to the seniors enrolled in my Positive Psychology course. I put up a calendar of the months of April and May and announce that only six weeks remain until graduation, bringing to light that their college careers will soon come to an end. My announcement is usually met with forlorn eyes, audible gasps, and woeful groans. One year a woman seated in the back of the auditorium exclaimed, "I hate you!"

Though it stirs panic and distress throughout the lecture hall, I continue to make this announcement each year because I know it will help my students end their experience on a high note. When Dr. Jaime Kurtz reminded a group of graduating seniors at the University of Virginia how little time they had before graduation, they ended up using their remaining time more efficiently, savoring every collegiate experience that came their way.[1] They spent more time with their friends, felt more gratitude for their college experience, took more pictures, visited more of their favorite spots on campus and in the nearby community, and engaged in more activities and organizations. Once they got over the initial shock of their impending graduation, they actually ended up significantly happier than a control group who had been made to feel graduation was still a long time away. As Kurtz explains, "Not surprisingly, reflecting on the fact that a treasured experience is soon coming to an end is not likely to produce an immediate boost in positive affect. What it does seem to do is endow the short time remaining with special value."[2]

Sure enough, that special value helped many of my students make the most of their final six weeks on campus:

> "I have gone to so many new places in these past few weeks. From going out dancing to experiencing nature to playing random sports, I am trying to do as much at WashU as possible. Because I do feel like I have limited time, I am actively pursuing all the opportunities thrown at me. Even if I do not do everything, I have been able to savor all the experiences I have had."

For another graduating senior, the reminder didn't affect what he did with his time, but instead how he valued it:

> "Over the past couple weeks I've been back to the Gateway Arch and tried to shoot every butterfly in the Saint Louis Zoo (with a camera, obviously). While I probably would've gone and done those things anyway, those acts took on some greater significance as I realized that I would be unlikely to have the opportunity to repeat them."

His experiences are similar to those of another of my students, who made a special trip to her favorite local BBQ joint, where she savored "every last sweet potato fry," knowing it would be her last time experiencing this in college. Time constraints on an experience can motivate us to check off more items on our bucket list and get more out of them as we do. We appreciate things more deeply when we are reminded they will not last forever.

This is the paradox of time: you might think that having more time is always better, but sometimes having *less* time is what serves us best of all. Tight deadlines prompt high-quality work, and limited time leads us to savor an experience more. Fortunately, even when it feels as if time is running out, we can make the time we do have feel more abundant. As we'll see, we can solve the time paradox not by giving ourselves more time, but by managing more carefully the hours that remain.

MAKING TIME SHORT

Deadlines stress people out. But they may be the key to productivity. Imagine that you were enrolled in a course that allowed you to choose one of two deadline options for its three required term papers:

1. The professor assigns firm deadlines for the papers, which are spaced roughly equally throughout the semester.
2. You set whatever deadline you want for each paper, so long as all three are handed in by the last day of class.

Most would find this an easy proposition. Going with the second option seems to be a no-brainer. Why not allow yourself as much time as possible? If something came up, you would have the flexibility to complete your work later, and if you finished it earlier, you could hand it in then. Although this line of reasoning makes the second option seem like the clear winner, the research suggests you may actually end up better off going with the first option.

Consider a study conducted by a professor at MIT who tested this with his own students.[3] He was teaching two sections of the same executive education course. The class content and requirements were identical for both sections. Each required the students to write three papers over the course of the semester. The only difference was in the paper deadlines. He assigned one group to be the "no-choice" section, in which the professor set the deadlines, like the first option above—the syllabus gave exact dates that each paper was due, at a rate of roughly one per month. The other was the "free-choice" section, in which students could choose their own deadlines, like the second option above—if they wanted to hand all the papers in toward the beginning of the semester, or wait until the last day to submit all three, the choice was entirely theirs.

At the start of the semester, the free-choice students had to tell the professor the deadlines they were setting for each of the three papers. Once these were established, they were binding, and late submissions would be penalized with grade reductions. Students who set early deadlines were offered no incentives (such as higher grades or feedback that would allow them to offer revisions). If anything, it seemed the greatest advantage would be for those who set later deadlines, because they would have more time to work. Plus, the option remained to submit papers earlier if they were finished before the self-imposed deadlines. For example, students could *plan* to submit a paper in early November, but tell the professor they were going to submit it on the last day of the semester. This would provide a buffer in case a cool Halloween party got in the way.

Although students in the free-choice condition seemed to have every advantage heading into the semester, the final grade book told otherwise. Not only did the students who set their own deadlines perform worse on the papers themselves, they also performed worse on the final project, due at the semester's end. But not all students in the free-choice section were at a disadvantage. Students in that section who established deadlines evenly spaced throughout the semester (roughly equivalent to those set by the professor in the no-choice section) performed just as well. In other words, it doesn't matter *who* sets the deadlines. What matters is when they occur.

Though they may send shivers down the spines of students during finals week, deadlines help us accomplish our goals efficiently. As one of my students has learned, tight deadlines are especially helpful for staying on task:

"Knowing that I have a limited time to complete a task forces me to approach it in the most efficient manner possible, which may mean that I don't have time to obsess over all the small details. Because I can be a perfectionist, I often take longer than I should to finish projects and papers when I have abundant time. This ends up costing me a lot of time and effort for an outcome that is likely not drastically different from what I would produce with less time."

It's not just academic performance that can be adversely impacted by the absence of deadlines. So can our bank accounts. Think about the last time you gave or received a gift card for a graduation or holiday. If it was in the last several years, there's a good chance it didn't have an expiration date. If it did, the date would have been at least five years after the card was issued. Thanks to the Credit Card Accountability Responsibility and Disclosure Act (Credit CARD Act) of 2009, "protections" for consumers include increasing how much time we have to spend gift cards. In some states they come with no expiration dates at all.[4]

Sounds great, doesn't it? If we want to make it more likely people will redeem a certificate, intuition tells us we should give them more time. When a group of eighty young adults were asked to imagine they had just received gift certificates to a local pastry shop, 68 percent said they would use it when it had an expiration date a full two months later, but only 50 percent said they would use it when the expiration was a short three weeks later.[5] This seems logical. More time should increase the likelihood we'll get something done. Right?

As we've seen in this book before, intuition is not always accurate. When the researchers gave actual gift certificates to a separate group of young adults—half with three weeks to use them and half with two months—they found a data pattern that flew in the face of the other students' predictions. Those with *less time* to redeem the certificates were the ones to actually use them. Even though the short-deadline group had only one-third as much time, they were *five times* as likely to cash in on their flaky croissants and chocolate éclairs. A whopping 94 percent of the students in the long-deadline group did not use the gift certificates at all.

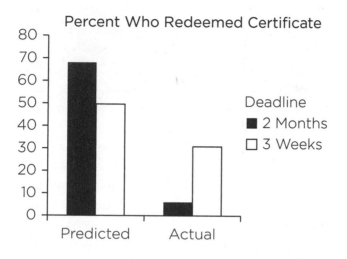

Most people *think* they are more likely to do something with more time, but the reverse is true. Like the MIT professor who found that students performed better with stricter deadlines, or my own students who savored college more when reminded that graduation was just around the corner, this study further highlights the notion that when we become aware of how short our time is, we make better use of it. With seemingly unlimited time to do something, we become careless, squandering time until opportunities we once had disappear. This helps explain why billions of dollars are lost each year in unused gift cards.[6] Without a deadline, the urge to use them is eliminated, and eventually they are forgotten about altogether. Deadlines call attention to time as a scarce resource, prompting us to use that time more effectively.

A SHIFT TOWARD SCARCITY

Just as abundant time can lead us to work less efficiently on a term paper and make us less likely to redeem a gift card, feelings of abundance more generally can prevent us from savoring even the food we eat and the vacations we take. For example, the more restaurants adults in Belgium have tried, the less likely they are to savor a spaghetti Bolognese dinner—a popular (though "ordinary") dish. The more foreign countries Americans have visited, the less likely they are to say they would savor "common" domestic vacations to places like Florida, California, and New York.[7]

In a study led by Jordi Quoidbach, a professor at Pompeu Fabra University in Barcelona, French adults were asked to imagine they had won a free trip to an "ordinary" vacation destination like nearby Italy. Those with the most expansive travel histories reported the lowest pleasure in anticipation of this Italian excursion. As the authors of this study explain, "Accumulating these fabulous life experiences could also have the paradoxical power of undermining their hedonic benefits."

This is not to say that those who have enjoyed rich travel experiences or been to many fine dining establishments are doomed to dull experiences in the future. Luckily, these researchers found one way to help even the most seasoned traveler enjoy a new experience. One summer day, the researchers stationed themselves outside Boston's Old North Church, monitoring how much time tourists spent inside. As they were entering the historic attraction, the researchers presented the tourists with checklists of vacation destinations and asked them to indicate how many they had visited. Half of them were shown lists of "common" locations like New York, Chicago, Las Vegas, and Orlando, and the others were shown lists of "exotic" locations like Tokyo, New Delhi, Sydney, and Bruges.

On average, people presented with the checklists of "common" destinations spent 30 percent less time inside the historic church. Those who were presented the list of "exotic" locations, however, having checked off fewer destinations, felt less well traveled. As a result they spent more time inside, taking time to read the plaques along the centuries-old pews, admire its pipe organ, and relish the other distinctive characteristics of the national landmark.

The study authors explain that "a wealth of pleasurable life experiences may impoverish people's ability to savor more ordinary pleasures, . . . [but] making individuals aware of the limits of their experiential background may propel them to savor their present experiences." If we are reminded about all the other experiences we have racked up, we don't need to savor the opportunity that's right in front of us. We have many others in our memory banks to relive. On the other hand, taking a moment to consider experiences we *haven't* had can remind us how precious those opportunities are, and prompt us to savor the occasion before us. After looking at the list of "exotic" locations, one of the visitors to the Old North Church told the researchers, "Seeing all of these countries, I felt like I traveled so little. It made me want to go on any vacation right away." Quoidbach and his colleagues explain that "exercises and activities aimed at decreasing feelings of abundance could help people maintain their capacity to savor small pleasures even after experiencing the best life has to offer—thereby allowing them to have their cake and savor it too."[8]

The next time you're about to head out to a concert, dinner with friends, or a road trip to a friend's wedding, take a moment to think about the concerts you haven't gone to, restaurants you haven't tried, or trips you've had to stay behind for. Though this might sound like a dire thought experiment, calling to mind opportunities you've had to miss may lead you to appreciate those you do have even more.

PERFORMING AT OPTIMAL LEVELS

An impending deadline leads us to work harder than we would otherwise, partly due to the physiological arousal it creates. As the deadline approaches, anxiety releases adrenaline into the bloodstream, enabling us to work harder and faster. When a deadline is far away, there is little anxiety, and in turn little arousal to light a fire under our feet. Of course, too much anxiety can be so stressful that it interferes with our ability to perform high-quality work.

Ultimately, we want to achieve an optimal level of arousal. Either too much or too little can lead to inefficient work. This interaction between arousal level and performance is represented by the Yerkes-Dodson law, so named for the two psychologists who first tested the idea more than a hundred years ago.[9] Their original study involved observing rats as they attempted to make their way through confusing mazes. Each time a rat made a mistake, it received a weak electric shock. Initially Yerkes and Dodson expected a linear relationship between the two variables: the stronger the shock, the quicker the rat would learn the maze. But when they dropped the rats in the mazes and began modifying the voltage levels, they found their hypothesis was only partly correct. As predicted, increasing the shocks from weak to medium improved performance—the moderate increase in arousal gave the rats the jolt they needed to find the maze's end quickly. But increasing the voltage from medium to strong brought performance *down*, back to the same level as when the shocks were weak. With arousal too high, the rats were overwhelmed with anxiety, unable to focus on which turn would bring them out of the maze. Yerkes and Dodson had discovered a happy medium when it comes to arousal. Some is good, but too much can be a barrier.

The students at MIT who chose to turn in all three papers on the last day of class were setting themselves up for the strong-voltage, high-arousal condition. Because they could put the assignments off until the last minute, they experienced high arousal from having to write three papers at once, which interfered with their ability to do good work. For the other students, evenly-spaced deadlines ensured they would be working on only one paper at a time, and that the accompanying arousal would be more moderate, closer to the optimal level.

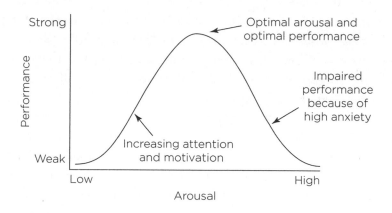

It can be helpful to keep this concept of optimal arousal in mind as we plan when to start an assignment in the face of a deadline. One of my students used this model to find an optimal timeline for beginning his assignments:

> "For many years I have tried forcing myself to do work as soon as possible, but I find that when I do, I lack focus; knowing I have a lot more time to finish it, I put in 50 percent effort and leave most of it for later. This results in me spending a lot more time than necessary working on a single assignment. Instead, if I wait to do it two or three days before the due date, I feel the time crunch and power through it efficiently."

If he began any sooner, he wouldn't have enough arousal to maintain focus; if he began any later, he would be too stressed to produce good work. He found his optimal level and used it to his advantage.

FINDING OUR OPTIMAL LEVEL

Optimal levels of arousal keep us working at our highest efficiency, making the best use of our time. In addition to impending deadlines, arousal can come from simply having other people around us or consuming stimulants like coffee and soda. You may be wondering, How much arousal do I need to be at my "optimal level"? To answer this question it's important first to know something about your personality. In particular, we need to know where you fall along the extroversion-introversion continuum.

The popular press gives a lot of attention to this distinction, including a recent *Onion* article poking fun at those at the low end: "Only 20 Minutes until Introverted Man Gets to Leave Party."[10] The difference between introverts and extroverts typically becomes evident in the activities and settings they prefer. Extroverts, who are enthusiastic by nature, like to do their studying in a crowded coffee shop, with a vanilla latte in reach and high-level chatter in the background. Introverts, who are more quiet and reserved, prefer the solitude of the library and the silence that makes a zipping backpack sound loud. Extroverts love socializing at crowded parties with high-energy music. Introverts prefer entertaining a small number of close friends over dinner at home.

These differences ultimately arise from how different people respond to external stimulation. Introverts are more sensitive to arousal and respond more strongly to any stimulation they encounter. This is why they do their best work when there is less going on around them. Too much noise in the background becomes like a twenty-page term paper due tomorrow that you haven't even begun: that much arousal sends the person off the Yerkes-Dodson chart, interfering with their ability to do good work. Extroverts, however, have a higher optimal level. Because they are less sensitive to arousal, they need *more* stimulation to reach their ideal setting. This is why they

When Plans Get Cancelled...

like studying in a crowded coffee shop with many people nearby and plenty of caffeinated beverages available. All that stimulation brings them to their optimal levels and peak performance. Without it they're like people trying to study for a quiz that will be administered in two months: there's not yet enough arousal to feel motivated. When you are searching for an environment that will allow you to be at your best, the first thing to consider is whether you are an introvert or an extrovert. Based on that, choose a setting that will bring you to your optimal level of arousal.

It's important not to get too caught up in this distinction. First of all, these are generalizations and do not capture the full complexity of any individual's personality. We need to remember that introversion and extroversion are on a continuum, even though they are typically represented as polar opposites. Most people fall toward the center of

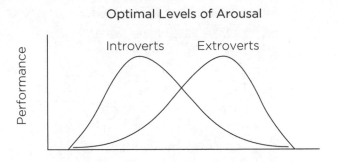

the continuum, exhibiting characteristics of both extremes. Plenty of introverts prefer studying in large groups with a pot of espresso brewing in the background, and you don't need to search very far to find extroverts who enjoy a quiet Friday night at home. But on average, extroverts tend to do their best work with higher levels of stimulation than introverts.

Second, someone's optimal level of arousal does not restrict that person from functioning in an environment outside their optimal range. People often find themselves in situations that force them to act out of character, and most people adapt fairly easily, at least for a short time. An introvert might have a job that requires interacting with colleagues and managers in high-energy group settings. An extrovert might have to work on projects in isolation all day with very little stimulation in the environment. But neither is necessarily at a disadvantage. People can still produce good work in nonoptimal environments if they also have the opportunity to create what's called a restorative niche.

TIME TO RESTORE

Psychologist Brian R. Little describes a restorative niche as "a place or setting...where individuals who are acting out of character may escape in order to restore their first natures."[11] As an example, many professors are highly introverted, but they are required to perform a highly extroverted behavior: delivering intellectually stimulating lectures in front of large groups of young adults. The stress associated with having to speak in front of that many people, and fitting in the entire lecture within a given time, is enough to push arousal to uncomfortable levels, especially for an introverted faculty member. The solution is to allocate time after that will let the high arousal return to its natural baseline. This is why many professors have office hours immediately following class—this allows an introvert time to restore their true nature with a quieter environment. Of course, it's not just professors who need this time. Students do as well:

> "I am an introvert, and therefore I require quite a lot of 'recovery time' after or before social situations. It was not until recently that I realized that I begin to feel very anxious if I have too many social situations coming up, or I know that my friends want to go out until the late hours of night and I won't have some time to myself too. This anxiety has grown, not lessened, as I have gone through college and I have become more aware of it. This 'recovery time' doesn't necessarily mean being alone in bed with Netflix anymore. For me it means a more relaxed setting, with or without friends. For instance, watching TV with my apartment-mates, chilling with the boyfriend, eating dinner with a friend or alone, or just sitting and chilling and really doing nothing."

Likewise, for the extroverted student who has to sit through hours of lectures on a given day, it is important to build in time to "restore" by elevating arousal levels—hanging out with a large group of friends, playing a team sport, or enjoying an extra-large coffee. First, know your nature and which environments are best for you. Then carve out a restorative niche for those circumstances that require deviating from your optimal environment.

So far in this chapter we have seen the benefits of time scarcity. Short deadlines move us toward an optimal level of arousal that can produce high-quality work (and make us more likely to redeem gift cards). Being reminded that time is short or being made to feel that our experiences have been scarce can prompt us to savor our time and experiences more. Knowing these things can help us manage our time more carefully. But what about those circumstances we all find ourselves in where we actually want to increase how much time we have?

WHEN "FREE TIME" EQUALS "ME TIME"

One semester around midterms (when time feels the most scarce), I asked my students to tell me what they would do with an extra half hour in their day. Most of their responses were what you might expect:

- "Watch TV"
- "Take a nap"
- "Lounge in my apartment"
- "Plan out the take-home midterm I have due Friday"
- "Do nothing"
- "Catch up on e-mails"
- "Get a coffee and read a *New Yorker* or *Atlantic* article online"
- "Mindlessly skim sites like *BuzzFeed* or Facebook"
- "Start studying for the four tests I have next week. I'd probably also text my girlfriend and ask her to come give me a hug."

None had difficulty coming up with something. When exams and paper deadlines are on the horizon, extra time is something that college students dream about. My true purpose in asking this question, however, was to find out not precisely *what* they would do with their time, but instead *who* would be involved. As it turns out, fully 89 percent said they would spend that time doing something for themselves, like most of the responses above. Only 11 percent would have used it for someone else, such as by running errands for a friend, proofreading a paper for a classmate, or performing some other random act of kindness for another person.

At first glance this makes sense. During a time of year when most college students are pressed for time, an extra thirty minutes should logically translate into completing a necessary task or taking a much-needed break. Recent research has found, however, that the 11 percent who identified a prosocial option would actually have been the best off in the long run.

Let's take a moment to unpack the stress-laden midterm season. The reason students' stress levels skyrocket is that they feel there is not enough time to complete all the required studying and projects. Stress isn't necessarily created by the objective amount of work or the actual amount of time you have. Instead stress comes from the *perception* that the work can't be done in the time allotted. In the same way that researchers altered tourists' experience of Boston's Old North Church not by changing their actual travel histories, but by changing their perception of their travel histories, a person can change their stress level simply by changing their perception of how much time they have on their hands.

MAKING TIME FEEL ABUNDANT BY GIVING IT AWAY

One study asked college students to spend fifteen minutes editing an essay written by a local at-risk high school student.[12] This was supposed to be the second part of a one-hour study. The first task lasted forty-five minutes, and the remaining time had been allocated for helping the nearby youth. After completing part one, half the participants were given a red pen and an essay to edit. The others were told that all the essays had been edited and they could leave, spending the fifteen minutes however they wished. All the participants in this study had this fifteen-minute block cleared on their schedule, but half of them were given that time back. In effect, this study examined what happens when college students get unexpected free time, a gift that nearly anyone would want.

Before they left the lab, whether on time or fifteen minutes early, they were presented with a brief series of questions. One asked them to report how much free time they felt they had, and another asked how much time they would be willing to commit to future research. Logic tells us that the students dismissed early should report the largest perceptions of free time. After all, they had *just been given* free time. However, it was the students who spent time helping the at-risk youth who subsequently felt they had the most time on their hands. In a similarly contradictory fashion, students who stayed for the full hour also committed to spend 30 percent more time on future studies than those dismissed earlier.

Why would the people with less free time report they had more of it and then be the most willing to sign up for additional work?

CONFIDENCE TO SOLDIER ON

The results of this study ultimately are due to self-efficacy, our confidence to carry out our work and achieve our goals. One way to increase such confidence is by being effective at something—anything, including helping a young student with an essay for fifteen minutes. Based on their findings, the authors who conducted this study offer the following advice:

> "Be effective by helping others. Decompressing in front of the television or getting a massage might be fun and relaxing, but activities like these are unlikely to increase feelings of self-efficacy. Indeed, people's choice to spend additional leisure

time on themselves may partly explain why the increase in leisure time in modern life has not increased people's feelings of time affluence....Spending time prosocially is more effective in relieving the pressure of time. When individuals feel time constrained, they should become more generous with their time—despite their inclination to be less so."[13]

When we accomplish one task, we become confident that we can accomplish other tasks. The narrow time window that once felt overwhelming suddenly becomes more manageable. Think back to chapter 3's discussion of why exercise is such an effective intervention for depression. The feeling of accomplishment from completing a workout increased the patients' self-efficacy, which told them they were in control of their well-being, helping to boost their emotional health as well. Or recall the admiral we met in the previous chapter who made his bed with meticulous precision every morning. By starting with this routine, he was gaining just enough self-efficacy to carry out everything else he needed to do that day. It's not that he was actually adding time to his day—if anything, folding perfect corners was depleting his time—but the self-efficacy he gained from his impeccably made bed gave him confidence to complete the next task waiting for him.

Doing things for others is a particularly good way to increase that sense of self-efficacy. During finals week a few years ago, I received an e-mail from a student who had taken my course the semester before. She'd taken the lessons from this research to heart and experienced the benefits herself:

"Like many other students, I am swamped with work. I have four assignments due tomorrow and left most of it for the day before. I am also an RA in one of the dorms and have wanted to make my residents little 'good luck on finals' packages for a while. But the time flew by and I still hadn't made the packages and I still had too much work to do. Then

I remembered one of the studies we learned about in class,
in which the people who helped others actually felt they had
more time. So I decided to go for it and make the packages
for my floor. Instead of feeling upset that I didn't give my
residents something before finals started, I feel great knowing
I made them feel special. Even though I spent way too much
time making them, I am satisfied and happy that I did it.
So what if I have to stay up a couple of more hours? Those
positive feelings are motivating me to get work done!"

Apparently this boost to self-efficacy gave her enough motivation
to also e-mail me this gratitude note that night, providing a triple win:
one for her residents, one for her former professor, and one for herself. So one way to increase a sense that our time is more plentiful is
by making ourselves feel effective. Remember that stress comes from
feeling like we won't be able to complete everything we need to. Helping others increases our self-efficacy, which gives us confidence that
we have what it takes to keep making progress on our to-do lists.

THE MYTH OF MULTITASKING

Another way to make our time feel more plentiful is by cutting out the
many hidden time drains that might be slowing us down. According
to a recent Gallup poll, 73 percent of young adults between the ages
of eighteen and twenty-nine check their phones at least a few times
an hour, and 22 percent say they check every few minutes.[14] Another
survey reports that 76 percent of adults reply to e-mails at work within
one hour, and nearly one-third reply within fifteen minutes.[15] And
these people apparently think others should be returning the favor—
more than half say they expect a response to *their* e-mails within an
hour. That may also explain why the majority also said they check
work e-mail outside of standard work hours several times a day. As

frequently as people use this type of communication, you might think responding to e-mails with such speed increases someone's productivity and helps their company work more effectively. But is this really true? What are the psychological consequences? And does it actually help people feel more productive?

Psychologists at the University of British Columbia found out by manipulating how frequently a group of young adults checked their e-mail.[16] For an entire week, one group was told to check their in-boxes as often as they could, keeping them open throughout the day and turning on any notification systems such as chimes or pop-ups that would let them know when new messages had arrived. The other group was told to check their e-mail only three times per day, keeping their in-boxes closed at all other times, with notifications and alerts turned off. All participants tracked their daily moods, along with how distracted they felt and how productive they were.

By the end of the week, those who had been checking e-mail only periodically reported lower levels of both daily distraction and overall stress. Importantly, they did not feel any less productive during the day than those checking their e-mail constantly. If you are able to do so, keeping your inbox closed more often may be one way to alleviate stress. Even if you can't shut off e-mail for hours at a time, you might try it at least during those times when you are tackling your most important work.

Although some people balk at this finding, claiming that they work more efficiently by responding to e-mails as quickly as they receive them, think back to the early studies from this chapter on deadlines. When time is scarce and we feel somewhat anxious, we work more efficiently. When you respond to each e-mail individually, it doesn't have a sense of urgency about it; you can take your time rereading, editing, and modifying small details that don't actually change the final message. It's kind of like a student who begins a term paper months before it is due and ends up obsessing over the minutia. On the other hand, if you check your in-box only periodically throughout the day and find twenty-five e-mails each time you do, the sheer volume of messages will create that anxiety-bearing arousal that can be so effective in motivating efficiency. You'll quickly delete those from LISTSERVs or vendors that offer no real value to your work that day, and cut to the chase with those requiring your attention. There's no time to agonize over precise word choice when you've still got another ten unread e-mails expecting your response.

SWITCH COSTS: THE INVISIBLE TIME SINK

Of course, many will contend that they don't linger over e-mails as they come in—being curt and glib is no problem. They know how to dash off a fast reply, even to the only e-mail vying for their attention. In that case, the loss of time isn't from the e-mail itself, but from a still more insidious time sink that psychologists call a switch cost: the expenditure of time and energy required to go back and forth between two tasks.

Let's imagine you're working on a big research paper when you suddenly hear the chime of your e-mail alert. That sound effectively hits the pause button on progress toward your paper as you decide whether it's important enough to respond to or another throwaway Facebook notification you can delete. Either way, it takes time to make the decision and then redirect attention back to your paper.

Some people believe they can actually do two things at once, circumventing the switch cost altogether by thinking about their work and the e-mail they're composing simultaneously. *Time* once ran an article referring to children of the nineties and early 2000s as "genM." This isn't an abbreviation for "millennial generation" (although that is their colloquial title), but instead for "multitasking generation."[17] The magazine featured stories of kids who "studied" while simultaneously listening to music, watching TV, browsing Amazon, posting to Facebook, and texting.

But in reality, multitasking doesn't actually exist. Our minds are capable of attending to only one piece of information at a time. If we think we are doing two things at once, all we are actually doing is switching back and forth so quickly that we create the illusion the two events are happening simultaneously. It's like an animator's flip-book. Each individual page shows a character in a slightly different pose, and when the images are flipped in fast succession, it appears they are shifting their posture or walking around. They're not actually doing these things, but the pages are moving so quickly it appears that they are. Whether we realize it or not, what we call multitasking is actually a dynamic process that shifts attention back and forth between two (or more) tasks, which does, in fact, incur a switch cost.

Let's demonstrate this with a quick activity. Of the shapes below, how many are circles and how many are triangles?

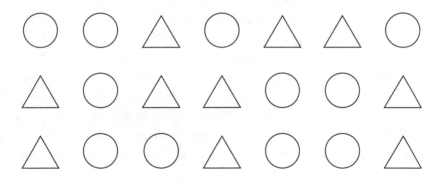

You should have found eleven circles and ten triangles. (If not, go back and try again!). You could have taken a few different approaches to find the correct answer. One way is to look at each shape individually, moving from one side to the other, keeping two running lists in your head. The mental dialogue would be like this: "One circle, two circles, one triangle, three circles, two triangles, three triangles, four circles…" I found it mentally exhausting making it through even the first row that way.

Another way—the approach most people take—is to count *all* of one shape, and then *all* of the other. Recognizing that this activity actually consists of two separate tasks and tackling each one individually produces faster speed and fewer mistakes. There are no switch costs here, as there are with the first approach.[18] When we attempt to complete a project with e-mail and phone alerts going off all around us, we are taking that first approach (the one that left me mentally exhausted) to our work. Whether it's responding to e-mails while studying or to text messages while driving, the act of leaving one task midstream to pick up another is costly in both time and accuracy.

PUTTING DIVERSIONS IN THEIR PLACE

One study tested the cost of technology interruptions by having students read passages from a college textbook that were being displayed on a computer monitor.[19] The activity was self-paced, allowing students to scroll through each page and advance to the next when they were ready. Some of the students received periodic instant messages ostensibly from another student asking them questions you might expect from a new friend, like, "What do you like to do in your spare time?" (This was a study done in the early 2000s, when AOL Instant Messenger was still a thing; it is the equivalent of text messaging today.)

The computers measured the total amount of time students took to read the passages overall, as well as how much time they spent reading and responding to the IMs. As you might expect, the students who were responding to IMs took longer to make their way through the passages: an average of forty-five minutes compared to only thirty-seven for those completing the task without anything else vying for attention. This is not surprising given that it takes additional time to respond to IMs.

However, students on average spent a total of only three minutes reading and responding to the IMs. When we subtract that from the total time it took to finish the passages themselves, we're left with forty-two minutes, still significantly longer than students in the IM-free condition. This tells us that the total amount of time they took to complete the task was not simply the sum total of how long it took to read the passage and respond to the IMs.

The difference is due to the switch costs, the additional time it took readers to reorient themselves to the passage after each quick diversion. It's the equivalent of counting the shapes in their exact order with two running tallies simultaneously, or responding to all incoming phone notifications while studying, or, yes, even keeping e-mail open throughout the day and responding to each message as it appears. Each time you pause a project to check Instagram, e-mail, or texts from bae, you have to stop where you are, redirect attention from one task to another, complete the other task, and then figure out where you were on the original task to get the wheels turning again. It's far better to recognize those are *separate* tasks and to complete them one at a time. Breaks are important. Diversions keep us motivated. But be mindful of where you place them. If you are growing restless, do what you can to keep working until you reach the end of a section or another clear stopping point before you get up and walk around or scroll through social media. Otherwise, when you come back you'll have to pay a switch cost, squandering time as you figure out where you were so you can keep going. And if something important does lure you away midstream, at least write down where you are leaving off and what your next step is, to minimize the time it takes to get back in the swing of things.

SOLVING THE TIME PARADOX

When you are feeling pressed for time, take a step back and think about how you can make the most of the time that *is* remaining. Set deadlines for your work—use the adrenaline rush from the time pressure to kick yourself into high gear. Align your environment with your optimal level of arousal—if you can't do that, at least schedule time for a restorative niche so you are able to return to a normal state and be efficient with your time in the future. Before you begin anything requiring your full attention, turn off your phone, close your e-mail, and block out any other distractions that might lure you away from the task at hand—although it might feel more efficient to be able to complete other tasks as they come up, the added switch costs will accumulate, slowing down your overall progress.

And when you are in the midst of an experience you are enjoying, take a moment to acknowledge that it will eventually come to an end. Acknowledging the impermanence of a beautiful sunset, a road trip, or even the college years can lead us to savor those experiences more. For anyone reading this chapter six weeks before your graduation, I understand if you hate me now. But you'll thank me come graduation day.

9

Managing the Inevitable Bad Day

Angry customers can be a nightmare for a business. Most would do anything to avoid them. But one company in Dallas, Texas, seeks them out. They welcome fuming, red-faced customers with open arms, and provide them access to their own private rooms that might contain a couch, end table, flower vase, and TV. But instead of being handed a cool beverage and the invitation to put their feet up, smell the flowers, and enjoy a TV show, they are handed a baseball bat and suited up in protective gear. These customers have just entered the Anger Room, which deems itself "a place where you can let your hair down, gear up, and destroy real-life mocked rooms that simulate an actual workplace, living area, or kitchen."[1] For twenty-five dollars, customers get five minutes to turn their anger into a pile of broken glass and splintered wood, one swing at a time. "We all get angry," the company claims, "so why not do everything you've dreamed of doing when you're mad."

It's true that we all get angry. But if you dream of unleashing that fury on unsuspecting office printers, your dignity may take a hit as well. While it may seem well worth the twenty-five dollars to walk out of the Anger Room feeling lighter, research shows that destructive forms of catharsis actually do more harm than good. There are far more productive techniques for recovering from a bad day that can leave you happier in the long run. You can leave the baseball bats behind for this chapter.

ASYMMETRICAL EMOTIONS

Try this: think of as many words as you can that could be used to describe different emotions. Go ahead and find a piece of scrap paper, and jot down as many as you can.

Once you've got your list, count up the total number of emotional states that are positive and the total number that are negative. In all likelihood, negative emotions appear on your list more than their positive counterparts. I find this pattern year after year when I do this activity with students in my classes. Most people have an easier time thinking of ways to feel bad than to feel good. The same pattern holds true around the globe.[2] When researchers from the University of Amsterdam gave this task to hundreds of young adults in six different countries, four words emerged consistently at the top of each country's list: sadness, fear, anger, and joy. Three negative and only one positive.

Part of this effect is a simple matter of linguistics. The more prominent an idea is in a culture, the more words there tend to be for it. For example, Alaska Natives have fifty words for snow. The Sami people in Russia and Scandinavia have a thousand words for reindeer.[3] When it comes to the nearly six hundred emotion words in the English lexicon, the majority—62 percent—are negative. So one reason people usually call to mind more negative words than positive words is that we have more negative words to choose from. There are more ways to talk about what we find fearful and upsetting than what we find joyful and uplifting.[4] A similar skew toward negativity appears in almost every language.

Another reason you likely listed more negative than positive emotion words is that this skew toward negativity seems to be part of our human nature. Psychologists have traveled all corners of the world and found a set of basic human emotions that transcend race, society, or class. Four of them are negative: anger, disgust, fear, and sadness, and only one is positive: happiness. Even in cultures that are illiterate and do not have words that label them specifically, people express these emotions and can detect them in others. (And if those five emotions sound familiar to you, you may be recalling the cast of the Pixar movie *Inside Out*. The screenwriters consulted with leading psychologists to align the characters with cross-cultural research on the topic.)

Whether we're talking about emotion words that are more prominent in language or basic emotional experiences common to the human species, feeling bad simply comes in more varieties than feeling good. We call this pattern the positive-negative asymmetry effect.[5]

There is also an asymmetry in how long different emotions stick around. A study conducted by Dr. Randy Larsen tracked the emotional ups and downs of college students for a semester, and found that the negativity of bad events stayed with the students significantly longer than the positivity of good events.[6] When they felt good about something in the morning, that happiness started to wear off by the afternoon. Negative emotions, however, tended to stay with the students much longer, still affecting them later that evening and even into subsequent days. This phenomenon is just as much biological as it is psychological. Some negative emotions are associated with the release of cortisol, a stress hormone that travels through the entire bloodstream, keeping its effects in our system for extended periods. The distress from a bad exam grade or the animosity brewing from a roommate dispute sticks around much longer than the positivity from an A on a big paper or a dinner out with friends. And it's all due to a pesky neurochemical taking its sweet time traveling through the entire circulatory system.

The underlying mechanism of the positive-negative asymmetry effect may have its roots in our cave-dwelling ancestors. In our evolutionary past, anyone who was not tuned into potential threats and looming danger was jeopardizing their survival. Genes that put us on high alert for negative aspects of our environment were most likely to be passed on from one generation to the next. We now live in an environment that is arguably much less threatening, but we are left with a genetic code hypervigilant to anything that could be harmful. We are hardwired to give more attention to the good than to the bad.

RECOVERING FROM THE ASYMMETRY

Given the potency of negative emotions, and how much longer they stay with us, it is understandable that places like the Anger Room exist. People need coping mechanisms for life's unavoidable rough moments. Even if they're not paying to destroy someone else's old stuff, many people still believe the best way to overcome anger is to scream, yell, or throw something to "get it out of their system." This commonly held belief has prompted the scientific community to ask, is this really effective?

There was only one way to test it: find a bunch of young adults and make them really mad. In an experiment performed at Iowa State University, Professor Brad Bushman angered a group of six hundred college students by giving them critical feedback on essays they had written about their personal views on abortion. One thing that reliably makes people angry is when their deeply held beliefs about controversial issues are criticized. Regardless of the perspective they took or the strength of their arguments, all students received identical feedback from a purported fellow student in the next room: "This is one of the worst essays I have read!" They were also told their essays had poor writing style, and that they lacked organization and originality. It was an attack on both their personal convictions and their ability to articulate them.

Of course, no one actually read the essays. Bushman reused the same disparaging feedback for all six hundred participants. He didn't care what they thought about abortion. He just wanted to get their blood boiling. In the next phase of the experiment, one half of the participants were told to release their anger by hitting a punching bag that was conveniently located on the other side of the room. They were even told to envision the person who had just attacked their views as they swung away. The other half were told to sit and wait quietly until the experimenter returned with instructions for the final task. The design of this study ensured that everyone was left alone in the room for the same amount of time; the only difference was how they spent that time. Half vented their anger, half just sat there.

In the final part of the study, the students completed an emotion questionnaire gauging the amount of anger they were currently experiencing. Next they were told they would play a competitive reaction time task against the person who had delivered the piercing feedback about their earlier writing. This person, they were told, was on his own computer in the next room. On each trial they each would have to press a key as fast as possible. The person who pressed it first would get to deliver a noise blast through the other person's headphones. The winner got to determine both the length and loudness of each blast. From Bushman's perspective, "Each participant controlled a weapon that could be used to blast the other person if the participant won the competition to react faster."[7] If they wanted to get back at the jerk who had insulted them earlier, now was their opportunity.

Remember that this other person didn't actually exist—the participants were actually just playing a computer, which was rigged so that the real participant would win half of the twenty-four trials. This allowed Bushman and his colleagues to see whether the twelve noise blasts they delivered to their partners differed based on which condition they were in. If the folks at the Anger Room are correct, and venting your anger "gets it out of your system," then we should expect to see lower ratings on the anger scale and less intense noise blasts during the competition from those students who had attacked the punching bag. But the results came back the exact opposite: those who had vented reported significantly *higher* levels of anger, and administered noise blasts that were louder and longer than the other participants'. Venting, in reality, does not release anger, but instead makes it worse by attaching itself to feelings and behaviors later on.

Many people hear about this study and respond in disbelief. "Wait a minute!" they say. "When I become angry, I scream, yell, or find another way to let it out of my system. Then it's over and I feel so much better." Yes, it is true that *eventually* we will feel better. That's the beauty of the passage of time. As we saw in chapter 2, one of the characteristics of human emotion is hedonic adaptation: sooner or later we return to baseline. What goes up must come down. That's also the case for negative emotions. When anger rises, it must come back down...eventually. How quickly or slowly it returns to baseline, however, depends on how we respond to our initial fury. Venting, it turns out, *slows down* our descent. Screaming or punching a bag prolongs the anger, delaying our emotional system's natural return to a calmer state. As Bushman explains, "Venting to reduce anger is like using gasoline to put out a fire—it only feeds the flame."

So if venting is not effective at reducing negative feelings, what should we do instead? Bushman offers four practical strategies:[8]

1. **Delay.** The participants who sat and did nothing for two minutes after they were angered were significantly less angry and aggressive later in the experiment. Allowing the simple passage of time by counting to ten or a hundred can bring us back to baseline before we act out with preemptive rage. Sending an angry text or e-mail in the moment won't make you feel better, and most likely won't solve the underlying problem.
2. **Relax.** Emotions have a physiological component. Deep breathing and other relaxation techniques can reduce the arousal and calm the emotion.
3. **Distract yourself.** Ruminating on negative experiences often intensifies their negative effects. Shifting attention to something

else like watching a TV show or running errands interrupts that negative thinking cycle. Distractions keep us from "feeding the flame."

4. **Do something incompatible with anger.** Perform a random act of kindness, search YouTube for babies laughing, or help someone in need. Activities like these prevent anger from being maintained.

The late dean of Arts and Sciences at Washington University, James McLeod, was known for his calming presence and his ability to help even the most irate individuals do something incompatible with their anger. When students, faculty, or administrators would complain about an unfair policy or difficult colleague, he would listen, offer sage advice, and then, as his visitor was getting ready to leave his office, say, "Now, I want you to take a moment to think of someone who could use your assistance and go help that person." Few among us could remain upset much longer after that.

When we are feeling upset or angry, there is often a temptation to bring others into our distress—either by yelling at the person who caused the problem, or by complaining to the first person we can find, text, or call who might offer sympathy over our misfortune. Each time we do this, we are doing the same thing as the participants who vented their anger by hitting a punching bag—we're maintaining our anger by reliving it over and over. It's not that we should never share our problems with others, but we have to be careful about the manner in which we do that.

In fact, as we'll see, putting our emotional experiences into language may be the best coping mechanism of all—if it's done correctly.

WRITING THROUGH THE DISTRESS

A fine line exists between venting and what's called emotional disclosure. If we bring someone else in just so we have an audience to shower us with pity as we wallow in despair, we're merely venting. But sharing our troubles with a close friend to seek understanding about what has happened and processing things from a calm, rational perspective is emotional disclosure, a much healthier alternative. This kind of reaction to distress positions us to gain insight from the experience, recover from its residual negativity, and move forward.

One of the most effective techniques for emotional disclosure also happens to be one of the simplest: putting pen to paper. In the words of one student, "Usually when I get stuck in a bad mood, the same thoughts keep swirling around my head. Journaling is a way for me not only to validate my thoughts, but also to stop ruminating on the same things. It is a space for me to be completely honest about what I'm thinking and try to figure out why I'm thinking that."

Consistent with this student's experience, a large and growing body of research has shown the value of putting our emotional experiences into words. In one study psychologist James Pennebaker asked undergraduates at Southern Methodist University to think about the "most traumatic and upsetting experiences" of their entire lives—especially those they had not previously disclosed to others—and write about the "deepest thoughts and feelings"[9] they had about these experiences.

They did this for four days in a row, spending twenty minutes in each session evoking psychological turmoil from their pasts. You might wonder if Professor Pennebaker was some sort of sadist. The short-term impact was, not surprisingly, upsetting. Immediately after the writing exercise, many students were distraught. Some left the experiment in tears. But the experiment didn't end there. This study kept tabs on these young adults, tracking their happiness levels, physical well-being, and academic performance for the next several weeks.

Even though earlier in the semester they had walked out of the experiment despondent after having dug up such painful memories, the long-term effects of this task landed them in a much happier state. Weeks later they were now on the upswing, with improvements across the board: they reported boosts in mood, fewer doctor visits, and higher grades.[10] They also were more socially integrated, talking to their friends more, laughing more, and focusing on more positive things about the present moment.[11]

Though difficult at first, translating a painful experience into language appears to carry benefits psychologically, physically, cognitively, and even socially. As Pennebaker explains, "The inhibition or active holding back of thoughts, emotions, or behaviors is associated with physical work that, over time, can become manifest in disease."[12] In other words, when bad things happen to us, their effects can be long lasting. In a way we always carry the stress and damage from those events with us, which can take its toll on all aspects of our well-being. Ignoring that damage won't make it go away. But writing it out can position us to move beyond it.

WHY DOES WRITING WORK?

Mother Teresa once said, "Kind words can be short and easy to speak but their echoes are truly endless." Although it may take only a few moments to say something nice to someone else, those moments could stay with that person for the rest of their life. The same is true of traumatic experiences: even if they're short lived, their effects can be unending. Writing about the trauma is one way to release it, as one of my students learned herself:

> "If I'm mad at someone or if I'm anxious about something, it just continues to build in my head over time. Even something innocent, like a small fight about whose turn it is to do the dishes, can really eat away at me. I've learned that if I take fifteen or twenty minutes to journal, it makes all the difference. When I write out whatever it is that's bothering me, it's almost as if it's leaving my system. I no longer feel like

I'm harboring those feelings, because I've released them on the page."

Remember, if we don't work through negative feelings appropriately, we always carry them with us—even if we are not consciously thinking about them at a given point. It requires both psychological and physiological work to keep those feelings bottled up. The stress such inhibition causes can increase blood pressure, heart rate, and the likelihood we'll get sick. Confronting these emotions by actively processing them has an "undoing" effect on this inhibition. Writing about them enables us to let them go. This explains why participants in Pennebaker's writing studies showed not only an increase in their mood, but also a decrease in doctor's visits. Writing can be an important step, emotionally and physically, in allowing suffering to leave our system.

WRITING TO UNDERSTAND

When bad things happen, we become motivated to understand why. Of course, gaining insight into anything—including unfortunate events—requires the ability to organize our thoughts. We must structure them in a way that helps us make sense of what has happened. This structure turns out to be a particularly important component of using writing to overcome psychological distress. One student describes how she uses writing to organize and understand emotional situations:

> "When I get upset, I write about it. This is how I process the things that upset or distract me. I want to have an idea about what I'm feeling and whether those feelings are rational. Writing is the best way to stop the snowball of irrational thinking and get myself moving in a more adaptive direction. To put things in writing implies a degree of formality and

requires a considerably more organized thought process. The more cognitive side of me is incredibly persuasive, and my emotion-driven self generally begins to come to the light when the reality of a situation is spelled out for me."

The act of writing forces us to take a step back and reflect on the experience using a rational perspective and an ordered sequence of events. The participants in Pennebaker's study who were the most self-reflective, emotionally open, and thoughtful in their writing experienced the greatest benefits.[13] In particular, those who increasingly used words and phrases suggesting they were gaining insight into their suffering—like "I have come to terms with" or "I now realize"— showed the greatest long-term health benefits. The stories they formed in the process of writing out their emotions helped them draw links they otherwise might have neglected. The insight they gained by identifying causes and reasons for what had happened allowed them to develop a rational perspective.

When writing is used as a vehicle to gain such causal insight into the past, it can be an important first step in letting go of the trauma, putting it behind us, and diminishing its impact on us going forward. Pennebaker and Kate Niederhoffer, his former PhD student, explain it this way: "Constructing a story facilitates a sense of resolution that gives individuals a sense of predictability and control over their lives— allowing them to be 'in sync' with their core selves."[14] Assembling the past in story form restores a sense of inner tranquility that was disrupted by the traumatic event and associated emotional upheaval.

One of my students told me he used writing as a coping mechanism a few weeks after breaking up with his girlfriend:

"I sat down and wrote three full pages describing my own emotional pain, regrets, and desires. It felt cathartic and I cried in the process, but by the time I signed my name at the bottom, I felt so much better. Writing the letter forced me to be honest with myself and be true to my feelings. The funny thing about reflecting upon emotions within your own mind is that emotions and facts tend to get muddled very quickly. On paper, words stick and they don't blend together."

As fate would have it, he and his ex-girlfriend started talking again the very night he wrote out his feelings. Even though he didn't show her the letter, it served him well. "I knew exactly what to say to her and how to be honest with her," he said. And two weeks after that conversation took place, the student told me they were "potentially unofficially back together."

PUTTING THE BRAKES ON OUR EMOTIONS

In the thirty years since Pennebaker first found evidence for the benefits of writing about adversity, hundreds of other studies have replicated the results with diverse populations. Cancer patients,[15] people recently fired from their jobs,[16] and young adults navigating the college transition[17] have all benefited from writing out their emotional sufferings. One question that often arises is whether there is something special about writing, or if merely talking about one's problems can provide similar benefits. Sure enough, verbalizing a past trauma in any way—talking about it with a friend or therapist or even speaking into an audiorecorder—can boost mental and physical well-being.[18]

Part of the benefit comes from the neural processes associated with putting feelings into words. When we come into contact with negative emotional information, the amygdala becomes more active—the same brain structure that goes on overdrive when we don't get enough sleep. The amygdala makes us more sensitive to negative information and can exacerbate fear and anxiety. Interventions for quelling the unpleasant effects of something—such as past trauma—are often aimed at decreasing activity in this brain region.

A study by Dr. Matthew Lieberman and his colleagues at UCLA discovered one such strategy for calming the fear response—labeling emotional reactions with words. Undergraduates came into his lab and viewed a series of faces as they flashed on computer monitors before them. Each of the faces wore an expression associated with an emotion, such as anger, fear, or happiness. On some of the trials the students were instructed to describe the facial expressions in words (such as the stimulus on the left below); on others they were told simply to indicate the person's gender (the stimulus at right).

As they were completing the task their brains were scanned, allowing the scientists to see which parts became most active. They found that the amygdala was significantly less active when the participants were giving labels to the emotional expressions.[19] This is exactly what we want to have happen: when the amygdala is less active, the world around us is less threatening.

"In the same way you hit the brake when you're driving and you see a yellow light, when you put feelings into words, you seem to be hitting the brakes on your emotional responses," Lieberman says. "Putting our feelings into words helps us heal better. If a friend is sad and we can get them to talk about it, that probably will make them feel better."[20] Emotions, if left to their own devices, can run rampant in our minds, blow things out of proportion, and escalate in intensity. A more productive and healthy way to deal with them is writing about them or talking them out.

Think back to the students we met in this chapter—the young woman who felt her troubles leaving her system when she released them on the page, the student who put her emotion-driven self in proper perspective when she spelled out her situation, and the young man who gained insight into his true feelings by writing a letter in the aftermath of his breakup. In all cases, writing put the brakes on their amygdalae, preventing their emotions from getting the best of them. Giving their emotions a label, spelling them out, and sequencing the events provided the mental clarity they needed to restore their moods.

Even if you don't consider yourself an expert writer, keep in mind that grammar, syntax, and sentence structure don't count here. It's not an assignment your English teacher will be grading. When something is bothering you, set a timer for fifteen minutes. Recount as much of the experience that led up to the emotion as you can from start to finish. Describe how you felt each step along the way. Use whatever format feels natural for you, whether e-mail, text, a note on a phone app, or good old-fashioned paper and pencil. You don't have to send what you write or share it with anyone. If it feels unnatural at first, remember that writing becomes easier the more we do it, just like gratitude, exercise, or meditation. The simple act of writing can be a powerful antidote to our most tumultuous emotions.

———

When my nephews were little and would become fussy or irritable, my older sister would respond with a simple phrase: "Use your words." Instead of enabling their meaningless groans by trying to guess what they wanted, she prompted them to verbalize their unrest. This way they articulated their precise needs and allowed those nearby to satisfy them.

"Use your words" is good advice for all of us when we are feeling upset and having that inevitable bad day, week, or semester. Although blowing off steam by yelling, screaming, or throwing things may be tempting at first, those behaviors only prolong negativity. Putting pen to paper or talking things over with a trusted friend can help us gain insight into the experience, put it behind us, and get on with our lives. That's far better for our well-being than suiting up in protective gear and smashing old TVs and office furniture. It'll save you twenty-five dollars too.

10

Social Connection

They sat in the third row, just behind the thirty-yard line. Any closer and they would have needed shoulder pads and helmets. The Seattle Seahawks were taking on the Arizona Cardinals at home in CenturyLink Field, and a college sophomore had wanted to give her father the experience of a lifetime.

"Seahawks tickets are ridiculously expensive," the Seattle native confessed. Even though she'd had to scrape together her earnings from a summer internship to purchase them, she knew this experience would be something special for her dad. "He had never been to a Seahawks game, and I just knew that he wouldn't shell out the cash for it." But for her it wasn't about the seats themselves or how much they cost. "It was about the feeling that I could finally give back in whatever small way I could to my dad, who has given me everything my entire life. This was an experience that he hadn't had yet. I felt so special that I was able to do something for him for once."

She could have spent that money on any number of high-quality gifts for her dad: an HDTV, a charcoal grill, or an upgrade to a new smartphone. Those would have offered function, utility, and convenience. But none would have offered as much *happiness* as the Seahawks tickets. "It was a perfect way to give my dad and me a great bonding experience that we would remember for many years to come," she said. "And even though the Seahawks lost (their first home game loss in two years), it was still the best present I've ever given."

In chapter 2 we saw that money doesn't buy happiness. The more we have, the more we want. Well, there's a caveat. It's true that once our basic needs are met, having more money won't make us any happier. But the way we *spend* our money can translate into well-being. In most cases money spent on life experiences like a concert or trip brings more happiness than the same amount of money spent on material goods like a laptop or new TV. Experiences outlast the time and space in which they occur by giving us something to look forward to, memories to relive, and stories to share in the future. Perhaps most importantly, experiences connect us to other people, strengthening our social ties, which is foundational to our happiness.

THE GIFTS THAT KEEP ON GIVING

In a study at Cornell University, students were asked to reflect on how much happiness they derived from either experiential or material purchases they had recently made. Experiential purchases not only brought more happiness than material goods, they also led the students to spend more time mentally revisiting them.[1]

When I gave my own students a similar reflection exercise, one told me about her experiences studying abroad in Europe during her junior year.

"I had the opportunity to travel to eastern Europe and learn about the Holocaust and my Jewish roots, as well as the recent history of the Cold War. I also experienced exciting cultural events such as Carnival in Cádiz and St. Patrick's Day in Dublin. I tried new foods, learned about different languages and cultures, and discovered the dos and don'ts of traveling. I went to museums, where I learned about different types of art and how they reflected different time periods and cultures. I met interesting people and did adventurous things that I would have not otherwise had the opportunity to do, such as caving in Budapest."

Each time she thinks back to her semester abroad, she gets to relive those adventures. "Although it is not something I literally carry with me, I will always carry everything I learned and all the amazing memories I made while traveling that semester."

Part of the reason experiences provide more happiness than material goods is the way they live on in our memories. The happiness we get from material possessions like a new car, bigger TV, or upgraded phone quickly fades. As we saw in chapter 2, we adapt to their features, and before long we are less excited to share them with others. Unlike material purchases, experiential memory is not subject to hedonic adaptation. Memories remain with us, and our ability to share them intensifies the original happiness they brought the first time around. This explains why the students at Cornell spent so much more time revisiting experiential purchases than reviewing material purchases. Each trip down memory lane allowed them to dip into the wellspring of happiness they'd first encountered during the initial experience. And because of the nature of human memory, they probably got even *more* happiness from the memory each time they did.

THE WINE EFFECT

Human memory is imperfect. Instead of operating like a camcorder, perfectly recording an event that we can later replay, it *reconstructs* memories when we recall them. This system of remembering can lead to errors not only in the exact details, but also in how we felt about them.

To demonstrate this phenomenon, one study asked students at the

University of Canterbury in New Zealand to rate their happiness in daily text messages during vacations they took over semester break.[2] A few weeks after the new semester resumed, the students were asked to think back and report how much happiness they *remembered* experiencing on vacation. Although you would expect people to recall their vacations accurately, the happiness they recalled afterward was significantly higher than the happiness they'd reported in daily text messages during the trip itself. If they rated their happiness at six *during* the trip, they gave it a seven when they were *thinking back* a month later. The process of reconstructing the memory involved looking back with rose-tinted glasses.

Think back to the last vacation you took. What events or images come to mind? You might call up specific instances like the great meal you enjoyed with your travel companions, the stunning artwork you encountered at a world-renowned museum, or the amazing sunset that took your breath away. Your first thoughts probably did not include all the long lines you had to wait in, the large crowds you had to push through, or an argument you may have had at the airport.

In the moment, those small nuisances will drive down an individual's happiness rating. But when we talk about the trip with others after the fact, we generally focus only on the most exciting highlights. Over time the nuisances and inconveniences fade into the background. Our overall evaluation of the trip becomes inflated because we are basing it not on a continuous record, but instead only on the key memories that defined the experience.[3]

This explains why my student who studied abroad in Europe derives so much happiness looking back on her adventures. Each time she shares them with another person, she is replaying those key memories, reinforcing the happiness they brought in the first place. In this way our memories are a bit like good wine. They get better with age. Or at least with each retelling.

STRENGTHENING SOCIAL CONNECTIONS

If you are meeting someone for the first time, maybe on a date, at a party, or on your first day at a new job, it can be hard to know what to say to draw someone in and pique their interest. Or on a job interview, when the executive behind the desk asks you to "Tell me about yourself," what's the best way to respond? Of all the topics you could choose, which will make the best impression?

A team of researchers at the University of Colorado examined this question by inviting pairs of previously unacquainted students into their lab to discuss recent purchases they had made.[4] Half the students were instructed to talk about material goods such as a new outfit or mobile device. The others were told to talk about life experiences such as a road trip with friends or a concert they had attended. By the end of the exchange, the students hearing about their partner's weekend getaway or concert experience found the conversation more enjoyable and had a more favorable impression of their partner compared to those discussing a new smartphone or laptop. Here we find another benefit of life experiences: they strengthen social connection not only during the experience itself, but also when we invite others in by sharing the memories after the fact.

As a bonus, stories about experiential purchases are more resistant to social comparison than those about material purchases.[5] As we saw in chapter 2, social comparison is one of the fundamental barriers to our happiness. By constantly looking over our shoulders to see how what we've got measures up to what everyone else has, we place serious limits on our happiness potential. Life experiences are much harder to compare than material goods. If you get the latest iPhone, you can place it right next to someone else's and know immediately whose has more storage, takes better pictures, and has a faster processing speed. There will be a clear winner. Experiential purchases by their nature are much harder to make side-by-side comparisons of. If

I went to Fort Lauderdale for winter break and you went to Maui, we might be able to compare how much each of us spent, but there is no means of quantifying the experiences themselves for a direct comparison. Who's to say that lying under palm trees on a beach in Hawaii is any better than enjoying the foliage and ocean views in southern Florida? When it comes to experiences, it becomes nearly impossible to judge whose was "better," which effectively shuts down social comparison.

The moral of the story: the next time you are about to head into a situation where you will be meeting people for the first time, take a few minutes to think back to the vacation you took last summer or the concert you saw over the weekend. Not only will you get to enjoy the happy memories again, but you'll be making positive social connections as well. Your conversation partner will enjoy learning about your life experience without either of you falling into the trap of social comparison that talking about material purchases would unlock.

THE ANTICIPATION EFFECT

Calling to mind an experience after it has happened is not the only way to feel happiness about it. Thinking about it beforehand can do the same, and that is another reason experiences, over things, are so valuable for our well-being. They give us something to look forward to. Multiple studies have found that anticipation itself is pleasurable, a source of "free happiness," according to psychologist Elizabeth Dunn and her colleagues.[6]

We receive an advance on the happiness in store for us down the road by directing attention toward the tunes we'll rock out to at an upcoming concert, or thinking about the stops we'll make during next summer's cross-country road trip. Some studies find that the happiness from anticipating an experience can be even greater than the happiness we get from the experience itself. According to Dunn, the anticipatory joy is "unsullied by reality."[7] Just as we recall past vacations by playing back key memories that defined the experience, we envision what the future has in store by focusing on big moments we have to look forward to. Our mind jumps from one upcoming adventure to the next, skipping over inconveniences or nuisances that may rear their heads along the way.

Remember, the happiness we get from experiences is not bound by the time and space in which they occur. This is why it may be advantageous to have many small experiences instead of only a few large ones. In the New Zealand study that tracked students' happiness levels throughout their vacations, the trip's length had no bearing on happiness. Those who took a quick weekend getaway experienced just as much happiness on average as those who luxuriated for a full two weeks. What matters more than a vacation's length is that we have something to look forward to, and key memories to look back on, with stories to retell and connect with others over.

As we saw in chapter 2, we adapt easily to what we have. Part of the happiness we get from an experience comes from the novelty of being in a new environment. Eventually we adapt to that environment, no matter how exciting it was at first. It's kind of like the thrill of a first kiss or watching a child take her first steps. Those things can happen only once, and each subsequent instance, though exciting, is not quite as wonderful as the first one. Even small experiences bring that "first-time" excitement at their start. Therefore, if you have the choice between one extravagant multiweek vacation or a handful of smaller trips throughout the year, go with the latter. You'll have multiple experiences to look forward to, and multiple sets of memories to look back on.

Last spring I asked my students to write about the best gifts they've ever received. One told me about her seventeenth birthday, sitting around her parents' dining room table, surrounded by family, cake, and gifts—all the ingredients for a truly happy birthday. It was shaping up to be a lot like her previous happy birthdays, until her sister furnished a golden envelope that would set this one apart.

As she opened the envelope, something fell into her lap: airline tickets to Los Angeles and weekend passes to Disneyland. "It was by far the best gift that I have ever received," the student recalled.

But it wasn't the thought of seeing Sleeping Beauty Castle or taking a ride on Space Mountain that excited her. It was the opportunity for a special trip down memory lane.

"When we were younger, my sister and I had several opportunities to visit Disneyland together, and those vacations were some of the best memories we ever had together. Although we both had grown into young adults, my sister wanted to recreate the magic and excitement of those childhood adventures. And it was the nostalgia and memories that came along with this gift that made it so special; it was not just a single object or material item—it was an entire collection of special experiences between the two of us."

Take a moment to think about some of the happiest moments from your life. In all likelihood they involve other people. Most life experiences—whether it's a Seattle Seahawks game or a trip to Disneyland—are shared with others and provide an opportunity to strengthen the relationships we have with them. It's the most important way experiences make us happier. Having high-quality relationships is a key predictor of our overall well-being, on emotional, physical, and cognitive levels.

When Ed Diener and Martin Seligman studied 222 college students at the University of Illinois, they found that the happiest 10 percent all had one thing in common: rich and satisfying social relationships. In fact, these psychologists note strong relationships may be a "necessary condition" for high levels of happiness. High-quality friendships provide a support structure during life's challenges, along with a means of helping us celebrate life's joys. Friends also become partners in happiness-boosting life experiences, or at the very least listening ears when we want to relive the highlight reel.

Beyond emotional support, high-quality relationships also provide a buffer against physical ailments. Researchers at Carnegie Mellon University and the University of Pittsburgh School of Medicine have found that people with thriving relationships are substantially less likely to contract disease than people whose relationships are marked by enduring patterns of chronic stress.[8]

Our social ties can even affect the length of our lives. A longitudinal study at UC Berkeley followed a group of adults over nine years, measuring preexisting conditions and behaviors that could affect mortality, such as smoking, alcohol consumption, physical activity, socioeconomic background, and preventive doctor's appointments.[9] By the end of the study, one variable had predicted mortality more strongly than any other: connection to others. Weak social ties increased the likelihood of death over any other demographic variable or behavior.

Cultivating relationships with others who share our interests and values is one of the most important behaviors for us to incorporate into our lives. For our physical health, strong social support systems provide a buffer against illness and mortality. And when it comes to increasing our happiness, nothing offers a greater return on investment.

SOCIAL SHARPNESS IS MENTAL SHARPNESS

The benefits of strong connections extend even beyond health and happiness. One of my students is a member of the varsity soccer team, and her teammates have become not only the quintessential support system, but also a group that motivates good cognitive behaviors.

"We're forced to be together at practice, but it is by choice that we eat together, go out together, and study together," she said. Observing her teammates' good study habits primes her to tackle her own work: "Even on game days when we're on the road, you can go into the hotel lobby and see a group of us getting some early-morning studying in. In this way, they motivate me to stay on top of my studies, even when the easy choice would be to get away from school for the entire weekend and only focus on soccer." Her teammates model good study habits, and the group rises together as a whole.

Some research has even found that meaningful social interaction itself can sharpen our minds. Consider a study in which students from the University of Michigan completed a series of tasks assessing their cognitive functioning.[10] Some of the tasks involved making decisions about whether strings of geometric shapes were the same or different. Others involved a working memory task that required them to recall information from sentences read aloud to them. For example, they might hear the sentence, "John wrote a note with a crayon," and then be asked, "Who wrote?" Both of these activities require the capacity to hold multiple pieces of information in mind simultaneously and recall them later. The speed and accuracy with which participants complete them provide a measure of their mental sharpness.

The researchers wanted to see what kind of pretest activities would strengthen the students' performance on these tasks. Beforehand, some of them spent ten minutes engaged in intellectual activities that involved reading comprehension tasks and crossword puzzles. Others spent those same ten minutes watching TV. Not surprisingly, the students who had been practicing cognitive tasks earlier in the experiment performed better on the subsequent working memory tasks and puzzles.

What may be surprising is how a third group of students performed. These students were assigned to a pretest activity that involved interacting with another study participant. For ten minutes they shared different perspectives on social and political issues. On the face of it, it seemed they weren't practicing cognitive skills at all. They were simply socializing. How did this affect performance on the subsequent puzzle task? These students went on to perform just as strongly as those who had spent the preceding time completing reading comprehension tasks and crossword puzzles. Along with its benefits for health and happiness, it turns out we can add enhanced intellectual capacity to the list of reasons relationships and shared experiences are so important.

The authors of this study note that social interactions may provide cognitive benefits because they require perspective taking, planning, inference generation, and other cognitive processes that strengthen mental acuity:

> "Social interaction and relationships not only sharpen our knowledge and social skills but also strengthen the cognitive processes that underlie those skills, which may then ready people for greater connection and effectiveness in dealing with others. Thus, an important outcome of social interaction appears to be mental sharpness, which in itself may play a central role in helping us enjoy the many other benefits that come from being socially connected."[11]

This study also showed that the effects are not merely about spending time in the presence of another person. In fact, students in the first two conditions—those doing intellectual activities and those watching TV—were completing their tasks with another student in the room. Those other two conditions, however, did not involve substantive interactions between each participant and his or her partner. So it's not just a matter of being in the presence of other people; socialization brings its greatest benefits when we are meaningfully engaged with them.

SUPERORDINATE GOALS

For my student on the soccer team, four years as a varsity athlete not only provided a support system that motivated her on and off the field, but also taught her a lot about how to work collaboratively with the diverse individuals who make up the team.

> "Every single member of our team is different and unique in their own ways, and they all inspire me to want to be better on a daily basis. Our differences make it work, and we find a way to come together to have the time of our lives while working toward our dream of a national title."

Coming together and working toward a common goal is especially beneficial for boosting cognitive performance. In another study at the University of Michigan, researchers introduced individual participants to a stranger and instructed them to spend ten minutes getting to know this other person.[12] Participants knew they would be playing a game with that person later in the experiment and this was their opportunity to learn more about them.

Some of the students were told they would be playing something called the Community Game and the other person was their partner; their goal would be to work with their partner to collectively earn as much money for the community as possible. Others were told they would be playing the Wall Street Game, and the other person was their opponent; their goal would be to compete against this person to earn as much money for themselves as they could. Immediately following the ten-minute "getting to know you" activity, all participants were given a series of puzzles and problems designed to measure their cognitive abilities. Who performed the best? The students who had spent ten minutes speaking with someone they saw as a partner and with whom they shared interests and goals.

When goals require collaboration to benefit the entire group instead of one particular person, psychologists refer to them as superordinate goals. We adopt a different mindset when interacting with someone we believe to be a comrade rather than a future foe. As the authors of this study explain, "Competitive goals can limit the degree to which executive functions are exercised, presumably because competition triggers withdrawal and self-protection, thus reducing the amount of mental engagement with the other person."[13] Superordinate goals, on the other hand, involve dedicated effort from each individual member because all are motivated to contribute to the greater good of the group.

As for my student whose soccer team worked together toward such strong superordinate goals, her dream came true. Within less than six months of her sharing that story with me, the team was crowned national champions of NCAA's Division III women's soccer. Chalk one up to the power of community.

BEING SOCIAL BY BEING PROSOCIAL

The benefits that come from the power of community don't necessarily have to involve people you know well. One of my students learned this himself just a few weeks before Christmas in the checkout lane of his local supermarket. As he began to put his groceries on the conveyor belt, he heard the cries of three young children accompanying their mother. Their cart pulled up behind his. "I could tell she was having a rough time handling them all among the chaos of the holidays combined with the regular difficulties of being an adult and having children."

That's when he recalled a YouTube video featuring a benevolent stranger paying for the groceries of the person in line behind them. He'd always wanted to try it out for himself. Plus he had just received his paycheck. "I instantly knew that this was the perfect opportunity."

His offer was met with astonishment. The young mother's face said it all. "It was a look of complete surprise, as if she could never have imagined something like this happening to her so randomly." She denied him at first, but he persisted and she accepted.

After expressing her heartfelt gratitude, the young mother walked away with her groceries paid for, and the young man walked away with extra spring in his step. "The best part about the whole ordeal is that I got as much out of it as she did."

Studies confirm that helping others is another way to help ourselves. Earlier in this chapter we saw that our happiness is affected by how we spend our time and money. A nice meal out or a trip to a new place will bring much greater joy in the long run than acquiring a new computer or pair of sneakers. But it's not only a matter of *what* we buy; it also matters *on whom* we spend our time and money. Investing in others, in fact, is another key way to actively maximize our own personal happiness.

In one study researchers doled out small amounts of cash to students at the University of British Columbia one morning, with instructions to spend it by five that evening. Some of the students were told to spend it on other people or give it to a charity; others were told to spend it on themselves by paying a bill or personal expenses. When the researchers followed up with the students later that day, they found that those who'd spent the money on someone else felt significantly happier than those who'd spent it on themselves.[14] It turns out the puppets from *Avenue Q* had it right all along: when you help others, you can't help helping yourself.

IN GIVING, WE RECEIVE

American author Henry James once said, "Three things in human life are important: the first is to be kind; the second is to be kind; and the third is to be kind."

One of my students personifies kindness as a volunteer at St. Louis Children's Hospital. One day, a father of one of the patients approached her and asked why she volunteers.

"I do it for the kids," she replied.

"Thank you for making each day just a little bit better," he said.

This simple interaction reminded her why volunteering is such an important part of her life. "It is amazing how the little things in life can make such an impact on someone else, even if it is just playing a game with a child and allowing the parents to go out for coffee," she said. "Even a smile is enough to brighten a child's day." Although she acknowledges that she is providing these children and their families a service, she feels that what she gains is even greater. "Children have the ability to teach adults to be spontaneous, be courageous, make mistakes, and, most of all, approach life with enthusiasm. As a volunteer, you learn that compassion is the key to everything since you do not necessarily know what the patient is going through. You have not walked in their shoes to know. But you do get the opportunity to walk with them and make a difference, even if it is small, in that patient's day. Volunteers are given the greatest gift, the ability to help others."

Helping others has been associated with many benefits that enhance the well-being of the giver. On a physiological level, it can decrease the release of adrenaline and cortisol, the body's stress hormones, and increase the production of endorphins, the body's natural feel-good chemicals.[15] These are the same chemical messengers that contribute to a "runner's high" during a race. People all around the world who serve their communities see benefits to their well-being. According to a report of more than a thousand adults living in Australia, those involved with humanitarian organizations tended to be the happiest.[16] The Institute for Volunteering Research in the United Kingdom reports that citizens who volunteer improve their mental health by finding direction and meaning in their lives and widening their social networks.[17]

One of the concerns with these data sets is that they are correlational in nature. Perhaps people who do humanitarian work were happier in the first place. To control for this possibility, one study randomly assigned people to perform good deeds for others, and compared them to people who were assigned to perform good deeds for themselves.[18] Participants could choose any activities they wished, but had to fall in line with one of three conditions to which they were randomly assigned:

1. *Other-Kindness:* Acts of kindness, generosity, and thoughtfulness—both large and small—for others. These acts of kindness did not need to be for the same person, the person might or might not be aware of the act, and the act might or might not be similar to the acts listed below.
   Examples:

   - "Helped elderly person with using their ATM at kiosk"
   - "Made my girlfriend coffee and breakfast"
   - "Walked a stranger with my umbrella to her car because it was raining and she did not have her own umbrella"

2. *World-Kindness:* Acts of kindness that made the world a better place. They did not necessarily need to involve other people, but they were to be efforts to contribute to the world or humanity at large.
   Examples:

   - "Picked up litter"
   - "Donated clothes to Salvation Army"
   - "Rescued a hummingbird the cat had got. Sat with the bird while my husband found a box for it"

3. *Self-Kindness:* Things out of the ordinary that the participant did for themselves with a little extra effort. Although the acts might involve other people, they were to be things that the participant did explicitly for themselves, not others.
   Examples:

   - "Treated myself to a good lunch (I usually pack a lunch)"
   - "Went for an extended run, something I used to do at least a couple times a week but haven't in some time"
   - "Went shopping"

Participants across all the conditions performed three activities of their choice each week for the next month. In addition to reporting which three acts of kindness they performed, they also reported how much positive and negative emotion they had encountered.

Two of the conditions—other-kindness and world-kindness—fall into the category of prosocial behavior, acts of kindness for the benefit of others. By the end of the study, those who had been performing the prosocial acts reported more positive emotion, less negative emotion, and spikes in life satisfaction and purpose that lasted even after their month of kind acts had ended. Whether the kind acts were targeted toward other people or the world more generally, the increases in well-being were similar. Any kind behavior targeted toward something outside of ourselves is beneficial, not only for the recipient but also for the person performing the act. According to the researchers, these prosocial activities put the participants on an upward spiral: "As people do nice things for others, they may feel greater joy, contentment, and love, which in turn promote greater overall well-being and improve social relationships."[19]

The irony, of course, is that the activities participants chose in the self-kindness condition were presumably intended to provide a boost to their happiness and overall well-being, and yet it was the participants in the other-kindness and world-kindness conditions who experienced the largest long-term personal benefits. The researchers offer the following suggestion based on their study: "People who are striving to improve their own happiness may be tempted to treat themselves to a spa day, a shopping trip, or a sumptuous dessert.... [But] they might be more successful if they opt to treat someone else instead."[20] If you really want to be kind to yourself, the best way is by being kind to someone *else*.

RANDOM ACTS OF KINDNESS

Part of the happiness my benevolent student in the grocery store experienced by way of his act of other-kindness toward the young mother in line behind him came from the spontaneous nature of the act. "I definitely think that there is a greater amount of gratitude expressed to deeds done out of nowhere compared to those that are planned."

Indeed, research has found that both the giver and the receiver of an act of kindness get more psychological benefit when it is unexpected. In a study at the University of California, researchers asked young adults to think of kind acts they could do for others.[21] Below are some examples the students came up with:

- "Taking out the trash in my [shared] apartment"
- "Letting a friend borrow a book for class"
- "Cooking dinner for my roommates"
- "Letting several cars merge in front of me on the freeway"

Some of the students were instructed to perform the same act each week over the next two months. If they chose polite driving, they were told to make that part of their regular routine each week of the study. Others were told to vary their acts. If they took out the trash one week, they should cook dinner the next. The following week should involve something different still.

Which students would be better off? Did it matter only that they were doing nice things, or did the amount of variety in the acts of kindness matter? By the end of the study, the students who had been varying their acts of kindness saw the biggest gains in their happiness. As the authors of the study explain, "Attending to variety in one's actions may be a powerful happiness enhancing strategy.... Varying how one does a 'positive' activity may be crucial in determining whether that activity continues to have enhancing effects on people's well-being."[22]

One of my students has found for herself how changing up random acts of kindness can be an important happiness booster.

"Making other people happy makes me happy, be it baking for them (I'm a hella good baker) on a bad day, going out and getting ginger ale and their favorite snacks when they're sick, buying food for homeless people on the corners, or just picking up some extra Cadbury Creme Eggs from the grocery store just because I know they'll automatically put a smile on someone in particular's face. Doing these things for others is something I enjoy and do willingly. I'm not a saint, though—I do get something out of doing all the good deeds for others: I feel better about myself."

BENEFITS TO OUR REPUTATION

Acts of kindness also influence how others perceive us. In a study conducted by researchers at the University of Kent at Canterbury, high school students from the South of England were split into groups of three. Each student was given a hundred pence (one pound) and told that they could keep some for themselves and contribute the rest to the group fund. The total amount the three students contributed to the group would be doubled and split among the participants. You can see the dilemma each student faces: they are guaranteed to keep the entirety of what they put toward their private funds, but if everyone acts generously and contributes a large amount toward the group, each person goes home with an even larger reward.

After each group member decided what to keep and what to contribute, all three were given feedback sheets that detailed the spending decision of each group member. This enabled everyone to see who was generous and who was miserly. Next they answered a series of questions about how they felt about each group member.

On average, the altruistic individuals—those who offered the highest proportion of their money to the group—were rated as the most respected, held in the highest esteem, and were most likely to be chosen as group leaders for a future task.[23] None of the students had known each other ahead of time, which means they based their impressions primarily on what percentage of money each person offered. In a similar study with students at the University of Kent, the most altruistic participants were rated highest in prominence, respect, and influence within the group. Benevolence apparently enhances reputation and status. According to the study's authors, "Niceness pays because in a world where people can choose with whom they want to interact, altruists create more opportunities for themselves than do selfish people."[24] By reaching outward instead of protecting inward, altruists create more chances for meaningful social connections.

PUTTING THE SOCIAL IN PROSOCIAL BEHAVIOR

Virtually all forms of prosocial behavior increase authentic happiness. Some research has found special benefits that come specifically from the *social* component of prosocial behavior. In a study led by a researcher at Simon Fraser University in Canada, college students were given $10 Starbucks gift cards.[25] That by itself would make most students pretty happy, but this study found that the way the students *used* the gift card affected how much happiness it brought. Some spent it entirely on themselves; others gave the card to another person to use on their own. But the students who got the biggest boost to their happiness incorporated the best of both worlds: they brought a friend along, using the gift card to treat both themselves *and* the other person.

When you are going to do something for someone else, make it a social experience. Remember, experiences make better gifts than material possessions because they present opportunities for social connection. When one of my students was considering a holiday gift for his girlfriend, he could have given her a necklace or pair of shoes. Instead he saved up and took her on a nature vacation they could enjoy together. "This gift left memories that we still both treasure today," he said. "There were so many beautiful views that we saw as we hiked along trails that scaled mountains, traversed forests that lined the ocean, and, after a week of fun and exploration, we ended with a show of a magnificent sunrise. We still love to reminisce about the delicious blueberry pie and the delightful popovers topped with ice cream after a long hike with those beautiful views."

When he first made the travel arrangements, his primary intent was to increase the happiness of his girlfriend. But just like the students at Simon Fraser who shared their Starbucks gift cards with someone else, he came out ahead himself. "The funny thing about this gift that I gave is that I benefited from it too. Not only did I get to provide her with an enjoyment that she still thinks about to this day, but also I got to enjoy it with her."

––––––––––

If we had to predict a person's happiness from only one piece of data, we would use the strength of their social relationships. Connecting with others gives you experiences to look forward to, memories to look back on, and a support system that provides benefits for your physical, emotional, and intellectual well-being. As you make decisions about how you spend your time and money, create opportunities to cultivate relationships with others. Even if you're not able to buy someone tickets to see their favorite sports team or visit their favorite vacation destination, performing a meaningful act of kindness for another person and sharing that experience with them can create just as much happiness. The social connection it brings will be the greatest gift of all, both for them and for you, and is arguably the most effective way to make each of you happ*ier*.

Putting It into Practice

This crash course in the science of happiness has, I hope, provided a tool kit of strategies and interventions that can bolster your psychological health and happiness. Over ten chapters we have reviewed more than a hundred studies conducted on thousands of young adults from all over the world. When I teach these topics at Washington University, I often get questions from students about how they are supposed to incorporate them all. "I understand that all of these things can improve my well-being," a student once told me. "But if I'm going to start doing them *and* get a full eight hours of sleep each night, I'll need at least thirty hours in the day."

For that student, and for you, I'd like to offer seven practical approaches for putting this research into practice, even in a busy day with only twenty-four hours.

I. Find the strategies that work for you and your lifestyle

When I was in graduate school, I enrolled in cooking classes at a local kitchen conservatory in an effort to force myself to put down my research and get off campus. One of the most important things I took away from the cooking classes was not the proper technique for chopping vegetables or deboning a chicken (which I'll admit I still can't figure out). The true value I gained from each class was a sense of whether the time and effort that went into preparing each dish was justified by the end result. For example, I learned that seafood lasagna requires hours of preparation and a list of hard-to-find, expensive ingredients; I have never made seafood lasagna again. On the other hand, I also learned that pasta primavera with sun-dried tomatoes and fresh garden vegetables takes hardly any effort, looks beautiful on the plate, and tastes great. It has since become one of my weeknight staples. Of course not all my former classmates feel this way; some make seafood lasagna weekly, some prefer the eggplant parmesan, and others found their niche with the Tuscan grilled chicken. (I still can't figure out how that guy learned to debone a chicken so easily.)

The idea is that certain strategies you read about in this book will work better for you than others. Try them out. See what feels natural. See which ones, after a few weeks, lead to the biggest changes in your mood and thought patterns. Stick with those and give them priority. If exercising is something you just can't get yourself to do, or if it comes with side effects that you find outweigh any boosts to your psychological well-being, just accept that it might be your equivalent of my seafood lasagna. Hold off on that one and spend a few minutes each week making entries in a gratitude journal instead. After a series of trials and errors you will get a sense of which strategies you enjoy the most, which ones you are most capable of incorporating into your life, and which offer the biggest happiness boost.

II. Be proactive in implementing the strategies that work for you

Maintaining psychological health involves incorporating positive behaviors into your life on the front end. People who have the best physical health didn't get that way by waiting until they were sick to exercise or eat right. The small, everyday decisions like choosing salad over French fries and going on a jog a few mornings each week accumulate to create physical fitness that makes the sick days few and far between. And when illness strikes, these generally healthy people recover more quickly.

The same goes for the strategies outlined in this book: pick your favorites and proactively make them part of your regular routines. One of the titles we initially entertained for this book was *Proactive Happiness*, which the publishing team liked for the *active* part. Psychological health requires that kind of preemptive energy. It may be tempting to think that if you're already feeling good, there is no need to meditate, exercise, or practice gratitude. But just as you shouldn't wait until you have a cold to take care of your physical health, you shouldn't wait until you're sad to work on your psychological health. Maintaining these behaviors even on the good days builds psychological capital that can both extend the positivity we are feeling and help us recover more quickly from rough patches.

III. Create habits

To the extent that happiness is your goal, create implementation intentions (which you read about in chapter 7) around your happiness strategies. Go out for a run at the same time each day. Go to bed at the same time each night. Identify a particular time and space where you meditate. Create rituals around the time you spend with friends. It's as easy as planning a weekly lunch date with a classmate or colleague and sticking to it. Or finding a TV series your friends all like and getting together each week to watch another episode. Those regular, ongoing forms of socialization take very little time and effort to plan or execute, but yield big payoffs in happiness.

Take time also to identify the environmental characteristics that might get in the way and develop contingency plans to address them. *If* you get tired midway through your run, *then* what will you do to regain motivation? *If* you find that you've gone two weeks without meditating, *then* what will you do to get back on track? *If* you find yourself obsessing over the perfect Instagram picture, *then* what will you do to put your phone down and savor the experience in real time?

IV. Focus on the activities' intrinsic value

Find enjoyment in the strategies themselves and learn to appreciate the sense of accomplishment that comes from completing them. Even activities that might seem unpleasant at first, like exercise or getting up early to make your bed, carry value. Recognize how they are strengthening your willpower muscles. Importantly, don't do the activities only because they are "supposed to" bring happiness. Suffering through them, hating every minute, but doing them because they have become a necessary evil, could backfire. In that case you might undermine their happiness potential and paradoxically become *less happy*.

It's a bit like shooting a bow and arrow. One of the most common mistakes novice archers make is concentrating so much on the target that they disregard the overall muscle movements that are important for hitting the bull's eye. Ironically, they would be more successful if they focused a little less on hitting the bull's eye and a little more on the process that can get them there. Think of happiness as the target. Don't focus so desperately on achieving it that you lose sight of the inherent worth of the activities themselves.

V. Keep your expectations realistic

One of the biggest barriers people experience on the road toward becoming happ*ier* is the misguided notion that within a short time, their lives will suddenly be transformed into the perfect lives they see everyone else living on social media and they will magically step into a state of everlasting bliss. But happiness doesn't work that way. To extend the earlier analogy of physical fitness, someone who wants to lose weight does not achieve that goal immediately after running on a treadmill one time. It's the repetition of that behavior, along with ongoing modifications to diet and other forms of physical activity, that promote physical fitness. The same applies for increasing happiness. Writing in a gratitude journal one time is not enough to thrust you suddenly into a state of euphoria. Instead the repetition of that behavior, along with others I've outlined in this book, leads to gradual increases in well-being.

Remember the happiness formula:

$$\text{Happiness} = \frac{\text{What We Have}}{\text{What We Want}}$$

In the pursuit of happiness, establish realistic expectations. Don't overinflate the denominator by assuming that the gains will be automatic. Instead, emphasize the numerator by celebrating the small steps you have taken in the pursuit of happiness. Remember, it's not necessarily about becoming happy, it's about becoming happ*ier* over time, even amid setbacks and bad days along the way.

VI. Give yourself permission to be human if you fall back into old habits

Even if you start with the best of intentions by incorporating some (or many) of these strategies into your life, you will probably go through stretches of time when they fall to the wayside. That's OK. I don't know anyone who maintains their regimens for psychological well-being perfectly. What's important is that you pick yourself back up and keep at them. When the demands of life prevent you from getting enough sleep, exercise, meditation, or socialization, bring awareness to the fact that your overall well-being may take a hit...and that's also OK. It's part of being human.

An idea that I introduced in the first chapter of this book bears repeating here: no one is happy all the time. Inevitably, we all have days when we are distressed, unmotivated, or otherwise just plain grumpy, no matter how much exercise we get or how many good things in our lives we choose to focus on. There will be days when you question whether these strategies are having any effect at all. Just remember that when we are feeling down, we do not have the mental capacity to make important judgments about ourselves and our lives. Such negativity can cloud our thinking. Write things out, talk things over with a friend, and when you are feeling better, slowly return to the strategies that you have found to work so far.

Most importantly, when you fall upon the inevitable bad day, don't deny yourself the sadness or despair sweeping over you. Otherwise those negative emotions become like that polar bear you were told not to think about in chapter 1, rebounding with even greater intensity.

VII. Surround yourself with good people who will help you achieve these behaviors

As I mentioned in the introduction, in the early stages of writing this book I had dinner with my friend James who asked me what motivated this project. He helped me put into words why I was writing it— a book for the young adult version of myself—and why its messages were relevant. In its final stages, I had lunch with my friend Ruth (the physiologist you met in chapter 3), who asked me what it had been like to work on this project over the previous two years. I told her that this experience provided an opportunity both to reflect on my own personal journey so far and also to consider the behaviors I can still work on to continue becoming happi*er*. (I had plenty of time to describe the contents of this book as we left the restaurant that day since we had parked as far from the entrance as we could!)

One of the most effective ways I have stayed on track with these strategies is by sharing them with others. (And this kind of "sharing" is not about posting to Facebook, Twitter, or Instagram.) As the Beatles once sang, "I get by with a little help from my friends." The strategies I have gotten the most out of have often involved the people who mean the most to me. Some of my favorites include going on trips with friends, sharing my meditation practice with Ginny, taking walks with Ruth, and spending time with my extended family at our annual Spedinifest (a holiday we invented just to have another excuse to get together each year...think *My Big Fat Greek Wedding,* Italian style). As an introvert I practice many strategies on my own as well, but incorporating others when it feels right (or when home-cooked Italian food is involved) creates accountability and enhances the positivity each has the potential to bring.

———

In the end, likes and follows, shares and retweets aren't enough to sustain well-being—but a life filled with close relationships and gratitude, a healthy body, and a sound mind can be the keys to authentic happiness.

Acknowledgments

"Chance favors the prepared mind."
—Louis Pasteur

I am indebted to so many people who helped prepare my mind to capitalize on the incredible chance events and encounters that ultimately led to this book.

To my extraordinary agent, Melissa Edwards, thank you for being my advocate, guide, and sounding board through every step of this process, responding to every call and e-mail with lightning speed. To my wonderful editor Brittany McInerney, thank you for gracing this book with your exceptional talent for narrative style and for bringing sage advice to the many decisions we had to make along the way. Tareth Mitch, Linda Duggins, Sadie Kleinman, Susan Benson Gutentag, and the entire team at Grand Central Publishing, thank you for the brilliant ideas and careful edits you contributed, as well.

To my awesome students at Washington University, thank you for motivating me to consider the real-world implications of this research with your questions and stories during class and office hours. Special thanks to those who read and offered feedback on early drafts of this book: Jonathan Nazha, Dante Chao, Max Helfand, Scarlett Ho, Danielle Kahn, Lian Steinberg, Hyun-Ji Yang, Albert Wu, Jan Mazur, Corey Meehan, Clare Kim, Ben Abramowitz, Hannah Graves, Laura

Zimmermann, Maria Dorfman, Melissa Geisel, Pooja Jairam, Taylor Pitcher, Elan Baskir, Jeremy Reisman, and the brothers of the Missouri Beta chapter of Sigma Phi Epsilon. I am especially indebted to Binil Jacob, Audrey Schield, Judah Silver, and Julia Winemiller, whose thorough edits improved the style and structure of this book inestimably. It is humbling to call myself an alumnus of an institution that has students as talented as each of you.

To my colleagues at Washington University and other mentors I have met throughout my life, thank you for lending your support and professional expertise in countless forms to this project: Zvjezdana Prizmic-Larsen, Gerry Everding, Ruth Clark, Ginny Fendell, Sarah Cunningham, Barbara O'Brien, Rob Patterson, Micah Zeller, Lisa Wood, Todd Braver, Jill Carnaghi, Jill Stratton, AnneMarie Watts, Kathy Drury, Matt DeVoll, Karen Coburn, Eric Brende, Chuck Kretschmer, Margy Weisman, Henry Biggs, and Gary Braun.

To my amazing friends, thank you for supporting me, encouraging me, and providing much-needed diversion from my writing: Ryan Bailey, Jason Lake, Colin Keller, Buz Hargraves, Kathy Wildman, Ron Gibbs, Kalen Furrer, Jim Mourey, James Croft, Pooja Agarwal, Geoff Maddox, Danielle Bristow, Katharine Pei, Daniel Faris, Pan Sukpaladisai, Justin Lerner, Scott Hampton, Nisa Qais, Jeff Grim, Nate Lucena, Lance Frutiger, James Compton, and Avi Silber. Heartfelt gratitude to Ryan Cook and Josh Gruenke in particular for unwavering friendship and encouragement through each step of this project.

Pam and Bob Schmidt, thank you for encouraging me to apply to Washington University when I was a senior in high school. Linda Churchwell-Varga, thank you for advocating my admission to WashU that spring and opening the door to a world of opportunities I never even dreamed were possible. Randy Larsen, thank you for teaching me not only how to study the science of happiness, but more importantly, how to live it. I hope to inspire my own students the same way that you have inspired me.

To my parents, Sam and Mary Lou, thanks for dedicating your

lives to raising five kids and exposing us to all those crazy, fun-loving, wonderful cuginos at every holiday and celebration (not to mention the spedini and cuccidati!). Is it any wonder your middle child grew up to be a psychologist? To your question from my freshman year of college, "What are you going to do with *that* major?," I hope this book finally provides an answer. Uncle Joe, Aunt Angie, and Aunt Carmella, thank you for being such wonderful role models. Joey, Vince, Samantha, and Jake, thank you for being my buddies and sidekicks. Oh, and Julie, Mike, Matt, and Christine—you guys are all right, too.

Notes

Introduction

1. Contrera, J., "13, Right Now," *Washington Post*, May 25, 2016. Retrieved from http://www.washingtonpost.com/sf/style/2016/05/25/13-right-now-this -is-what-its-like-to-grow-up-in-the-age-of-likes-lols-and-longing/?utm _term=.3c13154ac0f8.

Chapter 1. The Holy Grail of Young Adulthood

1. Snyder, T.D. & Dillow, S.A. (2015). Digest of Education Statistics 2013 (NCES 2015-011). National Center for Education Statistics, Institute of Education Sciences, U.S. Department of Education. Washington, DC.
2. Kim-Prieto, C., Diener, E., Tamir, M., Scollon, C.N., & Diener, M., "Integrating the Diverse Definitions of Happiness: A Time-Sequential Framework of Subjective Well-Being," *Journal of Happiness Studies* (2005) 6 (3) 261–300.
3. Conklin, J.E. (2008). *Campus Life in the Movies: A Critical Survey from the Silent Era to the Present.* Jefferson, NC: McFarland and Company.
4. Ibid., 3.
5. https://www.nami.org/Press-Media/Press-Releases/2004/Mental-Illness -Prolific-Among-College-Students.
6. Twenge, J.M., Gentile, B., DeWall, N., Ma, D., Lacefield, K., & Schurtz, D.R., "Birth Cohort Increases in Psychopathology among Young Americans, 1938–2007: A Cross-Temporal Meta-Analysis of the MMPI," *Clinical Psychology Review* 30 (2010): 145–154.
7. QuickStats: Suicide Rates for Teens Aged 15–19 Years, by Sex—United States, 1975–2015. *Morbidity and Mortality Weekly Report* 66 (2017): 816.
8. National Alliance on Mental Illness (2012). *College Students Speak: A Survey Report on Mental Health.* Retrieved from https://www.nami.org/collegesurvey.

9. Wang, S.S., "Is Happiness Overrated?" *Wall Street Journal*, March 15, 2011. Retrieved from https://www.wsj.com/articles/SB10001424052748704893604 576200471545379388.

10. Wilson, C., "Final Word: Happiness Is Overrated. You Can Bank on It," *USA Today*, April 10, 2012. Retrieved from http://usatoday30.usatoday.com/ life/columnist/finalword/story/2012-04-10/final-word-happiness-overrated -craig-wilson/54160464/1.

11. Winterson, J. (2011). *Why Be Happy When You Could Be Normal?* New York: Grove Press.

12. Ehrenreich, B. (2011). *Bright-Sided: How the Relentless Promotion of Positive Thinking Has Undermined America*. New York: Metropolitan Books.

13. Kirkey, S., "Refute of Happiness: How Our Obsession with Positivity Is Making Us Miserable—and Insufferable," *National Post*, October 16, 2015. Retrieved from http://news.nationalpost.com/life/refute-of-happiness-how -our-obsession-with-positivity-is-making-us-miserable-and-insufferable?lsa =95d7-515e.

14. Ben-Shahar, T. (2007). *Happier: Learn the Secrets to Daily Joy and Lasting Fulfillment*. New York: McGraw-Hill.

15. Snowdon, D.A., Kemper, S.J., Mortimer, J.A., Greiner, L.H., Wekstein, D.R., & Markesbery, W.R., "Linguistic Ability in Early Life and Cognitive Function and Alzheimer's Disease in Late Life. Findings from the Nun Study," *Journal of the American Medical Association* 275 (1996): 528–532.

16. Danner, D.D., Snowdon, D.A., & Friesen, W.V., "Positive Emotions in Early Life and Longevity: Findings from the Nun Study," *Journal of Personality and Social Psychology* 80 (2001): 804–813.

17. Fredrickson, B.L., "The Role of Positive Emotions in Positive Psychology: The Broaden-and-Build Theory of Positive Emotions," *American Psychologist* 56 (2001): 218–226.

18. Ingraham, C., "America's Top Fears: Public Speaking, Heights and Bugs," *Washington Post*, October 30, 2014. Retrieved from https://www .washingtonpost.com/news/wonk/wp/2014/10/30/clowns-are-twice-as -scary-to-democrats-as-they-are-to-republicans/.

19. Fredrickson, B.L., Mancuso, R.A., Branigan, C., & Tugade, M.M. "The Undoing Effect of Positive Emotions," *Motivation and Emotion* 24 (2000): 237–258.

20. Fredrickson, B.L., "The Role of Positive Emotions in Positive Psychology: The Broaden-and-Build Theory of Positive Emotions," *American Psychologist* 56 (2001): 218–226.

21. Ibid., 222.

22. Cloninger, C.R., "Mind, Body, Soul and Science: Researching Happiness at SLU and WashU" (Don Marsh, interviewer) [audio file], St. Louis Public Radio,

September 1, 2015. Retrieved from http://news.stlpublicradio.org/post/mind
-body-soul-and-science-researching-happiness-slu-and-wash-u#stream/0.

23. The effects held even when the researchers controlled for physical attractive-
ness, suggesting that physical beauty itself does not lead to life outcomes like
high-quality relationships and the capacity for interpersonal warmth, cheer-
fulness, and sociability. Rather, a high-quality smile that reflects inner happiness is far more valuable.

24. Carney, D.R., Cuddy, A.J.C., Yap, A.J., "Power Posing: Brief Nonverbal Dis-
plays Affect Neuroendocrine Levels and Risk Tolerance," *Psychological Science* 21 (2010): 1363–1368.

25. Ibid., 1366.

26. Hung, I.W. & Labroo, A.A., "From Firm Muscles to Firm Willpower: Understanding the Role of Embodied Cognition in Self-Regulation," *Journal of
Consumer Research* 37 (2011):1046–1064.

27. Riskind, J.H. & Gotay, C.C., "Physical Posture: Could It Have Regulatory
or Feedback Effects on Motivation and Emotion?" *Motivation and Emotion*
6 (1982): 273–298.

Chapter 2. The Common Denominator of Happiness

1. Kross, E. et al., "Facebook Use Predicts Declines in Subjective Well-Being in
Young Adults," *PLoS ONE* 8 (2013): 1–6. http://dx.doi.org/10.1371/journal
.pone.0069841.

2. Brickman, P., Coates, D., & Janoff-Bulman, R., "Lottery Winners and Acci-
dent Victims: Is Happiness Relative?" *Journal of Personality and Social Psychology* 36 (1978): 917–927.

3. Newmark, J., "Actress from Bourbon Savors Every Moment on Broadway,"
St. Louis Post-Distpatch, November 4, 2012.

4. Diener, E. & Biswas-Diener, R. (2008). *Happiness: Unlocking the Mysteries
of Psychological Wealth*. Malden, MA: Blackwell Publishing.

5. Sarkar, M., "How American Homes Vary by the Year They Were Built"
(working paper, United States Census Bureau, 2011). Retrieved from
https://www.census.gov/hhes/www/housing/housing_patterns/pdf/Hous
ing%20by%20Year%20Built.pdf.

6. Tversky, A. & Griffin, D., "Endowment and Contrast Judgments of Well-Being,"
in *Strategy and Choice*, ed. Zeckhauser, R.J. (Cambridge: MIT Press, 1991), 313.

7. Boyce, C.J., Brown, G.D.A., & Moore, S.C., "Money and Happiness: Rank
of Income, Not Income, Affects Life Satisfaction," *Psychological Science* 21
(2010): 471–475.

8. Lyubomirsky, S. & Ross, L., "Hedonic Consequences of Social Comparison: A Contrast of Happy and Unhappy People," *Journal of Personality and
Social Psychology* 73 (1997): 1141–1157.

9. Emmons, R.A. & McCullough, M.E., "Counting Blessings versus Burdens: An Experimental Investigation of Gratitude and Subjective Well-Being in Daily Life," *Journal of Personality and Social Psychology* 84 (2003): 377–389.

10. Seligman, M.E., Steen, T.A., Park, N., & Peterson, C., "Positive Psychology Progress: Empirical Validation of Interventions," *American Psychologist* 60 (2005): 410–421.

11. RefLearn, "Gratitude Visit™" (video file), July 8, 2008. Retrieved from https://www.youtube.com/watch?v=jyLYgR2nDkc.

12. Woollett, K. & Maguire, E.A., "Acquiring 'the Knowledge' of London's Layout Drives Structural Brain Changes," *Current Biology* 21 (2011): 2109–2114.

13. Maguire, E.A., Woollett, K., & Spiers, H.J., "London Taxi Drivers and Bus Drivers: A Structural MRI and Neuropsychological Analysis," *Hippocampus* 16 (2006): 1091–1101.

14. Hanson, R., "How to Trick Your Brain for Happiness," *Greater Good*, September 26, 2011. Retrieved from http://greatergood.berkeley.edu/article/item/how_to_trick_your_brain_for_happiness.

Chapter 3. A Healthy Mind in a Healthy Body

1. Velez, A., "Anna Kendrick's Shower Thoughts Are Just as Delightful as You Would Expect," *BuzzFeed*, (May 5, 2015). Retrieved from https://www.buzzfeed.com/alivelez/anna-kendricks-shower-thoughts-are-just-as-delightful-as-you?utm_term=.su0R0dBN2#.ouY86grwW.

2. Lou, D.W., "Sedentary Behaviors and Youth: Current Trends and the Impact on Health," Active Living Research, January 2014. Retrieved from http://activelivingresearch.org/sites/default/files/ALR_Brief_Sedentary Behavior_Jan2014.pdf.

3. "Physical Activity," updated February 2017, World Health Organization. Retrieved from http://www.who.int/mediacentre/factsheets/fs385/en/.

4. Winslow, R., "The Guide to Beating a Heart Attack," *Wall Street Journal*, April 16, 2012. Retrieved from http://www.wsj.com/news/articles/SB10001424052702304818404577347982400815676.

5. Fox, M., "Here's Just How Bad Sitting Around Is for You," NBC News, June 16, 2014. Retrieved from http://www.nbcnews.com/health/cancer/heres-just-how-bad-sitting-around-you-n132471.

6. Rocca, M., "Is Sitting the New Smoking?" (video), CBS News, August 24, 2014. Retrieved from http://www.cbsnews.com/videos/is-sitting-the-new-smoking/.

7. "Sitting Is the New Smoking: Ways a Sedentary Lifestyle Is Killing You," *Huffington Post*, September 24, 2014. Retrieved from http://www.huffingtonpost.com/the-active-times/sitting-is-the-new-smokin_b_5890006.html.

8. Park, A., "Sitting Is Killing You," *Time*, September 2, 1014. Retrieved from http://time.com/sitting/.

9. MacVean, M., " 'Get Up!' or Lose Hours of Your Life Every Day, Scientist Says," *Los Angeles Times*, July 31, 2014. Retrieved from http://www.latimes.com/science/sciencenow/la-sci-sn-get-up-20140731-story.html.

10. Biswas, A. et al., "Sedentary Time and Its Association with Risk for Disease Incidence, Mortality, and Hospitalization in Adults," *Annals of Internal Medicine* 162 (2015): 123–132.

11. Warren, T.W., Barry, V., Hooker, S.P., Sui, X., Church, T.S., & Blair, S.N., "Sedentary Behaviors Increase Risk of Cardiovascular Disease Mortality in Men," *Medicine & Science in Sports & Exercise* 42 (2010): 879–885.

12. Vankim, N.A. & Nelson, T.F., "Vigorous Physical Activity, Mental Health, Perceived Stress, and Socializing among College Students," *American Journal of Health Promotion* 28 (2013): 7–15.

13. "How Much Physical Activity Do Adults Need?" updated June 4, 2015, Centers for Disease Control and Prevention. Retrieved from https://www.cdc.gov/physicalactivity/basics/adults/index.htm.

14. Geist, W. "How to Work on No Sleep: Willie Geist," *Bloomberg*, April 12, 2012. Retrieved from https://www.bloomberg.com/news/articles/2012-04-12/how-to-work-on-no-sleep-willie-geist.

15. Puetz, T.W., Flowers, S.S., & O'Connor, P.J., "A Randomized Controlled Trial of the Effect of Aerobic Exercise Training on Feelings of Energy and Fatigue in Sedentary Young Adults with Persistent Fatigue," *Psychotherapy and Psychosomatics* 77 (2008): 167–174.

16. Ibid.

17. Williams, L.E. & Bargh, J.A., "Experiencing Physical Warmth Promotes Interpersonal Warmth," *Science* 322 (2008): 606–607.

18. Bargh, J.A., Chen, M., & Burrows, L., "Automaticity of Social Behavior: Direct Effects of Trait Construct and Stereotype Activation on Action," *Journal of Personality and Social Psychology* 71 (1996): 230–244.

19. Youngstedt, S.D. & Kline, C.E., "Epidemiology of Exercise and Sleep," *Sleep and Biological Rhythms* 4 (2006): 215–221.

20. Babyak, M. et al., "Exercise Treatment for Major Depression: Maintenance of Therapeutic Benefit at 10 Months," *Psychosomatic Medicine* 62, (2000): 633–638.

21. Klein, S. (2006). *The Science of Happiness: How Our Brains Make Us Happy—and What We Can Do to Get Happier.* New York: Marlowe & Company, p. 194.

22. Ratey, J.J. (2008). *Spark: The Revolutionary New Science of Exercise and the Brain.* New York: Little, Brown and Company, p. 7.

23. Klein, *The Science of Happiness*, 194.

24. Svrluga, S., "Lawsuit Filed against NCAA, University of North Carolina in 'Paper Class' Athletics Scandal," *Washington Post*, January 22, 2015. Retrieved from https://www.washingtonpost.com/news/grade-point/ wp/2015/01/22/lawsuit-filed-against-ncaa-university-of-north-carolina -in-paper-class-athletics-scandal/?utm_term=dd67db7bbb.9b.

25. "Judge Drops Ex-UNC Athletes' Lawsuit Over Sham Classes," February 19, 2016. Retrieved from http://www.espn.com/college-football/story/_/id/ 14808985/judge-dismisses-former-north-carolina-athletes-claims-school -academics.

26. Deacon, B.J., Abramowitz, J.S., Woods, C.M., & Tolin, D.F., "The Anxiety Sensitivity Index - Revised: Psychometric Properties and Factor Structure in Two Nonclinical Samples," *Behaviour Research and Therapy* 41 (2003): 1427–1449.

27. Broman-Fulks, J.J., Berman, M.E., Rabian, B., & Webster, M.J., "Effects of Aerobic Exercise on Anxiety Sensitivity," *Behaviour Research and Therapy* 42 (2004): 125–136.

28. Johnsgard, K. (2004). *Conquering Depression & Anxiety Through Exercise*. Amherst, NY: Prometheus Books.

29. Katz, M., "I Put in 5 Miles at the Office," *New York Times*, September 16, 2008. Retrieved from http://www.nytimes.com/2008/09/18/health/nutrition/ 18fitness.html?_r=0.

30. Koepp, G.A. et al., "Treadmill Desks: A 1-Year Prospective Trial," *Obesity* 21 (2013): 705–711.

31. Reiff, C., Marlatt, K., & Dengel, D.R., "Difference in Caloric Expenditure in Sitting versus Standing Desks," *Journal of Physical Activity and Health* 9 (2012): 1009–1011.

32. Kim, H. et al., "Effects of Oxygen Concentration and Flow Rate on Cognitive Ability and Physiological Responses in the Elderly," *Neural Regeneration Research* 8 (2013): 264–269.

33. Ekkekakis, P., Hall, E.E., VanLanduyt, L.M., & Petruzzello, S.J., "Walking in (Affective) Circles: Can Short Walks Enhance Affect?" *Journal of Behavioral Medicine* 23 (2000): 245–275.

34. Stroth, S., Hille, K., Spitzer, M., & Reinhardt, R., "Aerobic Endurance Exercise Benefits Memory and Affect in Young Adults," *Neuropsychological Rehabilitation* 19 (2009): 223–243.

35. Salas, C.R., Minakata, K., & Kelemen, W.L., "Walking before Study Enhances Free Recall but Not Judgment-of-Learning Magnitude," *Journal of Cognitive Psychology* 23 (2011): 507–513.

36. Schmidt-Kassow, M. et al., "Physical Exercise during Encoding Improves Vocabulary Learning in Young Female Adults: A Neuroendocrinological Study," *PLoS ONE* 8 (2013): 1–11. Retrieved from http://dx.doi.org/10.1371/ journal.pone.0064172.

37. Pontifex, M.B., Hillman, C.H., Fernhall B., Thompson, K.M., & Valentini, T.A., "The Effect of Acute Aerobic and Resistance Exercise on Working Memory," *Medicine & Science in Sports & Exercise* 41 (2009): 927–934.
38. Ekkekakis, P., Hall, E.E., VanLanduyt, L.M., & Petruzzello, S.J., "Walking in (Affective) Circles: Can Short Walks Enhance Affect?" *Journal of Behavioral Medicine* 23 (2000): 245–275.

Chapter 4. Sweet Dreams

1. Baltz, J., "Is Sleep Deprivation the New College Norm?" *Huffington Post*, April 4, 2016. Retrieved from http://www.huffingtonpost.com/jacqueline-baltz/sleep-deprivation-the-norm-college_b_9586402.html.
2. American College Health Association (2016), *American College Health Association-National College Health Assessment II: Reference Group Executive Summary Spring 2016.* Hanover, MD: American College Health Association. Retrieved from http://www.acha-ncha.org/docs/NCHA-II%20SPRING%202016%20US%20REFERENCE%20GROUP%20EXECUTIVE%20SUMMARY.pdf.
3. Scullin, M.K. & McDaniel, M.A., "Remembering to Execute a Goal: Sleep on It!" Psychological Science 21 (2010): 1028–1035.
4. "Study Shows How Sleep Improves Memory," June 29, 2005. Retrieved from http://www.sciencedaily.com/releases/2005/06/050629070337.htm.
5. Rasch, B. & Born, J., "Reactivation and Consolidation of Memory during Sleep," *Current Directions in Psychological Science* 17 (2008): 188–192.
6. Wagner, U., Gais, S., Haider, H., Verleger, R., & Born, J., "Sleep Inspires Insight," *Nature* 427 (2004): 352–355.
7. Ibid., 354.
8. Wrzus, C., Wagner, G.G., & Riediger, M., "Feeling Good When Sleeping In? Day-to-Day Associations between Sleep Duration and Affective Well-Being Differ from Youth to Old Age," *Emotion* 14 (2014): 624–628.
9. Gujar, N., McDonald, S.A., Nishida, M., & Walker, M.P., "A Role for REM Sleep in Recalibrating the Sensitivity of the Human Brain to Specific Emotions," *Cerebral Cortex* 21 (2011): 115–123.
10. Van Der Helm, E., Yao, J., Dutt, S., Rao, V., Saletin, J.M., & Walker, M.P., "REM Sleep Depotentiates Amygdala Activity to Previous Emotional Experiences," *Current Biology* 21 (2011): 2029–2032.
11. National Sleep Foundation, "Annual Sleep in America Poll Exploring Connections with Communications Technology Use and Sleep," press release, March 7, 2001. Retrieved from https://sleepfoundation.org/media-center/press-release/annual-sleep-america-poll-exploring-connections-communications-technology-use-.
12. Geist, "How to Work on No Sleep."

13. Morita, Y., Ogawa, K., & Uchida, S., "The Effect of a Daytime 2-Hour Nap on Complex Motor Skill Learning," *Sleep and Biological Rhythms* 10 (2012): 302–309.

14. Lavie, P. & Weler, B., Timing of Naps: Effects on Post-Nap Sleepiness Levels," *Electroencephalography and Clinical Neurophysiology* 72 (1989): 218–224.

15. Milner, C.E. & Cote, K.A., "Benefits of Napping in Healthy Adults: Impact of Nap Length, Time of Day, Age, and Experience with Napping," *Journal of Sleep Research* 18 (2009): 272–281.

16. Tietzel, A.J. & Lack, L.C., "The Short-Term Benefits of Brief and Long Naps Following Nocturnal Restriction," *Sleep* 24 (2001): 293–300.

17. Dinges, D.F., "Sleep Inertia," in *Encyclopedia of Sleep and Dreaming*, ed. Carskadon, M.A. (New York: Macmillan, 1993), 553–554.

18. Milner, C.E. & Cote, K.A., "Benefits of Napping in Healthy Adults: Impact of Nap Length, Time of Day, Age, and Experience with Napping," *Journal of Sleep Research* 18 (2009): 272–281.

19. Hayashi, M., Akiko, M., & Hori, T., "The Alerting Effects of Caffeine, Bright Light and Face Washing after a Short Daytime Nap," *Clinical Neurophysiology* 114 (2003): 2268–2278.

20. Fossum, I.N., Nordnes, L.T., Storemark, S.S., Bjovatn, B., & Pallesen, S., "The Association between Use of Electronic Media in Bed before Going to Sleep and Insomnia Symptoms, Daytime Sleepiness, Morningness, and Chronotype," *Behavioral Sleep Medicine* 12 (2014): 343–357.

21. Lemola, S., Ledermann, T., & Friedman, E.M., "Variability of Sleep Duration Is Related to Subjective Sleep Quality and Subjective Well-Being: An Actigraphy Study," *PLoS ONE* 8 (2013): 1–9. http://dx.doi.org/10.1371/journal.pone.0071292.

22. Fuligni, A.J. & Hardway, C., "Daily Variation in Adolescents' Sleep, Activities, and Psychological Well-Being," *Journal of Research on Adolescence* 16 (2006): 353–378.

23. Hamilton, N.A., Nelson, C.A., Stevens, N., & Kitzman, H., "Sleep and Psychological Well-Being," *Social Indicators Research* 82 (2007): 147–163.

Chapter 5. Attention Training

1. Wilson, T.D. et al., "Just Think: The Challenges of the Disengaged Mind," *Science* 345 (2014): 75–77.

2. Lyubomirsky, S., Sheldon, K.M., & Schkade, D., "Pursuing Happiness: The Architecture of Sustainable Change," *Review of General Psychology* 9 (2005): 111–131.

3. Killingsworth, M.A. & Gilbert, D.T., "A Wandering Mind Is an Unhappy Mind," *Science* 330 (2010): 932.

4. Parks, M., "It's Now Illegal to Text while Crossing the Street in Honolulu," NPR, July 29, 2017. Retrieved from http://www.npr.org/sections/thetwo-way/2017/07/29/540140824/its-now-illegal-to-text-while-crossing-the-street-in-honolulu.

5. Kushlev, K., Proulx, J., & Dunn, E. W., "Silence Your Phones: Smartphone Notifications Increase Inattention and Hyperactivity Symptoms," *CHI '16 Proceedings of the 2016 CHI Conference on Human Factors in Computing Systems* (2016): 1011–1020.

6. Ward, A.D., Duke, K., Gneezy, A., & Bos, M.W., "Brain Drain: The Mere Presence of One's Own Smartphone Reduces Available Cognitive Capacity," *Journal of the Association for Consumer Research* 2 (2017): 140–154.

7. Thích Nhất Hạnh (1990). *Present Moment, Wonderful Moment: Mindfulness Verses for Daily Living*. Berkeley: Parallax Press.

8. Whippman, R., "Actually, Let's Not Be in the Moment," *New York Times*, November 26, 2016. Retrieved from https://www.nytimes.com/2016/11/26/opinion/sunday/actually-lets-not-be-in-the-moment.html?_r=0.

9. Desrosiers, A., Vine, V., Klemanski, D.H., & Nolen-Hoeksema, S., "Mindfulness and Emotion Regulation in Depression and Anxiety: Common and Distinct Mechanisms of Action," *Depression and Anxiety* 30 (2013): 654–661.

10. Ibid.

11. Mermelstein, L.C. & Garske, J.P., "A Brief Mindfulness Intervention for College Student Binge Drinkers: A Pilot Study," *Psychology of Addictive Behaviors* 29 (2015): 259–269.

12. Joaquim, S. et al., "Direct Experience and the Course of Eating Disorders in Patients on Partial Hospitalization: A Pilot Study," *European Eating Disorders Review* 21 (2013): 399–404.

13. Fairfax, H., Easey, K., Fletcher, S., & Barfield, J., "Does Mindfulness Help in the Treatment of Obsessive Compulsive Disorder (OCD)? An Audit of Client Experience of an OCD Group," *Counselling Psychology Review* 29 (2014): 17–27.

14. Bei, B. et al., "Pilot Study of a Mindfulness-Based, Multi-Component, In-School Group Sleep Intervention in Adolescent Girls," *Early Intervention in Psychiatry* 7 (2013): 213–220; Caldwell, K., Emery, L., Harrison, M., & Greeson, J., "Changes in Mindfulness, Well-Being, and Sleep Quality in College Students through *Taijiquan* Courses: A Cohort Control Study," *The Journal of Alternative and Complementary Medicine* 17 (2011): 931–938.

15. Glick, D.M. & Orsillo, S.M., "An Investigation of the Efficacy of Acceptance-Based Behavioral Therapy for Academic Procrastination," *Journal of Experimental Psychology* 144 (2015): 400–409.

16. Teehan, S., "New SAT paying off for test-prep industry," *The Boston Globe*, March 5, 2016. Retrieved from https://www.bostonglobe.com/business/2016/03/04/new-sat-paying-off-for-test-prep-industry/blQeQKoSz1yAksN9N9463K/story.html.

17. Mrazek, M.D., Franklin, M.S., Phillips, D.P., Baird, B., & Schooler, J.W., "Mindfulness Training Improves Working Memory Capacity and GRE Performance while Reducing Mind Wandering," *Psychological Science* 24 (2013): 776–781.

18. Williams, M., Teasdale, J, Segal, Z., & Kabat-Zinn, J. (2007). *The Mindful Way through Depression: Freeing Yourself from Chronic Unhappiness.* New York: The Guilford Press, p. 34.

19. Ibid., 35.

20. Davidson, R.J. et al., "Alterations in Brain and Immune Function Produced by Mindfulness Meditation," *Psychosomatic Medicine* 65 (2003): 564–570.

Chapter 6. Failing Better

1. Ewalt, D.M., "By the Numbers: Kids' Dream-Job Salaries," *Forbes*, October 1, 2008. Retrieved from http://www.forbes.com/2008/10/01/kids-dream-jobs-lead-careers-dreamlife08-cx_de_1001salary_slide_11.html.

2. Pryor, J.H., Eagan, K., Palucki Blake, L., Hurtado, S., Berdan, J., & Case, M.H. (2012). *The American Freshman: National Norms Fall 2012.* Los Angeles: Higher Education Research Institute, UCLA.

3. "Medical School Applicants, Enrollees Reach New Highs," October 22, 2015. Retrieved from https://www.aamc.org/newsroom/newsreleases/446400/applicant-and-enrollment-data.html.

4. "Estimated Probability of Competing in Professional Athletics," National Collegiate Athletic Association, updated March 10, 2017. Retrieved from http://www.ncaa.org/about/resources/research/estimated-probability-competing-professional-athletics.

5. Baumeister, R.F., Campbell, J.D., Krueger, J.I., Vohs, K.D., "Exploding the Self-Esteem Myth," *Scientific American*, January 2005. Retrieved from http://cranepsych.edublogs.org/files/2009/06/Self_esteem_myth.pdf.

6. Seery, M.D., Holman, E.A., & Silver, R.C., "Whatever Does Not Kill Us: Cumulative Lifetime Adversity, Vulnerability, and Resilience," *Journal of Personality and Social Psychology* 99 (2010): 1025–1041.

7. Levin Coburn, K. & Treeger, M. L. (2009). *Letting Go: A Parents' Guide to Understanding the College Years.* New York: Harper.

8. Krauthammer, C., "Essay: Education: Doing Bad and Feeling Good," *Time*, February 5, 1990. Retrieved from http://content.time.com/time/magazine/article/0,9171,969312,00.html.

9. "About the Book," September 23, 2017, GenerationMe.com. Retrieved from http://www.generationme.org/about-book.html.
10. Brown, J.D. & Dutton, K.A., "The Thrill of Victory, the Complexity of Defeat: SE and Emotional Reactions to Success and Failure," *Journal of Personality and Social Psychology* 68 (1995): 712–722.
11. Ibid., 720.
12. Rowling, J.K., "Text of J.K. Rowling's Speech," *Harvard Gazette*, June 5, 2008. Retrieved from http://news.harvard.edu/gazette/story/2008/06/text-of-j-k-rowling-speech/.
13. Brown, J.D. & Dutton, K.A., "The Thrill of Victory, the Complexity of Defeat: SE and Emotional Reactions to Success and Failure," *Journal of Personality and Social Psychology* 68 (1995): 712–722., p. 173.
14. Seery, Holman, & Silver, "Whatever Does Not Kill Us," 1025–1041.
15. Seery, Holman, & Silver, "Whatever Does Not Kill Us," 1036.
16. Ibid., 1027.
17. Rowling, "Text of J.K. Rowling's Speech."
18. Dweck, C.S. (2006). *Mindset: The New Psychology of Success*. New York: Random House.
19. Ibid., 21.
20. Lieberman, M.D., "Self-Esteem vs. Esteemable Selves," *Psychology Today*, March 29, 2012. Retrieved from https://www.psychologytoday.com/blog/social-brain-social-mind/201203/self-esteem-vs-esteemable-selves.

Chapter 7. Willpower

1. Kim, E., "Here's the Real Reason Mark Zuckerberg Wears the Same T-Shirt Every Day," *Business Insider*, November 6, 2014. Retrieved from http://www.businessinsider.com/mark-zuckerberg-same-t-shirt-2014-11.
2. Baumeister, R.F., Bratslavsky, E., Muraven, M., & Tice, D.M., "Ego-Depletion: Is the Active Self a Limited Resource?" *Journal of Personality and Social Psychology* 74 (1998): 1252–1265.
3. Oaten, M. & Cheng, K., "Longitudinal Gains in Self-Regulation from Regular Physical Exercise," *British Journal of Health Psychology* 11 (2006): 717–733.
4. Ibid., 731.
5. Muraven, M., "Building Self-Control Strength: Practicing Self-Control Leads to Improved Self-Control Performance," *Journal of Experimental Social Psychology* 46 (2010): 465–468.
6. Muraven, M., Baumeister, R.F., & Tice, D.M., "Longitudinal Improvement of Self-Regulation through Practice: Building Self-Control Strength through Repeated Exercise," *Journal of Social Psychology* 139 (1999): 446–457.

7. Muraven, M., Gagné, M., & Rosman, H., "Helpful Self-Control: Autonomy Support, Vitality, and Depletion," *Journal of Experimental Social Psychology* 44 (2008): 573–585.

8. Ibid., 584.

9. Schmeichel, B.J. & Vohs, K., "Self-Affirmation and Self-Control: Affirming Core Values Counteracts Ego Depletion," *Journal of Personality and Social Psychology* 96 (2009): 770–782.

10. Muraven, M. & Slessareva, E., "Mechanisms of Self-Control Failure: Motivation and Limited Resources," *Personality and Social Psychology Bulletin* 29 (2003): 894–906.

11. Ibid., 897.

12. Yeager, D.S., Henderson, M.D., Paunesku, D., Walton, G.M., D'Mello, S., Spitzer, B., & Duckworth, A.L., "Boring but Important: A Self-Transcendent Purpose for Learning Fosters Academic Self-Regulation," *Journal of Personality and Social Psychology* 107 (2014): 559–580.

13. Galla, B.M. & Duckworth, A.L., "More than Resisting Temptation: Beneficial Habits Mediate the Relationship between Self-Control and Positive Life Outcomes," *Journal of Personality and Social Psychology* 109 (2015): 508–525.

14. James, W. (1890). *The Principles of Psychology* vol. I. New York: Henry Holt and Company.

15. Duckworth, A.L., White, R.E., Matteucci, A.J., & Gross, J.J., "A Stitch in Time: Strategic Self-Control in High School and College Students," *Journal of Educational Psychology* 3 (2016): 329–341.

16. Duckworth, A., "Facebook or Homework? How to Resist Distractions," (H. Kotb & K.L. Gifford, interviewers) [television broadcast], *Today*, October 7, 2013. Retrieved from http://www.today.com/video/facebook-or-homework-how-to-resist-distractions-52472387979.

17. Oaten, M. & Cheng, K., "Academic Examination Stress Impairs Self-Control," *Journal of Social and Clinical Psychology* 24 (2005): 254–279.

18. Oaten, M. & Cheng, K., Improved Self-Control: The Benefits of a Regular Program of Academic Study, *Basic and Applied Social Psychology* 28 (2006): 1–16.

19. Ibid., 7.

20. "Adm. McRaven Urges Graduates to Find Courage to Change the World," *UT News*, May 16, 2014. Retrieved from https://news.utexas.edu/2014/05/16/mcraven-urges-graduates-to-find-courage-to-change-the-world.

21. Ibid.

22. Duhigg, C. (2012). *The Power of Habit: Why We Do What We Do in Life and Business*. New York: Random House., p. 51.

23. Gollwitzer, P.M., Sheeran, P., Trötschel, R., & Webb, T., "Self-Regulation of Behavioral Priming Effects," *Psychological Science* 22 (2011): 901–907.

24. Ibid., 903.
25. Ibid.
26. Harris, P.R. et al., "Combining Self-Affirmation with Implementation Intentions to Promote Fruit and Vegetable Consumption," *Health Psychology* 33 (2014): 729–736.
27. Sheeran, P., Webb, T.L., & Gollwitzer, P.M., "The Interplay between Goal Intentions and Implementation Intentions," *Personality and Social Psychology Bulletin* 31 (2005): 87–98.
28. Ibid., 91.

Chapter 8. The Time Paradox

1. Kurtz, J.L., "Looking to the Future to Appreciate the Present," *Psychological Science* 19 (2008): 1238–1241.
2. Ibid., 1241.
3. Ariely, D. & Wertenbroch, K., "Procrastination, Deadlines, and Performance: Self-Control by Precommitment," *Psychological Science* 13 (2002): 219–224.
4. "State Gift Card Consumer Protection Laws 2013 Update," updated November 2013, ConsumersUnion. Retrieved from http://consumersunion.org/research/state-gift-card-consumer-protection-laws-2013-update/.
5. Shu, S.B. & Gneezy, A., "Procrastination of Enjoyable Experiences," *Journal of Marketing Research* 47 (2010): 933–944.
6. Teitelman, R. & Strauss, L.C., "Unused Gift Cards: Lost but Not Forgotten," *Barron's*, January 2, 2016. Retrieved from http://www.barrons.com/articles/unused-gift-cards-lost-but-not-forgotten-1451704473.
7. Quoidbach, J., Dunn, E.W., Hansenne, M., & Bustin, G., "The Price of Abundance: How a Wealth of Experiences Impoverishes Savoring," *Personality & Social Psychology Bulletin* 41 (2015): 393–404.
8. Ibid., 401.
9. Yerkes, R.M. & Dodson, J.D., "The Relation of Strength of Stimulus to Rapidity of Habit-Formation," *Journal of Comparative Neurology and Psychology* 18 (1908): 459–482.
10. "Report: Only 20 Minutes until Introverted Man Gets to Leave Party," *Onion*, March 12, 2014. Retrieved from http://www.theonion.com.
11. Little, B.R., "Free Traits and Personal Contexts: Expanding a Social Ecological Model of Well-Being," in *Person Environment Psychology*, 2nd ed., eds. Walsh, W.B., Craik, K.H., & Price, R. (New York: Guilford, 2000), p. 98. 87–116.
12. Mogilner, C., Chance, Z., & Norton, M.I., "Giving Time Gives You Time," *Psychological Science* 23 (2012): 1233–1238.
13. Ibid., 1237.

14. Newport, F., "Most U.S. Smartphone Owners Check Phone at Least Hourly," Gallup, July 9, 2015. Retrieved from http://www.gallup.com/poll/184046/smartphone-owners-check-phone-least-hourly.aspx.
15. Kelleher, D., "Survey: 81% of U.S. Employees Check Their Work Mail outside Work Hours [INFOGRAPHIC]," *TechTalk*, May 20, 2013. Retrieved from http://www.gfi.com/blog/survey-81-of-u-s-employees-check-their-work-mail-outside-work-hours/.
16. Kushlev, K. & Dunn, E.W., "Checking Email Less Frequently Reduces Stress," *Computers in Human Behavior* 43 (2015): 220–228.
17. Wallis, C., "genM: The Multitasking Generation," *Time*, March 27, 2006. Retrieved from http://content.time.com/time/magazine/article/0,9171,1174696,00.html.
18. Garavan, H., "Serial Attention within Working Memory," *Memory & Cognition* 26 (1998): 263–276.
19. Bowman, L.L., Levine, L.E., Waite, B.M., & Gendron, M., "Can Students Really Multitask? An Experimental Study of Instant Messaging while Reading," *Computers & Education*, 54 (2010): 927–931.

Chapter 9. Managing the Inevitable Bad Day

1. Anger Room home page, http://www.angerroom.com.
2. Van Goozen, S.H. & Frijda, N.H. "Emotion Words Used in Six European Countries," *European Journal of Social Psychology* 23 (1993): 89–95.
3. Robson, D., "There Really Are 50 Eskimo Words for 'Snow,'" *Washington Post*, January 14, 2013. Retrieved from https://www.washingtonpost.com/national/health-science/there-really-are-50-eskimo-words-for-snow/2013/01/14/e0e3f4e0-59a0-11e2-beee-6e38f5215402_story.html?utm_term=.63bc53f32dd5.
4. Averill, J.R., "On the Paucity of Positive Emotions," in *Advances in the Study of Communication and Affect* vol. 6, eds. Blankstein, K., Pliner, P., & Polivy, J. (New York: Plenum, 1980), 745.
5. Baumeister, R.F., Bratslavksy, E., Finkenauer, C., & Vohs, K.D., "Bad Is Stronger than Good," *Review of General Psychology* 5 (2001): 323–370.
6. Eid, M. & Larsen, R.J. (2007). *The Science of Subjective Well-Being.* New York: Guilford.
7. Bushman, B.J., "Does Venting Anger Feed or Extinguish the Flame? Catharsis, Rumination, Distraction, Anger, and Aggressive Responding," *Personality and Social Psychology Bulletin*, 28 (2002): 728, 724–731.
8. McRaney, D., "Catharsis," You Are Not So Smart, August 11, 2010. Retrieved from https://youarenotsosmart.com/2010/08/11/catharsis/.
9. Pennebaker, J.W., Kiecolt-Glaser, J.K., & Glaser, R., "Disclosure of Traumas and Immune Function: Health Implications for Psychotherapy," *Journal of Consulting and Clinical Psychology* 2 (1988): 239–245.

10. Pennebaker, J.W., "Writing about Emotional Experiences as a Therapeutic Process," *Psychological Science* 8 (1997): 162–166.
11. Niederhoffer, K.G. & Pennebaker, J.W., "Sharing One's Story: On the Benefits of Writing or Talking about Emotional Experience," in *Handbook of Positive Psychology*, eds. Snyder, C.R. & Lopez, S.J. (New York: Oxford University, 2002), 573–583.
12. Pennebaker, Kiecolt-Glaser, & Glaser, "Disclosure of Traumas and Immune Function," 244.
13. Niederhoffer & Pennebaker, "Sharing One's Story," 578.
14. Ibid., 576.
15. Rosenberg, H.J. et al., "Expressive Disclosure and Health Outcomes in a Prostate Cancer Population," *The International Journal of Psychiatry in Medicine* 32 (2002): 37–53.
16. Spera, S.P., Buhrfeind, E.D., & Pennebaker, J.W., "Expressive writing and coping with job loss," *Academy of Management Journal* 37 (1994): 722–733.
17. Pennebaker, J.W., Colder, M., & Sharp, L.K., "Accelerating the coping process," *Journal of Personality and Social Psychology* 58 (1990): 528–537.
18. Slavin-Spenny, O.M., Cohen, J.L., Oberleitner, L.M., & Lumley, M.A., "The Effects of Different Methods of Emotional Disclosure: Differentiating Post-Traumatic Growth from Stress Symptoms," *Journal of Clinical Psychology* 67 (2011): 993–1007.
19. Lieberman, M.D., Eisenberger, N.I., Crockett, M.J., Tom, S.M., Pfeifer, J.H., & Way, B.M., "Putting Feelings into Words: Affect Labeling Disrupts Amygdala Activity in Response to Affective Stimuli," *Psychological Science* 18 (2007): 421–428.
20. Wolpert, S. "Putting Feelings into Words Produces Therapeutic Effects in the Brain; UCLA Neuroimaging Study Supports Ancient Buddhist Teachings," UCLA Newsroom, June 21, 2007. Retrieved from http://newsroom.ucla.edu/releases/Putting-Feelings-Into-Words-Produces-8047.

Chapter 10. Social Connection

1. Van Boven, L. & Gilovich, T., "To Do or to Have? That Is the Question," *Journal of Personality and Social Psychology* 85 (2003): 1193–1202.
2. Kemp, S., Burt, C.D.B., & Furneaux, L. "A Test of the Peak-End Rule with Extended Autobiographical Events," *Memory & Cognition* 36 (2008): 132–38.
3. Ibid., 137.
4. Van Boven, L., Campbell, M.C., & Gilovich, T., "Stigmatizing Materialism: On Stereotypes and Impressions of Materialistic and Experiential Pursuits," *Personality and Social Psychology Bulletin* 36 (2010): 551–563.

5. Howell, R.T. & Hill, G., "The Mediators of Experiential Purchases: Determining the Impact of Psychological Needs Satisfaction and Social Comparison," *The Journal of Positive Psychology* 4 (2009): 511–522.
6. Dunn, E.W., Gilbert, D.T., & Wilson, T.D., "If Money Doesn't Make You Happy, Then You Probably Aren't Spending It Right," *Journal of Consumer Psychology* 21 (2011): 115–125.
7. Ibid., 120.
8. Cohen, S., Frank, E., Doyle, W.J., Skoner, D.P., Rabin, B.S., & Gwaltney, J.M., "Types of Stressors That Increase Susceptibility to the Common Cold in Healthy Adults," *Health Psychology* 17 (1998): 214–223.
9. Berkman, L.F. & Syme, L., "Social Networks, Host Resistance, and Mortality: A Nine-Year Follow-Up Study of Alameda County Residents," *American Journal of Epidemiology* 109 (1979): 186–204.
10. Ybarra, O. et al., "Mental Exercising through Simple Socializing: Social Interaction Promotes General Cognitive Functioning," *Personality and Social Psychology Bulletin* 34 (2008): 248–259.
11. Ibid., 257.
12. Ybarra, O., Winkielman, P., Yeh, I., Burnstein, E., & Kavanagh, L., "Friends (and Sometimes Enemies) with Cognitive Benefits: What Types of Social Interactions Boost Executive Functioning?" *Social Psychological & Personality Science* 2 (2011): 253–261.
13. Ibid., 256.
14. Dunn, E.W., Aknin, L.B., Norton, M.I., "Spending Money on Others Promotes Happiness," *Science* 319 (2008): 1687–1688.
15. Brooks, A.C. (2008). *Gross National Happiness*. New York: Basic Books.
16. Vinson, T. & Ericson, M., "The Social Dimensions of Happiness and Life Satisfaction of Australians: Evidence from the World Values Survey," *International Journal of Social Welfare* 23 (2014): 240–253.
17. Paylor, J. "Volunteering and Health: Evidence of Impact and Implications for Policy and Practice," London: Institute for Volunteering Research, 2011.
18. Nelson, S.K., Layous, K., Cole, S.W., & Lyubomirsky, S., "Do unto Others or Treat Yourself? The Effects of Prosocial and Self-Focused Behavior on Psychological Flourishing," *Emotion* 16 (2016): 850–861.
19. Ibid., 856.
20. Ibid., 859.
21. Sheldon, K.M., Boehm, J.K., & Lyubomirsky, S., "Variety Is the Spice of Happiness: The Hedonic Adaptation Prevention (HAP) Model," in *The Oxford Handbook of Happiness*, eds. Boniwell, I. & David, S. (Oxford: Oxford University Press, 2012), 901–914.
22. Ibid., 911.

23. Hardy, C.L. & Van Vugt, M., "Nice Guys Finish First: The Competitive Altruism Hypothesis," *Personality and Social Psychology Bulletin* 32 (2006): 1402–1413.
24. Ibid., 1412.
25. Aknin, L.B., Dunn, E.W., Sandstrom, G.M., & Norton, M.I., "Does Social Connection Turn Good Deeds into Good Feelings? On the Value of Putting the 'Social' in Prosocial Spending," *International Journal of Happiness and Development* 1 (2013): 155–171.

About the Author

Tim Bono, PhD, is a psychologist and lecturer at Washington University in St. Louis. He has won several teaching awards and thousands of students have taken his popular courses on the Psychology of Young Adulthood and the Science of Happiness. He is an expert consultant on psychological health and happiness for a number of national media outlets, including CNN, *Fast Company*, The Associated Press, and several public radio stations.